PORSCHE

42

PORSCHE
SPECIAL EDITIONS

MATT STONE

CarTech®

INCLUDES 930 TURBO FLACHBAU, GT1, RUF, SINGER VEHICLE DESIGN, IROC RSR, CLUB AND ANNIVERSARY SPECIALS, AND MORE

CarTech®

CarTech®, Inc.
6118 Main Street
North Branch, MN 55056
Phone: 651-277-1200 or 800-551-4754
Fax: 651-277-1203
www.cartechbooks.com

Edit by Bob Wilson
Layout by Connie DeFlorin

ISBN 978-1-61325-700-5
Item No. CT684

Library of Congress Cataloging-in-Publication Data Available

Written, edited, and designed in the U.S.A.
Printed in China

10 9 8 7 6 5 4 3 2 1

Parting shot (final page):
Photo courtesy Porsche Cars North America.

DISTRIBUTION BY:

Europe
PGUK
63 Hatton Garden
London EC1N 8LE, England
Phone: 020 7061 1980 • Fax: 020 7242 3725
www.pguk.co.uk

Australia
Renniks Publications Ltd.
3/37-39 Green Street
Banksmeadow, NSW 2109, Australia
Phone: 2 9695 7055 • Fax: 2 9695 7355
www.renniks.com

Canada
Login Canada
300 Saulteaux Crescent
Winnipeg, MB, R3J 3T2 Canada
Phone: 800 665 1148 • Fax: 800 665 0103
www.lb.ca

TABLE OF CONTENTS

ACKNOWLEDGMENTS

At (or certainly near) the top of any thank-you list for this project is Herr Tobias Mauler of Porsche AG and the Porsche museum and historical public relations, who unselfishly opened the factory photo archive and provided countless historical and significant photos and valuable bits of information. It is with no sense of irony that I say that I couldn't have done it without him.

Additionally, thanks to Bob Wilson and the gang at CarTech Books, who brought this project from an idea, pages of text, and piles of photos to life as the book in your hands. Thanks to photographer Mel Stone Carlisle, whom I proudly admit is my daughter. She snapped photos and otherwise helped along the way. Thanks to Shelby Akin and Luke Vandezande of Porsche Cars North America. Thanks to another mega-talented photographer Evan Klein, who created our great cover; and other capable snappers Andrew Tipping, Dirk de Jager, Rich Chenet, and Bill Warner. Thanks to Armen, Beau, Tiffany, and everyone else at Galpin's Porsche of Santa Clarita, who hosted and facilitated our tasty cover shoot. Thanks to Kahn Media, Bob Clarke, Kirk Gerbracht, Deb Pollack, Nick Barnes (operations manager at Gunther Werks Group), and the Petersen Automotive Museum.

Everyone wants to hang out with the Cat in the Hat. Magnus Walker, like a Porsche Santa, is surrounded by a throng of fans at a recent Cars and Coffee event at the Petersen Automotive Museum in Los Angeles, as he hands out free samples of his own line of Urban Outlaw Hot Wheels toys. All anyone had to do to get one was to be there, raise his or her hand, and say thank you. Walker is no dilettante celebrity and is only too happy to meet his many fans, sign autographs, pose for social media photos, and talk cars. He's smart, friendly, and engaging.

Thanks to my wonderful wife, Linda, who always supports my book and automotive projects (and the rest of my life) in countless ways.

Thanks to the incomparable Magnus Walker, who is a notable Porsche shaman, collector, and style setter, for his insightful words and thoughts for this book's foreword.

Finally, to you, dear readers, thank you for reaching into your actual or metaphorical wallet to purchase, read, and hopefully enjoy this book. If you didn't do those things, I would have had no reason to write it.

FOREWORD

If the average person ran into Magnus Walker on the streets of Los Angeles, they might mistake him for a random homeless guy. That's not far from the truth when he was a young teen and came to California for the first time. He bounced from flophouse to flophouse and couch to couch and admitted he was often penniless. Walker couldn't be further from that notion today. He's intelligent to the extreme, a serial entrepreneur, highly thoughtful, and considered among the world's most prominent Porsche collectors. (Photo Courtesy Magnus Walker)

Have you ever wondered what the difference is between an R, a TR, an ST, an RS, an RSR or a 930 or 935? What's a few new stickers, and what's an actual performance upgrade? When is a car too much of a race car for the street, and why is a certain model not street legal? Have you wondered how "Race on Sunday, Sell on Monday" actually works?

To many, all Porsches are special. This book explains what makes certain models more special than others. Porsche is a bit like Heinz with its 57 varieties. They're all the same but different.

Walker with his famous 277 911 is backdropped by the downtown Los Angeles skyline. Magnus's fabulous vintage warehouse PorscheCave is in downtown Los Angeles's Arts District. Many of his popular social media videos have been filmed nearby in this historic area that combines an honest grittiness with just enough gentrification. (Photo Courtesy Magnus Walker)

The guy on the left is Magnus. The dog on the right is Willow. The dented Porsche in the back is assuredly waiting its turn to be an Urban Outlaw build and maybe even star in its own video or be the model subject of a future Hot Wheels toy. Walker's lair is clean but not glossy or polished. It's an authentic warehouse that houses an interesting guy and some fabulous machines. (Photo Courtesy Magnus Walker)

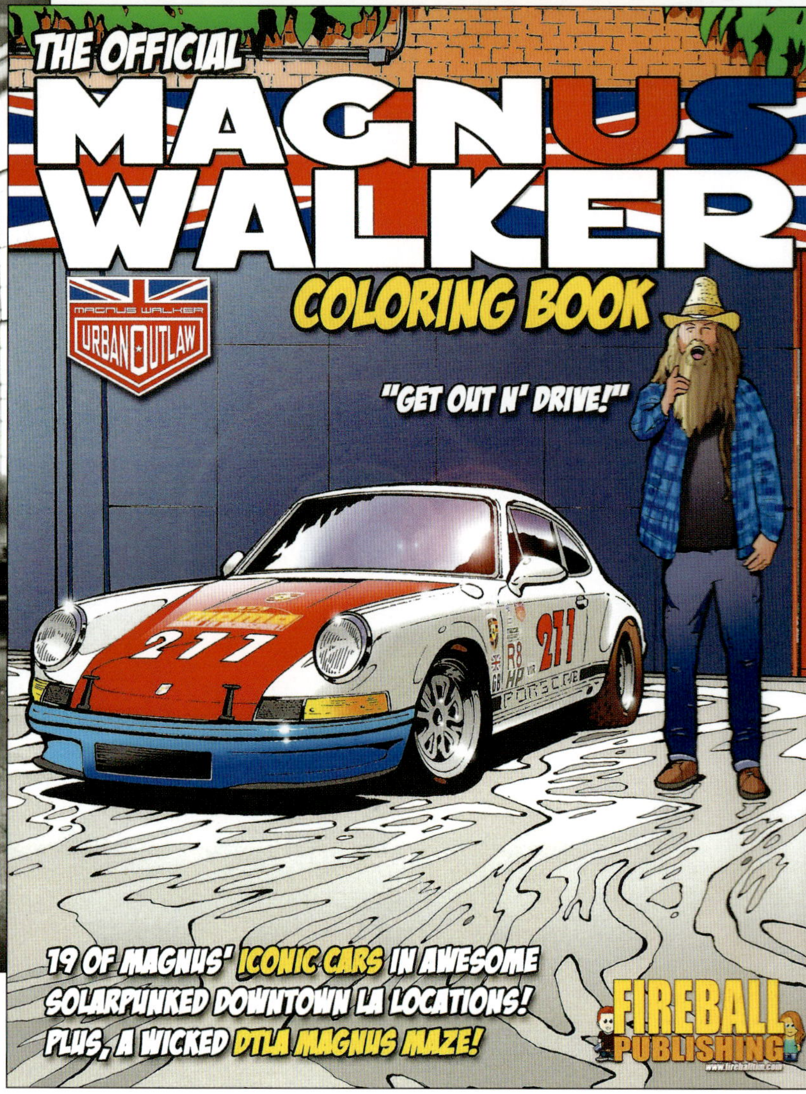

You need to be famous, or perhaps infamous, to rate your own coloring book. This fun piece of Urban Outlania is the work of also somewhat famous, or infamous, Fireball Tim that depicts 19 of Magnus Walker's cars in various iconic locations around town. It's fun for kids of all ages. (Photo Courtesy Magnus Walker)

The little company that began life on June 8, 1948, in Gmünd, Austria, and then moved to Stuttgart, Germany, quickly became a giant force in the automotive world in terms of speed, style, performance, reliability, and affordability.

I imagine many of us had a Porsche poster on the wall at some time in our lives. My first was on my bedroom wall back in the late 1970s. My love affair with the Stuttgart team began in 1977, when as a 10-year-old, I joined my dad at the London Motor Show. I saw a white Martini Turbo with red and blue racing stripes, fat tires, and a big wing. That was all I needed to start dreaming of owning and driving one.

Armed with brochures and posters upon my return to Sheffield, I wrote a letter to Porsche that explained how I wanted to design cars for them. Ironically, Porsche wrote back with words to the effect of, "Call us when you're older."

Forty-four years later, I've owned a few Porsches. I've raced, built, designed, driven, and shared the experience all over the world with fellow like-minded enthusiasts.

I'm a goal-oriented Porsche collector. It's more than just the 911 that appeals to me. I'm after examples of front-, mid-, and rear-engined cars both air- and water-cooled, so naturally this covers many models and variations throughout Porsche's 74-year history.

Every model has a story, so sit back, put your feet up, and get ready for the read of a lifetime. *Porsche Special Editions* is a deep dive down the slippery slope of Porsche addiction. After all, every Porsche is special and meant to be driven.

Cheers, and get out and drive!

Magnus Walker
Los Angeles, 2021

MAGNUS WALKER URBAN OUTLAW

INTRODUCTION

The notion of Porsche special editions seems easy to understand on the surface but is challenging to define. Most particularly ardent Porschephiles say that every Porsche is special. This is true to a great extent but not exactly what is meant in this context.

Porsche and other entities have designed, built, and sold limited production or otherwise special versions and variants of mainstream models. This can be compared to the Ford Mustang and Chevrolet Corvette Indy 500 pace car editions, just to name a couple. This notion

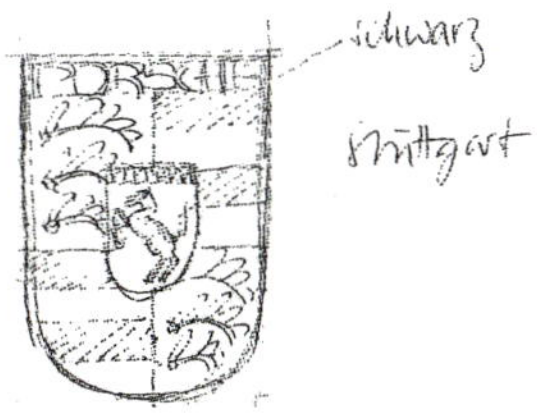

Heraldik made by Porsche oder die Entstehung eines Markenzeichens.

„Wenn es sich nur um ein Wappen handelt, das können Sie auch von uns haben!" Dieser Satz fiel 1952 in einem New Yorker Restaurant. Es war Ferry Porsches Antwort auf eine Anregung Max Hoffmans, dem ersten Porsche Importeur in Amerika. Wie viele andere Hersteller sollte Porsche auch ein Markenzeichen erhalten. Also nahm sich Ferry Porsche eine Serviette, einen Stift und begann zu zeichnen. Und zwar das Wappen des Landes Württemberg, in das er das Wappen des Standortes Stuttgart – ein springendes Pferd – integrierte. Darüber setzte er den Namen Porsche. Manchmal sind es die einfachen Ideen, die begeistern. Typisch Porsche eben.

Heraldry by Porsche: the origins of a trademark.

"If all you need is a badge, we can give you one too!" These words, spoken in 1952 in a New York restaurant, were Ferry Porsche's response to a request by Max Hoffman, the first Porsche importer in America. Since many manufacturers used an emblem on their cars, Hoffman believed that Porsche should too. With this, Ferry Porsche laid out a napkin, picked up a pencil, and began to draw. Within the arms of the state of Württemberg, he placed the black prancing horse of the company's home city of Stuttgart. Across the top, he wrote the Porsche family name. A simple idea, yet so inspirational. And still so typically Porsche.

Porsche's world-famous logo was first sketched in a New York restaurant in 1952 between Ferry Porsche and Max Hoffman, America's first North American importer. Prior to this, the cars were identified by small individual chrome letters that spelled out "P O R S C H E." Oddly enough, the prancing horse used in Porsche's new logo, which is also a major part of Ferrari's brand identification, is the official symbol of the city of Stuttgart, Germany. Additional symbols and colors further signify other regions germane to the company and family.

While nearly every Porsche vehicle qualifies as being special in one way or another, not all of them meet the mark for a special edition or model. (Photo Courtesy Corporate Archives Porsche AG)

Porsche's special edition models are often officially badged. Here, the "911 50" designation (left) indicates one of the limited production 50th-anniversary 911s, while the Heritage Design Edition (right) commemorates a run of special-option packages that honors the company's design traditions. (Photos Courtesy Corporate Archives Porsche AG)

can include anniversary, car club, racing team, championship, region-specific, and other unique models that are somewhat set apart from the normal production offerings. These are most often limited production runs ranging from a handful of cars to a few hundred and are the focus of this book.

However, I'm not including certain models, even though many are somewhat limited and very special, that ultimately stand as mainstream production pieces. As Magnus Walker suggested in this book's foreword, some of these special editions boil down to tape stripes, a unique color, and stickers or badges. Others are very special bespoke cars that involve genuinely limited production, considerable design, engineering, unique personality, and/or enhanced performance.

RUF's earliest days were rooted in Porsche service, modification, upgrades, and motorsport. It has since grown to be the world's foremost low-volume vehicle design and production company. It looks like testing at the Nürburgring is on this RUF Porsche's itinerary for the day. (Photo Courtesy RUF Automobile GmbH)

While they may not quite fit the rule and definition above, I've included a handful of factory and otherwise concept cars and design studies. This is primarily because it is often so interesting and compelling that they resulted from or led to more clearly defined special edition models, all of which demonstrate the factory's (and outside the factory) thinking and creativity.

Tuners and low-volume producers and models are even more of a challenge to define. Many individually owned and built hot rod or tuner Porsches are one-offs so they're not really editions, special or otherwise. Some tuner and custom outfits claim to produce their own limited edition model runs, and some of them were very limited, as in only one or two cars built. However, certain companies, such as RUF Automobile, legitimately develop and manufacture limited production, highly specialized machines that are without question small-run production vehicles, so I've included several of them here.

Another potentially sticky wicket from a definition standpoint is racing cars because so many Porsche racing cars stem directly from their street-bound equivalents. One example is the 356SL (Sport Licht or Sport Lightweight) machines that earned Porsche's first-class victories at Le Mans in the early 1950s. They are early 356 Gmünd Coupes architecturally but with thin, lightweight aluminum bodywork and some aero aids and other twists. They have lights and most of the other accoutrement of a street car, but three were built so I've included them. The 911 GT1 was a hyper car street machine that was intended to type-certify or homologate the GT1 variants for Fédération Internationale de l'Automobile (FIA) and other international sports car and endurance racing. It's a true super

When does a racing car become a street car, and vice versa? Quite often at Porsche. A small run of the Strasse (street) model GT-1 was required to qualify and certify this model as derived from a factory production product. Don't expect to see them on a street or highway near you any time soon, as they are rare and expensive. (Photo Courtesy Corporate Archives Porsche AG)

exotic that anyone with the notion and the money could buy. In addition, a litany of 911R and Carrera RS models hop back and forth over these blurred lines.

Porsche isn't universally consistent when it comes to addressing or publishing special edition model production numbers. Sometimes it commits to a given hard number at the time of announcement, and this is often memorialized on a special badge or plaque on or in the car. In other cases, Porsche produces a given model only for a select amount of time. In others, the company built as many as it could sell for as long as it could sell them. Recently, the company has gone more toward the first approach, understanding that the announcement of a unique, limited production model along with badging and serializing adds a certain specialness. It further generates demand and makes the customer feel a bit special too, invariably adding to its future value. When any kind of production or series numbers are available, I've listed them. When they're not available, they're not listed.

Given the task of making compelling selections that you will enjoy seeing and learning about, I made somewhat flexible judgements about what defines a special edition, including the most relevant and hopefully interesting vehicles and models. This is written with the understanding there can and should be friendly and passionate bar room debate about what is included and what is not.

Was there some semi-obscure special edition Porsche sold only in Zimbabwe or Sri Lanka that I missed? Assuredly. Please accept my mea culpa on that note. However, there is a bunch of fun miscellanies in Chapter 5 that hopefully compensates for any omissions. This has been a highly enjoyable pursuit for me, as I discovered Porsches that I previously knew nothing about or had never seen before. I hope you will enjoy it too. Just so you know, I too drink the Porsche Kool-Aid as a longtime fan and owner of several Porsches.

Again, my thanks.

Matt Stone
Los Angeles, 2021

Yes, that's me and my 1989 Porsche Carrera 3.2 Coupe as evidence that I speak Porsche and drank more than my share of brand Kool-Aid over the years. (Photo Courtesy Linda J. Stone)

Given Porsche's penchant for vehicle weight savings, it isn't a huge surprise that many Porsche racing cars wear a logo sticker instead of a few grams heavier metal and cloisonné badge as found on the street models. The fixation to save every ounce possible can be found on so many of the company's pure racing cars and includes see-through fiberglass and shift knobs made of balsa wood.

CHAPTER 1

FACTORY SPECIAL AND LIMITED EDITIONS

The birth and history of Porsche has been told well and often in several books and publications, but an understanding of its nature is relevant to the goal for this book.

Born in 1948, the company we now know as Porsche was, and to some extent remains, a family business. The foremost and original Dr. Ferdinand Porsche (1875–1951) was a considerable industrial designer and engineer. He was primarily a transportation designer and engineer prior to forming his own car-making business. He notably worked with or for Mercedes-Benz and the German government on various military projects.

Herr Porsche Senior is credited as the principal designer behind what is considered the first gas/electric hybrid car, which was called the Lohner-Porsche Semper Vivus of 1900–1905. His highest-volume contribution to transportation history was the original Volkswagen Beetle, also known as the "People's Car." The Beetle, internally designated the Porsche Type 60, was produced all over the world and sold in the tens of millions.

He was older and deep into his career when a volume-production sports car appeared that bore his own name. Even though his original design and production workshops were in Gmünd, Austria, Drs. Porsche (father Ferdinand and his son, also named Ferdinand) set up their new sports car company in Stuttgart, Germany, a suburb of Munich, which is not far from the primary factories and main offices of Mercedes-Benz and BMW.

The original Ferdinand Porsche is in either his own design studio or the Porsche studio in Gmünd, Austria. (Photo Courtesy Corporate Archives Porsche AG)

Porsche's first production model was the Gmünd 356. Its general architecture and powertrain design logically stemmed from the original Type 60 Beetle but with lightweight aluminum coachwork and the shape that defined the brand through the early 1960s. The most-commonly quoted production number is that 52 Gmünd-era cars were hand-crafted diligently and slowly from 1948 to 1951 before more productionized, steel-bodied cars began rolling off the lines in Stuttgart.

At the beginning, the company's in-house design department was very small and family driven by Ferdinand and his son Ferdinand, who went by "Ferry." Ferdinand Sr. is the company's namesake, and the brilliance of his engineering and design prowess underpins everything the company has done or became. However, it was Ferry Porsche who crystalized Porsche into a true worldwide automaker and motorsport mega power. He was most responsible for the 356.

Another in-house engineer and designer, Erwin Komenda, was of foundational significance on Porsche design throughout the 1950s and mid-1960s. He was a primary design influencer

The Lohner-Porsche is often credited as the first true gas/electric hybrid car. Electric motors and batteries drive the front wheels, while the two vertically mounted single-cylinder motorcycle engines power a generator to keep the batteries up to snuff. The model was called the Semper Vivus, which is Latin for always alive since the engines recharged the batteries to keep the motors moving. Think of this as the original HEV range extender. (Photo Courtesy Corporate Archives Porsche AG)

in the development of the Beetle and its many prototypes. He is generally credited with what became the 356, although it's fair to say that Ferdinand and Ferry Porsche were never far away from the birth of the cars and brand that bore the family name.

Ferdinand Porsche's son is also named Ferdinand, although he went by Ferry. It was not, nor is it now, common for Europeans to use the naming convention of senior or junior to descendants with the same name, so they often develop nicknames to distinguish them. (Photo Courtesy Corporate Archives Porsche AG)

Other designers and design firms recognized the potential in Porsche's lightweight, sporty, rear-engined, air-cooled mechanics and either designed modified bodies for the production machines or designed their own sporty bodies.

Prior to the 356, there was an interesting pre–World War II Porsche-badged car. It is widely acknowledged as the first true Porsche model. Although, with only three examples being hand-built primarily for the 1939 Berlin-to-Rome race, it's not considered to be high volume or production by any measure. It is interesting and relevant to any further production Porsche sports cars for its shape, proportions, and powertrain layout. The lines of the 356 (and nearly all future Porsches) are patently clear in the Type 64. The hand-formed aluminum coachwork of the Type 64 is curvier and swoopier than many

Herr Ferdinand the original is shown late in life with his hair thinning and growing gray next to one of his automotive offspring. This photo was likely snapped at the Gmünd works or in Zel Am See, Austria, the home of the family estate. (Photo Courtesy Corporate Archives Porsche AG)

Looking very much the part of a young president, chairman, or CEO, Ferry fully brought the 356 into meaningful production and established Porsche as a legitimate automotive producer. (Photo Courtesy Corporate Archives Porsche AG)

Jeff Zwart's 1948 Gmünd Coupe is number 50, which makes it a near unicorn in terms of collectible Porsche history. These cars are fairly aerodynamic and light, which is part of what makes them still feel so sporty and fun to drive, even with just 40 hp. (Photo Courtesy Kirk Gerbracht)

later production models due to its primary mission of being a race car.

It's helpful in framing this entire discussion to remember that the model 356 (in five somewhat-distinct iterations: hand-built Gmünd 356, 356 pre-A, 356A, 356B, and 356C) was produced from 1947/1948 to 1965/1966. Each iteration was distinct and evolved the development of its predecessor. Porsche itself didn't design or build many special edition–type models in the 1950s, but there were a few. There were also several others that were experiments or made in cooperation with

The unmistakably Porsche familial look and shape clearly defines the Type 64, even if the brand wasn't yet fully formed. The shallow nose elevation surely helped with aerodynamics. It's hard to believe that it predated the earliest 356s by approximately a decade. Just three were planned, and it is believed that just a single original example remains. (Photo Courtesy Corporate Archives Porsche AG)

The Type 64's proportions look slightly odd from this angle. Notice the car is wearing headlight blinder lenses that were used during World War II to make cars, and more particularly groups of them, less visible during nighttime bombing raids. The shallow nose and narrow greenhouse help reduce weight and aerodynamic drag, which are critical for a car with 35 or so hp. (Photo Courtesy Corporate Archives Porsche AG)

The aerodynamic wheelhouse covers further aid drag reduction. The vertical slat-like objects in the fenders aft of the front tires are semaphores, or Trafficators, that flip open and light up to indicate which direction a car is turning. It's the 1930s take on what we today commonly call turn signals. (Photo Courtesy Corporate Archives Porsche AG)

From this angle, the Type 64 somewhat resembles a large drop of Marvel Mystery Oil being blown in a wind tunnel. This is a modern photo from a Porsche 70th anniversary exhibit at the Los Angeles Petersen Automotive Museum.

other design and construction shops.

Once Porsche set up shop in Stuttgart, Germany, and productionized the 356 model line, the cars themselves were in a constant mode of evolution. Bumper, taillight, cooling grille designs, and interior trim details and options were constantly being fiddled with and updated. Not only did customer demand influence the makeup of the cars but so did the dealers, importers/distributors, and customers. The company was trying to grow into a legitimate, full-fledged automaker. It wasn't so big that it couldn't and didn't experiment with some short-run models that were more specifically tailored to certain ideas, flavors, and concepts. We'll call them the 1950s version of special editions.

The Porsche Museum defines this very special 1953-only America Roadster model as "a roadster that was significantly

This may be the most remarkable photo in this book. In front is the first 356 prototype, always called **Number 1*****, occupied by what appears to be Ferdinand and Ferry Porsche, in Austria during 1948, as they take a cruise around town. It wears a license plate and is road legal. Behind and just to the left in this photo is one of the Type 64s that must have provided recon support to this licensing and test drive. It's early Porsche history defined. (Photo Courtesy Corporate Archives Porsche AG)***

This is a better look at **Number 1*****. It's clearly a Porsche and a 356, although the proportions are somewhat different than the production cars. Much of the detailing is obviously familiar, and the Porsche factory owns this car, which is in marvelous condition and often taken out for exhibition runs. Not to brag, or maybe just a little, but I've ridden in it. (Photo Courtesy Corporate Archives Porsche AG)***

The three-quarter rear side angle view shows more interesting details of Number 1. *Here, you can clearly see the elongated rear deck engine cover that curiously has no visible cooling vents or louvers, as we've become so familiar with on any other rear- and mid-engine Porsche. Notice the dainty and somewhat ornate taillight trim features. The capital "A" badge on the lower left portion of the fender stands for Austria. Now that the car was road legal, Porsche as a carmaker was official. (Photo Courtesy Corporate Archives Porsche AG)*

The curvaceous, light, lithe, and perfectly proportioned 356 America Roadster was specifically developed as a road-legal racing car. Surely some were street driven, but most found their way to the track either as a production class racer or weekend club track toy. (Photo Courtesy Corporate Archives Porsche AG)

Check out the goggles. They are most likely motorcycle goggles with a bit of silver tape or perhaps military surplus pieces that Jack MacAfee wore as he ran his SCCA F Production America Roadster at Moffett Field in 1953. (Photo Courtesy Corporate Archives Porsche AG)

lighter than the 356-series models in production [and] at the same time was created exclusively for the North American market. The car achieved the ideal weight of 605 kg [about 1,330 pounds] thanks to an aluminum body with deep door cutouts, slot-in side windows, and a [removable] rain top. With its Spartan specification, this precursor of the 356 Speedster was specifically designed for motor racing use."

With its trimmer top and side roller windowless alloy body that is most easily identified by its rounded rump trim design, it looked light and near race ready even though it was fully equipped with lighting and normal instrumentation to make it legal to be sold as a street model. Built-in folding top and side windows? A radio and heater? Forget about it. Note the split windscreen sans framework along the top.

Some describe the America Roadster's overall look as playful. With a weight of just over 1,300 pounds, the uprated 70-hp 1,488-cc engine moved the car to a top speed of about 110 mph, which was much quicker than a stock, steel-bodied 356 Cabriolet. Only 17 were produced, and all but one had alloy coachwork. Some bought and owned them as a street sports car, but the majority of the cars were raced. Today, they

Racer and future Porsche distributor Johnny von Neumann is shown in an America Roadster at the Reno road course in 1953. (Photo Courtesy Corporate Archives Porsche AG)

The America Roadster was the last Porsche bodied by Dresden, Germany's Glaser Karosserie. Having said that, the company lost money on all of its projects with the marque, including the America Roadsters and approximately 250 356 Cabriolets, which likely put the company under. (Photo Courtesy Corporate Archives Porsche AG)

As you'd expect, a rather pristine 356 America Roadster is on exhibit at the Porsche Museum in Stuttgart. (Photo Courtesy Corporate Archives Porsche AG)

Ferdinand Alexander "Butzi" Porsche, Ferry's son, assumed control of Porsche's design efforts in 1962 and led the work that resulted in the 911/912 and set down the footprint for all future Porsche models. Handsome, erudite, and supremely intelligent, Butzi ultimately left this role to establish his own design firm, which today is known as Porsche Design and has created sunglasses, watches, fashion, and luggage. (Photo Courtesy Corporate Archives Porsche AG)

After Butzi worked through the Type 695 design concepts, clays, and models, which were never quite right, this proud papa ideated and made the Type 901 into reality. Always sharp and well turned out, Butzi was the quintessential definition of an automotive designer and executive. Porsche simply would not be what it is today without this important family member's talent and deep involvement. (Photo Courtesy Corporate Archives Porsche AG)

are as rare as the proverbial hen's teeth and are very expensive on the rare circumstance when one comes to market. As of this writing, $4,000,000 might buy a good one.

When hearing the name Continental, you most likely

This Type 695 prototype in the design studio appears to be an odd amalgam of the 356 Notchback, 912, and other Porsches never built. Handsome enough and with a somewhat practical and roomy greenhouse, it was judged not sleek or sporty enough to become Porsche's newest flagship sports car. (Photo Courtesy Corporate Archives Porsche AG)

think of a Lincoln of one era or another. This is correct. However, between the big V-12-powered Continentals of the 1940s and the elegant, hand-built Continental Mark II of 1956 and 1957, Porsche put the name and a Continental script badge on a very special and limited production 1955-only 356 Cabriolet. At the time, Porsche models were referred to by numbers: 356, Type 64, 550, 718, etc.

Porsche's East Coast importer and distributor Max Hoffman believed that American car buyers more strongly identified with cars that had names instead of number designations. It is rumored that once Ford and Lincoln decided to form its own premium Continental Division for 1956 that it contacted Porsche and "politely suggested" that it refrain from using the name on one of its sports cars. Stuttgart complied, which is why the last 356 Continentals were built in October 1955.

Unlike the flyweight America Roadster outlined above or the just-introduced 356 Speedster, the Continental was anything but a stripper designed for lighter weight or racing as its intention. The 356 Continental hinted at more European style and luxury overtones. The special 356 was nicely equipped with quality interior fitments, a fully padded convertible top, roll-up windows, a fully framed and full-height windscreen, windshield wipers, a radio, and handsome chrome trim throughout the car. It was powered by a 55-hp, 1500-cc version of Porsche's venerable flat-four overhead-valve engine with dual carburetors. All Continentals wear Reutter coach-

This unusual clay model shows two different rear treatments being considered along the Type 695 trail. It is common in the model-building trade to design and construct split models such as this so two different designs can be considered against each other without the time and cost investment of constructing two separate models. (Photo Courtesy Corporate Archives Porsche AG)

work, and although most identify this model as an open-bodied cabriolet, some Continental Coupes were also produced. Only 299 Continental Cabriolets and likely fewer coupes were built. Since Hoffman pushed for the Continental branding, his import dealerships ended up with most of them and were sold by Hoffman Motors, Ltd.

Beyond the 356 street models and various racing cars, Porsche's model expansion and growth began with the first seedlings of what became the 911s and 912s of the early 1960s. Its story began in 1952, when the still-very-young company began to contemplate life beyond the 356. There was early discussion around this time that Porsche needed a platform with more than two seats: either a 2+2 or some other form of four-seater. However, nothing much happened with it at this point because the 356 and its brand were still fairly fresh on the market and the company sold every car it could produce. Principal founder and senior namesake Ferdinand Porsche passed away in 1951, so this likely stunted some talk of new designs, products, investment, and direction.

Fortunately, this is one that got away. This 695 clay model explored the design with quad headlights, which were growing in popularity at the time, most particularly in North America. Cadillacs and Lincolns had switched over to quad light designs, and even Ferrari produced a dual headlights per side model. However, I can't imagine a modern 911 Turbo wearing this look with any panache. (Photo Courtesy Corporate Archives Porsche AG)

However, time marches on, and there was no question that Ferry would continue to lead and grow the company. Work on what initially became the 901-series Porsche began in 1959.

The lead designer was Ferry's son Ferdinand Alexander "Butzi" Porsche. The Type 695 was among the earlier concepts that made it past the drawing stage and into scale models and full-sized clay and metal concept cars. The 695 looked very Porsche. It shared some basic themes with the 356 and previewed what became the 911/912 shapes of which we're all familiar. There were several versions of this. The cabin was much more upright and glassier than the 356, and it was longer to accommodate more wheelbase and allow space for rear cabin seating. The longer horizontally opposed air-cooled 6-cylinder engine was under development.

The 356 was a rousing success, which put the company on the map as a major sports car producer and successful racing car builder and entrant, but more seating was needed to make the car practical. The original Volkswagen-derived overhead-valve flat-four engine had reached the practical limits of its development. Even though an exotic double-overhead-cam version of the engine was developed and produced considerable power, it was a high-winding, somewhat high-strung powerplant not ideal for sporty production street sports car use. This engine powered the 356 Carrera and an updated and slightly less complicated variant for the Carrera and Carrera 2 models.

Instead, a larger six was a much more viable option for what became the new 911. It had single overhead cams and two valves per cylinder to somewhat split the difference between the 356 primary overhead valve and the Carrera's four-cam engine architecture. However, to maintain a price-leader model, and for those who weren't concerned with

This display engine gives a good look at the famous 550 and 718 Spyder four-cam Carrera engine. On the left side of this engine, both sets of heads each with its own camshaft bank are visible. The all-encompassing aluminum shroud was a very important element of cooling this engine while it ran max revs on the racetrack. Though it was complicated, the engine proved to be very tough in long distance racing competition, and even ran 7,000- to 7,500-rpm shift points for hours on end.

the need for the higher-horsepower 6-cylinder version, the 356's overhead-valve four was used in an additional model to combine the new 901-series chassis and body architecture. We know this as the 912, which was produced between 1965 and 1969 with a one-year reprisal for 1976 as the 912E.

The most completed and fully realized versions of the 695 show a front visage that clearly predicts the first-generation production 911/912. The most noticeable evolution of production car versus the Type 695's design is the latter's much more upright greenhouse and the less fastback profile and engine cover. The concepts were built on lengthened 356 platforms, but the 695 retained the 356's outdated swing-arm suspension and did not yet utilize the new torsion-arm sprung rear suspension design ultimately developed for the 911.

In fact, one rear-angle photo of the final 695 model design wears "1600 Super" on its unvented or louvered rear deck to clearly indicate that a 75-hp 356 engine lies below. The flattish rear engine compartment certainly appeared long and large enough to contain the new flat-six engine, but it wasn't yet developed to this stage. All of the Type 695 concept and models roll on 356-style stamped steel wheels with chromed hubcaps, as the forged aluminum five-spoke Fuchs-style mag wheel had also yet to make an appearance.

The reasons that the Type 695 didn't become the 911/912 aren't abundantly clear, but most sources agree that its upright profile, roofline, and somewhat overly practical four-seat platform weren't sporty enough for Porsche at the time. Development then continued with a shorter wheelbase 2+2 seating configuration and the fastback profile we now associate with the 911. The 695 program ground to a somewhat endless halt in 1962 in time for the Type 901/911/912 design and platform to make its worldwide debut at the 1963 Frankfurt Auto Show.

What's the difference, you may ask, between a 901, a 911, and/or a 912? The ultimate first production nomenclature for what became the 911 was originally the Type 901, which was how a few hundred of the first production units are named and badged. However, Porsche immediately learned that French carmaker Peugeot held a trademark on a three-numbered badging sequence beginning with the number 9 and a zero in the middle. It had built countless models called the 902, 903, and so on and had plans to produce more and continue the same theme. Peugeot successfully defended its trademark, so Porsche added a "1" to the middle digit. Hence, what was a Porsche 901 became a 911, and what had been a 902 was called 912. It was a straightforward problem with a simple fix. Case closed.

1970–1971 911 ST

A few years after the development, production, and homologation of the 911R (see Chapter 3), Porsche produced a smaller, shorter run of a competition-based 911 in 1970/1971 called the ST, for Street Track. Most said it was decidedly more focused on the track aspect of that equation with the notion to compete on the World Rally stage.

Rallying was and remains a highly competitive international series run in several countries around the world. It usually consists of ever-changing and regularly treacherous passages of pavement, dirt, mountain hill climb, and possibly

Got lights? This 911 ST certainly does, which tips it off as a rally racer, being it's the 1970 Monte Carlo Rally. Driven by Gérard Larrousse and Maurice Gélin, the number 2 Porsche finished second overall to another 911 S. (Photo Courtesy Corporate Archives Porsche AG)

Looking every bit the rally racer, this 911 ST sports a racing dual-exhaust system, an interior roll bar, ancillary driving lights up front, and a pretty husky skid plate underneath. (Photo Courtesy Corporate Archives Porsche AG)

snow. It takes a fast, tough, highly versatile car to be competitive at these events. The standard 911 and the specialized 911R demonstrated that Porsche's now-foundational sports car had much of the right stuff but needed more. There was more power and wider rear fender flares with more aggressive rolling stock, and it was all with an eye toward keeping weight down to 2,100 to 2,200 pounds, aided by use of lighter weight steel body panels.

This is a serious skid plate. It reaches from the front bumper well back beyond the steering and front suspension. There's likely a similar installation aft to protect the engine, transaxle, and half-shafts. Notice the accessory fog light blank-off plates in the lower front fascia. All extra lighting is always mounted above the front bumper, as a small pair of lights in the lower factory location wouldn't last 10 minutes in most rally stages. (Photo Courtesy Corporate Archives Porsche AG)

This hard-working ST's alloy wheels are long gone in favor of a round of steelies with studded tires for the occasional snow-covered rally stage. Besides the usual bolt-on, high-powered lights up front, this entry also sports an extra set of air horns. (Photo Courtesy Corporate Archives Porsche AG)

Expert sources can't quite agree on how many ST models were factory produced. The two most common numbers are 23 and 24, but it's impossible to know how many were later cloned into a similar configuration. The picture is further confused by the fact that some STs were built from former street cars using a kit of components sourced from Porsche. The emphasis was clearly on World Rally competition, as many appear with a squadron of extra head, driving, and fog lamps mounted on the front hood, in or around the bumper area, or in replacement of the small metal grilles just inboard of the turn signal/running light clusters.

Bjorn Waldegaard and Lars Helmer are hard on the dirt in their ST at a rally in Austria in 1970. (Photo Courtesy Corporate Archives Porsche AG)

Wider wheels and tires are de rigueur. Sometimes they are the standard slotted steel wheel; the strong, forged Fuchs 5-spoked alloys; and occasionally, they have wider rear wheels of an entirely different design and brand in search of a wider footprint than Porsche offered at the time. To accommodate the beefier rolling stock, the fenders were flared slightly front and rear. Cabins were stripped clean of racetrack non-essentials and replaced with simple, lighter weight door cards and fabric door pulls.

By the time the first STs were produced in 1970, Porsche already enlarged its 911-type 6-cylinder engine well beyond the original 2.0 liters. The earliest STs ran a 2.3L six rated at 230 hp. Later, a torquier 2.5L ST engine came along that was credited with more like 250 hp. It was mission accomplished for the 911 ST, which proved to be a highly successful rally racer and somewhat set the tone for future GT class and rally-spec track 911s and certain street models. Original factory-built STs are rare as the proverbial dinosaur bones, and those with significant track or rally competition provenance cost a mint in the current marketplace.

1973 Carrera RS 2.7

This rather magic model fits many categories. It's a concept that evolved into a limited production special edition and a race-inspired street model that became a racing car. The Carrera RennSport 2.7 of 1973, much like the above-noted 911R, was an outgrowth and evolutionary higher performance development of the then-current 911S. The RS 2.7 was originally conceived as a model to homologate or type-approve a variety of weight-reducing measures. Only 500 of the larger, more powerful, mechanically fuel injected (MFI) engine were originally planned.

The demand for this GT class racing and rally competition model, as well as a more aggressive street 911, was so high that 1,580 were ultimately built. This Carrera model is most instantly recognized by its ducktail Bürzel, or rear decklid wing, the unique Carrera script running lengthwise above the lower rocker panels of the bodywork, and Porsche lettering on the rear decklid.

The RS 2.7 was produced in Touring and Lightweight configurations, although both were street legal and suitable as a high-performance street sports car. The available colors included black, Light Ivory White, Aubergine, Dalmatian Blue, Sepia Brown, and Lilac with brightly colored contrasting lettering graphics. Among the colors, black and Light Ivory White were the most popular, each with about a 10-percent take rate. Any list of all-time great and most significant Porsches always includes the Carrera RS 2.7, and many marque experts

This is a charming period European public relations shot of a new 1973 Carrera RS 2.7, which is what many consider to be the seminal model that distills the very best of what an early air-cooled 911 is all about. (Photo Courtesy Corporate Archives Porsche AG)

Besides its graphics and other defining features, the famous ducktail rear Bürzel spoiler most instantly screams Carrera RS 2.7. It provides a modicum of rear downforce and was further used on a few later Carrera models and reproduced in the aftermarket to don the engine covers of countless 911s and Carrera RS clones. It's as much a Carrera trademark as scissor-style doors are for the Lamborghini Countach. (Photo Courtesy Corporate Archives Porsche AG)

Porsche produced Touring and Lightweight versions of the RS 2.7. This is an immaculately restored example of the latter. It used thinner metal body panels, a minimum of sound insulation, and lighter glass to reduce weight. (Photo Courtesy Petersen Automotive Museum)

and fully entrenched enthusiast owners consider it to be the ultimate distillation of the best ethos of the early air-cooled 911-era machines.

It cannot be overstated the great lengths that Porsche went to improve and develop the performance of what to date was its highest performing 911 and the second 911 model intended to be highly track-worthy. To reduce weight of the Sport, or lightweight edition, several of the body panels used thinner gauge steel to save a few pounds where possible. Thinner, lighter weight glass was also employed. The interior door panels, which normally contained armrests, map pockets, insulation, and such, were replaced with simpler cardboard-like pieces that did away with the aforementioned components. The door handles were replaced with lightweight fabric pulls to save precious grams.

At this point in time, most 911s ran the same tire sizes front and rear, yet the Carrera RS 2.7 had modestly wider rear fender flares to accommodate slightly wider 15-inch wheels and tires to help quell the rear-engine machine's occasional tail-happy handling.

The RS 2.7-spec engine is very special. Other 1973 911 models ran 2.4L sixes, while the RS motor was punched up to 2.7 liters and given Bosch/Kugelfischer mechanical fuel injection. The result was a high-revving, raspy-sounding 210 hp available only with the 5-speed manual transaxle. Along with the body modifications and engine upgrade, the RS 2.7 boasted stiffer suspension turning and slightly larger brakes.

The Carrera RS engine evolved over and above the standard 911 S powerplant in several ways, including the 2.7L displacement and the Bosch mechanical fuel injection, which many have nicknamed MFI. Every cylinder got its own intake butterfly and fuel-injector nozzle. The result was more power and increased throttle response. (Photo Courtesy Corporate Archives Porsche AG)

The RS 2.7 was named Carrera in recognition of the brand's 1950s success at the Carrera Panamericana Mexican off-road race. This special model wasn't officially imported to or sold in the United States when new, although hundreds have made it to American shores.

It was a classic then, as it is now, and today it is highly sought after with clean, well provenanced examples ringing up big prices at the cash register or auction block. The mechanical fuel injection architecture continued in various 911s for quite some time, as did the rear ducktail wing look and the Carrera name. It's a giant among great Porsches.

This lovely period public relations photo of the Carrera RS 2.7 hints at the romance of the time, a great car, and a pair of enthusiasts enjoying it and the variety of aircraft around it. (Photo Courtesy Corporate Archives Porsche AG)

Mega Porsche-phile and enthusiast/collector Bruce Meyer is in his immaculate, highly original, and often-driven 1973 Carrera RS 2.7 at a great car show in the Hollywood Hills. Blue over Grand Prix White is one of the most popular RS 2.7 liveries.

1980 911 SC Weissach Edition

Considering how far and effectively the 911 SC evolved the 911 from the challenging years of 1975 to 1977 (when power was generally down, as the company dealt with emissions regulations), it is somewhat surprising that there weren't more special or commemorative editions during the SC's six-model-year run.

They are truly remarkable cars and embody what's great about a modern, air-cooled 911. There was one worthy of mention that was created for the U.S. market in 1980. It was a strictly cosmetic package that didn't involve more engine power or performance, but it didn't matter. It was distinctive looking and produced in limited quantity.

The Weissach Edition SC was available in metallic black or a silver called Platinum Metallic, and it was split about 50-50 among the production run. The Fuchs wheel centers were finished to match whichever body color the car was painted.

To add a further visual punch was a whale tail rear wing that was slightly smaller but very similar to the whale tail wing featured so famously on the 930 Turbo Carrera that came to market about five years later. There was also a black plastic lower front chin spoiler. The interior was finished in a special leather color called Doric Gray with burgundy piping, red/burgundy carpet, and beige leather seats. This special option group was called M439. The most commonly quoted production number is 408 units for this 1-year-only limited edition 911.

A subtle, elegant livery was used for this early special edition SC. The slightly warm silver teams handsomely with the body-colored wheel centers and Bordeaux-colored interior for a decidedly European luxury flair. (Photo Courtesy Corporate Archives Porsche AG)

The Weissach 911 SC's cabin was essentially stock in terms of features, save for the contrasting piped and colored leather upholstery. (Photo Courtesy Corporate Archives Porsche AG)

1987–1989 Carrera Club Sport

Think "less is more." As the 911 matured, it became more developed, more luxurious, and gained a little weight. Porsche rightly gauged the demand for a new somewhat simpler and lighter model that was still completely street legal and appropriate but also slightly adept for the occasional time trial or club track day event.

This is the single prototype from which the Carrera 3.2 Club Sport was developed, and it set the tone for this edition and all other Club Sports to follow. After its developmental testing duties, it was complete but somewhat used up until the Porsche Museum's Achim Stejskal spearheaded its immaculate restoration. He led a team of factory mechanics, technicians, and volunteers in restoring this historically important car for the museum's permanent collection. In spite of its many hard miles, it looks and drives factory fresh in every way. (Photo Courtesy Mel Stone)

The idea was straightforward and included the Turbo-style aerokit rear wing. It peeled off a few pounds, trimmed back the options and equipment levels a bit, added some unique yet tasteful graphics, and replaced the heavier leather interior trim with fabric. It was an instant track-day runner that could be happily driven every day. The idea was named Club Sport, and it was first offered on 1987–1989 Carrera 3.2 Coupes.

Porsche defined the Club Sport's austerity program thusly: "With reduced furnishings, the 911 Carrera Club Sport is trimmed for an even greater degree of sportiness. In fact, less is actually more, so the parts that have been omitted include

Given the body-colored wheel centers and whale tail rear wings, you might think this is a 930 Turbo prototype of some sort, but no. The Turbo had already been on the market for more than a decade by this time. Instead, this look and content established the Club Sport ethos. (Photo Courtesy Mel Stone)

Porsche toyed with the idea of a purpose-built three-dial instrument panel but instead stuck with a conventional 911 piece for the production run. (Photo Courtesy Mel Stone)

The standard Carrera 3.2 engine received no internal modifications and just had some reprogramming and a higher rev limit. It may have made a few more horsepower but wasn't rated as such. (Photo Courtesy Mel Stone)

A snazzy, modern art graphics package was developed for the Carrera 3.2 Club Sport. It was appropriate for the time and similar in philosophy for what Porsche had designed for the first Turbo Carreras. (Photo Courtesy Mel Stone)

rear seats, side and rear wall paneling, insulating material, and window levers. Compared to a well-quipped normal Carrera, the 911 Club Sport is a good 100 kg [about 200 pounds] lighter."

The engine management system was recalibrated for a slightly higher rev limit (6,840 rpm versus 6,350), although the engine wasn't officially re-rated in terms of horsepower. The 3,147-cc CS engine in European trim was rated at 231 hp, with U.S. 50-state versions at 217 (1987 and 1988) and 214 (1989). A 5-speed manual Getrag G50 manual transaxle was the only transmission offered. The Club Sport model was only served in non-sunroof coupe form with a restricted options list. It's rare to find one with air conditioning. The standard 15-inch Fuchs alloy wheels were in this case replaced with the normally optional 16-inchers. There was also a limited color palette to be had; most are white with red or gray graphics, although we've seen black Club Sports too.

This looks similar to the Turbo's whale tail spoiler, but the primary difference is in the shape and size of the rubber lip surround. The louvers on the horizontal surface certainly aided engine cooling, but it didn't need to feed cool air to an intercooler as it would on a later-generation 930 Turbo. (Photo Courtesy Mel Stone)

Another design touch taken from the Turbo is the black mudguard shark-fin appliqué in front of the rear wheels. (Photo Courtesy Mel Stone)

This handsome graphic says it all. Most well-used or used-up automotive development prototypes are junked or crushed when their prototype job is done. Thankfully not so for this important Carrera that set the tone and formula for many future Club Sport models. (Photo Courtesy Mel Stone)

Those who worked on the restoration signed the undersurface of the Club Sport prototype's front trunk lid. (Photo Courtesy Mel Stone)

Road & Track magazine's May 1988 issue, which featured the car on the cover, summarized the Carrera Club Sport: "It's a back to basics 911 targeted at the hard-core enthusiast. The sort of person who is active in the Porsche club and wants a no-frills car to drive in slaloms, solos, time distance rallies, and other club events. Now you know where the name comes from."

The Carrera CS acquitted itself well in *Road & Track*'s instrumented testing by running 0–60 in 5.7 seconds, which in today's terms may not sound overly impressive, but this was 1988. A time of 5.7 seconds was really hustling for a naturally aspirated, 3.2L 6-cylinder car with 217 hp that weighed about 2,600 pounds.

Only 340 of this Carrera Club Sport era were produced. Later, there were Club Sport versions of the front-engine, water-cooled Porsche 968, 944, 993, and 928S models as well.

The S on this Euro license plate signifies Stuttgart. At this angle, the Club Sport logo graphic appliqué reads quite clearly. Only the lack of the 930's fat fender flares indicates this isn't a factory Turbo. (Photo Courtesy Mel Stone)

Turbo-Look

When Porsche developed the original 930 Turbo Carrera, which came to market in most of Europe for 1975 and in North America for the 1976 model year, it established a whole new look and reputation for the design ethos of the original 901/911 that was first shown in 1963. Tall, narrow steel wheels and hubcaps were replaced with fat Fuchs forged alloys wearing aggressive, low-profile rubber. The ride height was lowered. Beefed-up, cross-drilled disc brakes directly connected to those on the all-conquering 917 prototype racers and hid just behind the massive new rolling stock. The front end got a black rubber lower lip spoiler, and the fenders were aggressively flared to wrap around the new wheels and tires. The Turbo's most defining feature is the fabulously fat whale tail wing that sits atop the engine cover.

A star was born. Posters were printed. Stories were told; some were real, and some were made up, exaggerated, or merely imagined about Porsche's legendary turbocharged 911 street car. Just by being designed and built, the 930 Turbo established the Look.

Low, squat, fat-fendered, and winged all defined the Turbo-Look. In the beginning, independent shops, owners, tuners, and occasionally dealers converted naturally aspirated 911s to look like Turbos. Some of the cars authentically looked the part; others looked like aftermarket boy-racer specials.

Porsche, seldom being one to not recognize or otherwise miss a consumer demand trend in the marketplace, decided that since it already produced all the parts needed to make a 911 look and drive like a 911 Turbo, it jumped on the proverbial bandwagon. Initially offered in 1984 as option 491, it was

It's the profile that inspires miles of smiles whether you're at the wheel or simply staring. The Turbo-Look's look, as defined by the flares, rolling stock, and spoilers front and rear, really give this 911 platform a decidedly husky stance.

The Turbo-Look has certainly got the look. The factory Turbo-Look option gave the Carrera 3.2 everything it needed to appear the part of a 930 except the turbocharger. It has the big rolling stock, flares, front and rear spoilers, brakes, and the stance. It fooled me and probably you too.

Only the subtle Carrera badge on the engine lid just below the big wing hints that there's no forced induction aboard.

officially called the Turbo-Look and included the purposeful addition of the hyphen between the two words to indicate that it was a factory-built car. This option package was of high content and particularly well thought-out. It gave a standard Carrera 3.2 what it needed to look every bit the part of a factory 930 Turbo without the turbocharger itself. The Turbo-Look package and concept was originally conceived and built for Carrera 3.2 models of 1984–1989, including the rare speedster, although elements of it later appeared on certain 964-generation cars.

According to the Turbo-Look registry (turbo-look.com), the hardware contained in this package is as follows:

- Wider 930 Turbo front and rear fenders (At first, they were panels factory welded onto the narrow-bodied cars' standard fenders but were later updated to new purpose-designed wide stampings.)
- Front apron black elastic rubber/plastic lower chin spoiler and fender spats
- 930 Turbo 3.3L rear wings with elastic rubber-lip rim
- Complete Turbo 3.3L braking system (derived from the 917)
- 930 Turbo anti-roll bars
- 16-inch Fuchs forged alloy wheels (7x16-inch front, 9x16-inch rear)
- Longer wheel studs
- Further 930 Turbo suspension tuning specifications

Considering the added cache and meaningful hardware included in the 491 Turbo-Look option, its cost of an additional $5,000 onto the sticker price was the bargain among all Porsche bargains. Today, a low-mileage Turbo-Look Carrera will bring approximately 10 times that amount in terms of additional value and sales price over a comparably equipped and condition narrow-bodied Carrera.

Unfortunately, there isn't a comprehensive, worldwide source that conclusively covers how many Turbo-Look wide-body factory-built cars were made. There are registries, forums, and websites that address the issue to a certain extent.

Although the Turbo-Look had a unique option code, such cars did not get model-specific vehicle identification numbers (VINs). The best we can offer at this juncture is a document that appears to be drafted on Porsche Cars North America (PCNA) letterhead. However, it is unsigned and undated. Considering that it comes from PCNA, I'm quite confident that it addresses North American models and production only.

Flachbau

The term flachbau means flat nose or slope nose. It was a style of modified 911 that, like so many other things, grew out of Porsche's all-conquering success in motorsport. The 911-based 935 racer dominated many forms of motorsport from 1976 to 1981 in single- and, most particularly, twin-turbocharged form. Various 935s and their evolution of models dominated global motorsport, capturing countless big sports car and endurance races and championships, such as the 24 Hours of Le Mans, the Sebring 12 Hour and Daytona 24 Hour races, plus FIA and International Motor Sports Association (IMSA) titles galore.

To make the 911 a winner on the world stage, Porsche had to substantially evolve and develop it not only from a power

Some aftermarket slant-nose conversion jobs look fairly credible if done properly, but none get it quite as right as this 1988 factory-built, all-steel Flachbau. If you think this example resembles the car on the cover, you'd be correct as it's a proud member of the Galpin Collection. (Photo Courtesy Evan Klein)

Galpin's screaming red zonker has it all: the perfectly proportioned box-style rocker panels, the cooling grilles that are cut into the front portions of the rear fenders, all the wings and things, immaculate rolling stock, original paint and interior, and very low original miles.

Some 911s with improperly modified suspension or all out-of-whack rolling stock either sit high or resemble low-riders. That's not the case with this Big Red. It sits tight, right, perfect, and truly ready to pounce.

and suspension standpoint but particularly aerodynamically. The car sprouted massive fender flares and huge rear wings. The front end, which was not aerodynamically efficient, was restyled to minimize its upright fenders and headlight design. The fenders were stripped clean of the headlights, and the fender line was brought down much closer to that of the front hood. Radical front facias were designed to further manage the wind, spoilers were incorporated, and high-powered head-lights were needed for the nighttime stints in long endurance races. This look was colloquially named slant-nose, or flach-bau in German.

It wasn't long before Porsche customizers began to develop this look for street 911 customers who wanted a truly unique and race-inspired look. These flat-nosed conversions were most commonly performed on 930 Turbo models, although more than a share of naturally aspirated 911SCs and Carrera 3.2 models ended up with them too. The earliest slant-nose conversions encompassed body panels handmade in fiberglass,

The "turbo" badge on the tail says it all, as does this prop-erly huge rear wing. In spite of all the Flachbau redesign work that takes place up front and along the rockers and fenders, there are no modifications to the rear aspect of this rare and expensive option.

This area of any given car is often an easy place to spot an aftermarket, fake, or poorly done Flachbau conversion. The black strakes are seldom this smooth and perfect, and the metal work inside the scoop isn't often this cleanly shaped.

If you've ever won-dered where the whole Flachbau thing and inspiration came from, look no further than this Interscope Racing IMSA 935. This is Danny Ongias at Laguna Seca in 1976/1977.

Things are serious business inside this marvelous 1988 Flachbau. Notice the special steering wheel that is identical to the standard Carrera 3.2 wheel, save for the recessed Porsche badge on the right side of the horn pad, which was a Turbo-only touch.

Some Turbo models wear factory dual exhausts, although this is a neat and great sounding, aftermarket stainless-steel system.

This is the view most pursuers are likely to see of this car as it disappears into the horizon in front of you.

Another quick tip that there's forced air under the hood is the huge and very effective intercooler that came along on second-generation Turbo models. This brought in a cooler induction charge, which reduced ignition detonation and added horsepower.

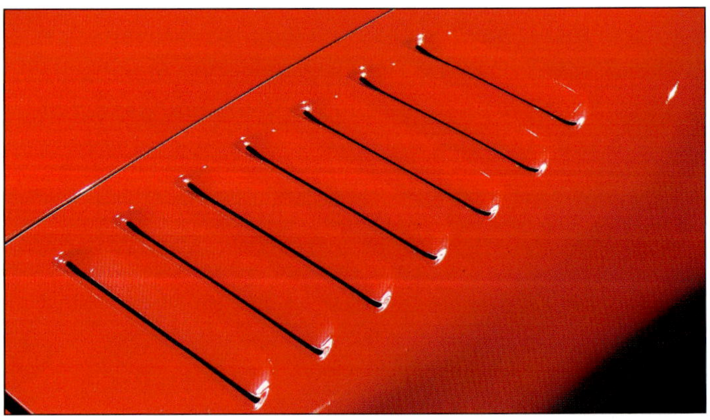

The inspiration of these front fender exhaust louvers comes straight from the factory 935 race cars. These vents are used to exhaust air from underneath the wheel well and fender area to help cool the brakes but also reduce lift and drag.

The Flachbau Turbo looks as shark-like today as it did in the late 1980s. Speaking of eye candy, check out the Turbo Cabriolet just visible behind the red car in Porsche of Santa Clarita's fabulous new showroom.

The boost gauge at the bottom of this factory tachometer is a quick tell that you're looking at a real Turbo and not an aftermarket-converted or naturally aspirated car.

Look how great the boxed rockers, welting, and rubber edges look on these factory Flachbau rocker panels. Cheap fiberglass pieces won't be finished this well.

although some of the most premium tuners and custom shops shaped them of steel. While of course all factory 935 race cars were coupes, it wasn't long before the aftermarket also gave this body treatment to targas and cabriolets.

Porsche is a company that seldom misses a worthwhile or potentially profitable bandwagon. It is believed that the first factory produced 935 Flachbau special was constructed in 1982 by the Special Wishes customer customization department (see

This is another place to quickly spot a factory Flachbau from aftermarket conversions, be they fiberglass or steel. Note the clean and sharp edges and surfaces of the metal stamping. Most cheap aftermarket fenders won't look this crisp.

Chapter 6).

The project began with a 930 Turbo body shell that was stuffed full of the latest parts and a modified 3.3L turbocharged flat six. The body was then treated to a very comprehensive and expensive conversion to a 935 for the street look, including a full flat-nose front-end treatment with pop-up hideaway headlights instead of the Lexan-covered headlights faired into the front spoiler that so many of the real race cars had.

Additionally, the special 935 with all the luxury touches also wore widened box-shaped rocker panels, wide rear fender flares that incorporated massive intake scoops, and a decidedly 935-esque rear wing. It was treated to a gold finish, BBS center-lock alloy wheels, and a metallic red paint called Brilliant Red. Among the bodywork, suspension, engine, and interior modifications, this machine wore more than 500 unique and, in some cases, handmade parts to make into this customer's vision of an ultimate 911.

This Blaupunkt stalk equalizer control is a bit of period campiness that was pretty high tech in the late 1980s and is very much the accessory to have in your Porsche.

This was the factory's first Special Wishes department Flachbau conversion. It very much resembles a 935 for the street, which was the idea. Note the IMSA–style box-flared rear fenders, gold BBS wheels, and the high-riding wing out back. It's one very expensive car that started a trend at Porsche.

Initially, factory-built Flachbau Turbos only came in coupe form, but targa and cabriolet models soon followed. Judging by the red and black interior trim on this car and its red-finished wheel centers, this example made a stop at the Special Wishes department before it was shipped from the factory. (Photo Courtesy Corporate Archives Porsche AG)

Some of the Porsche faithful objected to and griped about the notion of targa- and cabriolet-style Flachbau conversions inspired by the 935 racer because the factory racing teams never raced targas or cabriolets. Why should they produce 935-ified versions of those open cars? It didn't matter a bit to those who wanted an open-air version of that racy style. Porsche built them, they were very expensive, and they were in high demand. (Photo Courtesy Corporate Archives Porsche AG)

The car was featured in countless magazines and newspapers, and it made about as many international auto show appearances. The look really caught on with the 911 community. Porsche ultimately decided to develop the Flachbau look as a factory option (group number 505) for Turbos and naturally aspirated Carreras. The factory design wasn't quite as radical as some of the more daring aftermarket looks, and the factory-built machines featured steel bodywork instead of fiberglass. The option added about $30,000 to the base price of the underlying 911 Turbo.

Ultimately, for production, the look was toned down a bit to encompass less aggressive side scoops and flares as well as a more conventional Turbo whale tail wing. Porsche offered the Flachbau look on a variety of coupe and cabriolet models. It is estimated that 948 of these factory-developed slant-nose 911s were produced.

1988 944 Turbo S Silver Rose

There have been several special edition 924s over time but seemingly fewer special or anniversary edition 944 models. This is a bit of a shame in that the latter is a better performing, more developed evolution of the former.

One very special 944 that blended the best equipment upgrades with a decidedly eye-catching (if not somewhat controversial) paint color and interior trim combination is nicknamed the Silver Rose, of which 1,000 were produced for only the U.S. market. The dusty rose colored paint is itself called Silver Rose Metallic. The Silver Rose S had 16-inch Club Sport wheels, the M030 option code Sports Suspension package, and the 2.5L 944 turbo inline 4-cylinder cranked up to 250 hp backed only with a 5-speed manual transmission.

If you're not completely sure about the dusty rose metallic exterior paint scheme, it's quite elegant and attractive when clean and detailed and sitting in the right soft sunlight. The eye-popping rose- and burgundy-trimmed cabin used a special Tartan plaid red, blue, rose, and yellow seat insert fabric.

If the rose-tinted silver paint on the 944S didn't put you off, there's a chance that the eye-popping interior livery might have. At the end of the day, it worked, as these cars are rare, in demand, and command a premium price over a standard 944 Turbo. (Photo Courtesy Corporate Archives Porsche AG)

The 944 engine was a huge advance over the 924's Audi-based I-4. It had a pure Porsche engine that was much smoother and had much more power potential. It's at its 944 best in the special S model. (Photo Courtesy Corporate Archives Porsche AG)

Besides unique paint and interior schemes, the Silver Rose Turbo S had the best of the 944, including upgraded rolling stock and every spoiler or wing served on any 944. (Photo Courtesy Corporate Archives Porsche AG)

The rest of the car came well equipped and included air conditioning, a Blaupunkt audio system, rear window wiper, headlight washers, cruise control, and a removable electric tilt sunroof and antilock braking system (ABS). It took only 5.7 seconds to go 0–60. The Silver Rose edition option package was designated M758, and many 944 aficionados consider the Silver Rose Edition to be the ultimate expression of a factory-offered street-spec 944. By owning this car, you are one of 1,000 to demonstrate that a rose, by any other name, is a special Porsche 944.

2010 Cayenne S Transsyberia

Not every camper in Camp Porschephile was happy when the company introduced the Cayenne sport utility vehicle (SUV). The faithful cried out that "Porsche is a sports and a racing car company. It shouldn't be making trucks."

Love the idea or not, company CEO Wendelin Wiedeking clarified that the new model wouldn't cannibalize or otherwise marginalize the sports car lines; it would in fact help support and pay for their continuance. The Cayenne, like all Porsche models over time, was introduced in a couple of different model derivations, with S and GTS and other hotter versions to follow. That ultimately meant a special edition: the uniquely developed and trimmed Cayenne S Transsyberia bowed for the 2010 model year only.

When Porsche launched a new or special edition model, it often put on large-scale driving and appearance events, as was the case when the Cayenne Transsyberia edition came about. Given today's political environment, putting on such a grand affair in front of Red Square would not be so easy to accomplish, but it certainly was newsy and decidedly colorful. (Photo Courtesy Corporate Archives Porsche AG)

This was the start or the finish of a road rally event sponsored by Porsche to announce the Cayenne Transsyberia special edition. (Photo Courtesy Corporate Archives Porsche AG)

Among the many great things about this special Cayenne, the Transsyberia could talk the off-road rally talk and walk the walk as well. If you've never done any serious off roading in a Cayenne, you may be surprised at how capable it is in these tough conditions. (Photo Courtesy Corporate Archives Porsche AG)

Worried about your concours Porsche? Well, don't be with a Cayenne Transsyberia because this is what it was made for. (Photo Courtesy Corporate Archives Porsche AG)

An armada of Cayenne Transsyberias is lined up in front of the factory museum in Stuttgart. The cars closest to the cameras are black, and if you look at the far end of this photo, you'll see the other color offered: silver. (Photo Courtesy Corporate Archives Porsche AG)

This special edition's inspiration related to Porsche's previous victories in the Transsyberia rally. It was definitely more than just a trim package, although the branding was unique. The base colors offered were black, silver, or gray with orange or silver accents that extended to the gauge aces and trim on the leather and Alcantara GTS sport seats. All Transsyberia Cayennes had V-8s and came with air suspension and Porsche Active Suspension Management (PASM) with the traction control to bias the front/rear power delivery split 62 percent more strongly to the rear.

Transsyberia Cayennes are rather light on the ground. Only 600 were built worldwide and 119 of them went to North America. Many civilian Cayennes have been cloned into something that looks a lot like the factory-offered Transsyberia special, so if you're shopping one, dig deep into the window sticker or other paperwork to make sure you're looking at the real deal or pay less for one that's not.

2010 Porsche Cayenne GTS Porsche Design Edition 3

By this point in its history, Porsche was deservingly recognizing its own in-house homegrown design studios' capabilities, and in that process, began short production runs of various design editions. If the treatment is good for a 911 or other model, why not the Cayenne SUV, as per the Transsyberia edition previously noted.

Stealthy is this dark gray and black livery on the Cayenne GTS Design Edition. These colors beautifully emphasize this model's curves and lines. While the GTS model can and will be effective off road, it's primarily designed to carve up corners finished in pavement. (Photo Courtesy Corporate Archives Porsche AG)

Look close at the left-side black stripe on the hood to see the words Porsche Design die- or laser-cut out of the material. It's a handsome and conservative way to call attention to this special edition without shouting or tooling up and stamping out yet another metal badge. (Photo Courtesy Corporate Archives Porsche AG)

This next design special was developed more toward street and on-road high performance rather than the Transsyberia's greater rally and off-road targeting. Built upon the decidedly sporty Cayenne GTS model, which already offered more engine performance and sportier suspension tuning than other more average Cayennes, the GTS Porsche Design Edition wrapped the package in a very handsome Lava Gray with black accent stripes paint scheme that spoke understated sport and luxury with just a touch of menace. It also had color-matched 21-inch wheels, blacked-out bi-xenon headlights, and tinted windows. Available to customers at no additional charge was an extended roof-mounted spoiler similar to the one found on the Subaru WRX STI. Don't miss the Porsche Design Edition 3 graphics on the doors.

The theme continues inside with black leather seating trimmed with Porsche logos on the headrests, Alcantara inserts, and red stitching. The dashboard also has the red stitching in addition to some carbon-fiber accents, a numbered production plaque, and another Design Edition logo on the tachometer face. A standard 14-speaker Bose surround-sound system delivers your favorite tunes. Power comes from the naturally aspirated and highly responsive 405-hp, 4.8L V-8 engine that powers the standard Cayenne GTS, which is backed by Porsche's 6-speed Tiptronic S automatic transmission. A sport exhaust gives the DE3 a bit more bark, all rated by Porsche to hit 60 mph in 6.1 seconds. This one turned out to be quite the rare bird with just 100 examples coming to the U.S. It listed at $89,900, although that's largely fully equipped, as few options were offered or necessary.

2012 Brumos B59 Edition Carrera

This handsome 991-generation Carrera Coupe project was a joint venture between Porsche in Germany, Porsche Cars North America, the world famous Brumos Porsche racing teams, and the Brumos Porsche dealership.

Besides recognizing Brumos's long standing as a significant Porsche dealership and race entrant, it further and more directly commemorated the incomparable Hurley Haywood's five overall wins at the Daytona 24 Hours endurance race in Florida. This extremely limited special edition wears traditional Brumos team colors and Haywood's signature racing number 59. All were finished in Carrera White with the Brumos Red/Blue stripe design for the front hood and lower deck. The Brumos B59 was only offered in coupe form in 408-hp GTS spec and trim. The interior is full leather black with Alcantara accents and various white trim bits inside. The exterior mirrors are also painted black. The 19-inch Sport Classic Fuchs-style alloy wheels add

Much like the famous Gulf Blue and Orange or the Martini racing stripes, the Brumos Porsche racing livery is timeless and immediately recognizable. Besides the direct involvement from Brumos Racing stalwart Hurley Haywood in the design and development of this Brumos special edition, you also get one beautiful and fabulously equipped 911. (Photo Courtesy Kirk Gerbracht)

Among the many outstanding design features on the Brumos Racing edition Carrera are the use of a modern Fuchs-style wheel adapted to the larger wheel diameters and the modern ultra low-profile tires that came along since the early days of 15-inch Fuchs wheels. It's a perfect fit on these later 911s and very appropriate here. (Photo Courtesy Kirk Gerbracht)

a properly retro touch. The door sills are crafted of stainless steel and feature Haywood's engraved signature. Each car is numbered and badged accordingly. There were few options to include the Sport Chrono Package Plus: a shorter throw Sport Shifter, upgraded Sport Suspension tuning, a Bose Surround Sound system, XM radio, and heated front seats.

The manufacturer's suggested retail price (MSRP) for the B59 when new was $133,540, and only five were produced.

Late-Model Speedsters

Porsche's trim 356 Speedster of 1955 to 1958 is as seminal to Porsche's history as is nearly any other model. The original speedster was developed and produced at the behest of America's primary Porsche importer Max Hoffman, who at the time rightly felt there was demand for a lighter weight, somewhat stripped-down 356 that could be sold for around $3,000 and had potential in the Sports Car Club of America's (SCCA) production-based racing classes. Thus, the 356 Speedster was born in late 1954. Porsche got the cues just right on this one: a racier cut-down windshield, no roll-up windows, a removable folding convertible top, and a dearth of weight- and cost-adding features best left to the 356 Continental and other upmarket variants.

Hoffman was correct. Speedster demand lit up like a candle, and every sports car–type driver wanted one. James Dean had and raced one with success, as did Steve McQueen. Over its four-year production run, the speedster was offered with a variety of 1,600-cc overhead valve flat-four engines. In 1957, the speedster was available with the much more powerful, high revving Ernst Fuhrmann–developed Carrera double-overhead-camshaft engine that was virtually identical to what powered the purely racing focused 550 and 718 Spyder models. The Carrera-powered speedster is the most highly sought after and most expensive 356 Speedster today. It was replaced for 1959 by a tweener model called the Convertible D, which was more completely trimmed and outfitted than the stripped-down speedster with larger seats, a taller windshield, roll-up windows, and a more substantial top, but it was not as heavy or luxurious as the cabriolet model.

The quintessential 356 Speedster is Steve McQueen's 1958 Speedster, which was the first new car he ever purchased and the car in which he won his first SCCA race at Santa Barbara in 1959. His son Chad is at the wheel sporting a smile and flashing a victory sign. (Photo Courtesy Chad McQueen)

The original 356 Speedster was such a charmer and a success, it's little wonder that Porsche sought to recapture the magic with this concept design study, named the Speedster Studie, that spawned several generations of new-age 911 Speedsters. The smiling young man at the helm of this tightly canopied concept Porsche is notable F1 and sports car racing champion Jochen Maas.

Another look at the Speedster Studie clarifies the look and intent of this machine. It shows how much larger a later 911 is than a 356 as well as the different proportions. (Photo Courtesy Corporate Archives Porsche AG)

1989 Carrera 3.2 Speedster

A huge portion of Porsche legend, lore, and history rides upon the 356 Speedster's rounded shoulders. Model ranges of the post-1959 356B and 356C went speedster-less, and it wasn't until 1988/1989 that Porsche went back to the speedster well for a very special edition version of the then-current G-series Carrera 3.2 model, which was soon replaced by the 964-generation 911.

For 1989, there was a new speedster in town called the Carrera 3.2 Speedster, which wasn't completely true to the original model in that it had a built-in top, roll-up windows, and the wider fender flares borrowed from the 930 Turbo model. However, the important elements were in place: a lower height front windscreen, a bit of weight savings here and there, plus a handsome tonneau cover that hid the lighter weight, single-layer cloth top. The fold-down rear jump seats were jettisoned in the name of reduced weight and the interest in returning to a proper two-seat roadster configuration. Buyer demand was substantial, but many buyers asked for their cars with the Carrera's standard narrower bodywork, so that was ultimately added to the order sheet. All power output ratings and specifications remained standard Carrera 3.2 fare.

A total of 2,104 Carrera 3.2 Speedsters (option M503) were produced between January and July 1989. A total of 823

The 1989 Carrera 3.2 Speedster was the first among the new generation of 911-based Speedsters and credibly pulls off the look, especially in red with the cut-down windshield and body-colored rear tonneau cover. Factory Speedsters of this era had the fender flares and other trim of the Turbo-Look model. (Photo Courtesy Corporate Archives Porsche AG)

The removable soft top on 356 Speedsters was low to meet up with its reduced-height windshield to give the car a bit of a rakish chopped-top look. It was not different when the Speedster model and top was reborn as a 911 in the late 1980s. (Photo Courtesy Corporate Archives Porsche AG)

went to the U.S., and only 139 examples were produced in right-hand-drive format. Of the total, only 171 narrow-body versions were produced with the Turbo-Look being more popular.

1993 964 Speedster

The Carrera 3.2 Speedster, a low volume special edition, was a big halo model for the brand and an instant sell out. Porsche wisely calculated there was more water in the late-model speedster and reprised it for the 964-generation 911. Launched in 1992 as a 1993 model, the 964 Porsche Speedster was based on the Carrera 2 Cabriolet and available either in standard or lightweight trim called Club Sport. Unlike its predecessor, the 911 Speedster, the 964 Speedster was initially not available with the Turbo-Look wide bodystyle.

The 964 Speedster was intended to be a more focused driver's car and served as a hybrid between a 964 Carrera 2 Cabriolet and the 964 RS, which was not sold in the U.S. While it featured a softer suspension setup than the 964 RS, the 964 Speedster offered almost none of the comforts of a normal 964 Carrera 2 Cabriolet, though power windows were standard and air conditioning and a stereo were options. The manually folding pram-like top was a basic contraption that required practice to erect quickly. Porsche referred to it as strictly an emergency soft top for inclement weather. The hard composite tonneau cover featured a handsome double-hump design that emphasized the car's pure two-seater notion. The 964 Speedster wasn't offered in all-wheel-drive Carrera form, nor as a Turbo. The interior trim was much the same as standard 924s, save for the speedster model's lighter weight, shell-shaped bucket seats. Toward the end of the production run, 20 special examples were finished at Porsche Exclusiv's Werk 1 workshop with the optional Turbo-Look wide bodies. Porsche was targeting to build up to 3,000 964 Speedsters, but in the end, only 936 were produced during the two-year production run,

Body-colored wheels and trim on this 964 Speedy evoke a certain Mercedes AMG look that was very popular in the early 1990s. Who needs the top? (Photo Courtesy Corporate Archives Porsche AG)

The 964-era Speedster is without the wide Turbo-Look body, which some feel was more appropriate to the original 356 Speedster look. This one's been modernized firmly into the 1990s with its body-colored wheels and trim. The double-hump tonneau cover also lends a certain 550/718 Spyder vibe. (Photo Courtesy Corporate Archives Porsche AG)

which makes them more rare than the Carrera 3.2 Speedster by half and expensive by more.

1995/1998 993 Speedster

According to the highly authoritative speedsters.com, "Porsche never officially released a 993 Speedster model. However, two were known to have been built by the factory [that were] based on the cabriolet but with a low raked windscreen, lowered hood [folding top], humped rear end [tonneau cover], and a redesigned interior.

The first was a dark green Tiptronic S Speedster with 17-inch wheels for 911 designer Butzi Porsche in 1995 on the occasion of his 60th birthday. The second, in 1998, was in silver with manual transmission and 18-inch wheels for the American TV star and car collector Jerry Seinfeld."

The 997-edition Speedster seemed to coalesce the whole package and combined the chopped-top look with a modern version of the classic Fuchs 5-spoke wheels, double-humped rear tonneau cover, and a limited run of 356 units. It looks just right in Mexico Blue. (Photo Courtesy Corporate Archives Porsche AG)

This look at the top-down 997 Speedster emphasizes its great stance, husky rolling stock, beefy brakes, and how low the rear tonneau cover sits. It's certainly an amalgam of 356 and 911 Carrera themes, but a perfectly proportioned and beautiful one it is. (Photo Courtesy Corporate Archives Porsche AG)

It's easy to spot a special car built for Ferry Porsche as the late family doyen favored green cars, and many of his personal rides were variations of this hue. The 993 adapted nicely to the speedster style, this time without the more aggressive Carrera S model rolling stock instead relying on standard Carrera alloys. It somehow looks a bit more classic because of it. (Photo Courtesy Corporate Archives Porsche AG)

The site also noted that several 993 Speedsters have been created on a bespoke basis by several car owners and independent shops using 964 Speedster parts.

2010 997 Speedster

After perhaps missing an opportunity in not coming to market with a factory-offered speedster model from 1995 to 2009, Porsche redeveloped the concept for the water-cooled 997-generation Carrera. It employed the same recipe as previous modern-generation speedsters with a shorter and more steeply raked windshield and an overall racy stance with the convertible top smoothed and neatly integrated into the overall shape. The top is still of lighter weight and folded manually but hid nicely beneath the handsome double-hump composite tonneau cover.

All 997 Speedsters were based on the rear-drive-only 408-hp GTS-spec Carrera and featured Porsche's outstanding new double-clutch PDK gearbox, a limited-slip differential, sports exhaust system, carbon ceramic brakes, and active suspension management. Color choices were limited to Pure Blue or Carrera White. In recognition of the original speedster's 356 model designation, just 356 997-generation speedsters were produced worldwide.

This profile shot of the late Dr. Porsche's forest green metallic 993 Speedster demonstrates how the side windows needed to be shorter to mesh with the lower windshield header and the folding convertible top. (Photo Courtesy Corporate Archives Porsche AG)

2020 991 Speedster

Much like the 1989 Carrera Speedster was deployed to highlight and run out the last of the G-series 911s, the 991-generation Speedster was created to wrap up the 991-series production. Its design concept made its debut in 2018, which marked Porsche's 70th year as a carmaker. The speedster was the final variant of the 991-generation car and received the very latest and greatest of hardware and equipment offered on this era of Carrera.

It is common for big manufacturers to invest heavily into auto show reveal presentations. A new Porsche is always news. (Photo Courtesy Porsche Cars North America)

It is not uncommon for the folks who stage these big reveals to employ beautiful women to roll back the proverbial silk cover. Some may consider this out of fashion today, but with Porsche, it's always classy and in the best of taste. (Photo Courtesy Porsche Cars North America)

Black silk is removed, and the lights are on high as the current Porsche CEO Oliver Blume introduces the world media to the newest 991-generation Speedster. The number 48 on the side honors Porsche's official birth year. (Photo Courtesy Porsche Cars North America)

Even though the model platform generation had changed, the formula was much the same: a double-hump tonneau cover at the rear, cut-down windshield, and a Speedster badge on the engine cover. (Photo Courtesy of Porsche Cars North America)

With just 1,948 units produced, the number honored the first year Porsche began production. As of this writing, no current 992-generation Speedster has been shown or announced.

The One-off Peter Schutz Speedster/Coupe/Cabriolet

The late Peter Werner Schutz (April 20, 1930–October 29, 2017) was the president and CEO of Porsche between 1981 and 1987 and is recognized as the man who saved the 911. By the late 1970s, it was common knowledge that the old-school, air-cooled, rear-engine 911 would soon (by 1981) be retired and replaced by various water-cooled, front-engine platforms used in the 924 and 928.

Herr Schutz demonstrated his objection to the plan in a most clever and demonstrative way. While he was in the office of Engineering Chief Dr. Helmuth Bott, he noticed a chart that showed the evolution of the 924, 928, and 911 on the wall. The line for the 911 stopped at the end of 1981. Schutz picked up a marker, extended the 911's line off the end of the chart onto the wall, and instructed Bott to make it happen. And happen it did. The 911 SC, which was supposed to be the end of the line for Porsche's defining sports car model, so we received the improved Carrera 3.2 era, then the 964 and 993, and you know the rest from there. It is still current today.

Former Porsche CEO Peter Schutz's Carrera looked much like any other 911 Coupe if it wasn't for the visible but subtle body cutlines around its windscreen and the rear area of the roof. This special one-off also wears the wide fender flares and wider rolling stock of the Turbo-Look option, yet sans the Turbo whale tail wing aft. (Photo Courtesy Bill Warner)

A little unlatching and some snapping and the closed coupe becomes a tonneau-covered cabriolet. (Photo Courtesy Bill Warner)

A different racing-inspired windscreen and another hard tonneau cover, and the coupe that became a cabriolet becomes a speedster. Talk about some clever bodywork. (Photo Courtesy Bill Warner)

This decisive action made Schutz a bit of a folk hero around the halls in Stuttgart, particularly with groups of engineers who worked so hard to improve the 911 and felt it had a future beyond the last 91 SC. How right they were.

It was not at all uncommon for the company to build special one-offs as either company cars or out-and-out gifts to Porsche family members and senior executives. Pending his retirement to Florida, Herr Schutz was either offered, granted, or commissioned a very special 911 for his personal use. It is utterly unique in terms of Porsche bodystyles in that depending upon which roof, top, and windshield configuration was installed, it could serve as a closed coupe, cabriolet, or speedster. The unique Guards Red machine appears to have begun life as a Carrera 3.2 Cabriolet or a closed coupe when some clever and precise redesign work was done to the upper body and roof structure.

In fully closed coupe form, other than visible body cutlines, it looks for all the world like a standard 911 Coupe. This entire structure could be unhitched and removed. Much of the cabin area, including the front passenger seat and the rear area +2 jump seats, could be covered with a black cloth snap-on tonneau cover to make the car into a cabriolet. Further, the stock-height windshield could be removed and replaced with a shorter cut-down windshield like the original 356 Speedster and the front passenger seat and rear jump seat area covered with a body-color matching hard tonneau cover to make the car a close coupled single seater with a headrest bubble fared into the rear deck area of the hard tonneau.

There is no indication that this versatile, unusual, and attractive body configuration was designed or ever considered for production. At this point, it remains Peter Schutz's highly unique one-off.

1993/1994 964 RS America Coupe

For sundry reasons, Porsche didn't bring its 964-generation Carrera RS model to the United States market. Some felt its aggressive suspension tuning wouldn't appeal to North American drivers' tastes. Others were concerned that its lack of options and creature comforts would limit its marketability. The company still wanted a special edition 964 for its largest world market, which ultimately proved to be an amalgam of the Carrera RS, the 964 Turbo, and the standard 964 Carrera. It was appropriately called the 964 RS America and only produced in closed coupe form wearing a Turbo-esque rear whale tail wing.

The cabin was also stripped of its rear folding jump seats and leather trim and instead opted for lighter weight fabrics. There was also no power steering, cruise control, powered side mirrors, air conditioning, or sunroof. But the RS America got the goods when it came to suspension prowess upgrades.

North American RS buyers got something that European and other world market buyers did not: the huge Turbo whale tail aft. Of course, those other markets got a racier suspension and more power too. (Photo Courtesy Corporate Archives Porsche AG)

The RS America very much resembled what a 964-gen Turbo-Look would be if Porsche produced one. In this case, less was less. Less weight and otherwise great specs meant less weight, which translated to less money and more performance. A sharp-edged killer sports car on the street was also an ideal weekend track toy. (Photo Courtesy Corporate Archives Porsche AG)

The standard 964 cup-style wheels gave way to larger and wider 17-inch alloys and wider low-profile tires. The standard 964-spec engine, 5-speed manual gearbox, and brakes were employed and deemed good enough.

The weight savings cut about 77 pounds out of the RS America's curb weight compared to a standard Carrera 2 Coupe. The goal here of course was to focus the RS America as a more committed driver's car without making it too racy, which proved to be a success. Other options were few: air conditioning, a sunroof, audio system, and locking differential, although many RS Americas came stripped of any of those weight- or cost-adding add-ons. Standard color choices included red, black, and white with Midnight Blue and Polar Silver (both metallic) as optional.

The 3.6L, twin-plug flat six was rated at 250 hp, which was more than enough to push the modestly lightened RS America from 0–60 in 5.5 seconds and to a 164-mph top speed. Many of them ended up equipped with roll bars and other racy modifications for countless track-day laps. The RS America could also be seen as somewhat of a runout model for the 964-generation 911 as the new and substantially revised and updated 993-generation Carrera was cued up for 1995.

Something else the RS America accomplished perhaps without really trying was "less" for a change. It was indeed less as the RS America was the least costly 911 in the lineup in 1993. By adding lightness and simplicity, it effectively added less cost. Less weight, better performance, and lower cost was a rare quinella to be sure. Just 701 were produced.

2010 Carrera Sport Classic

As the 911 and associated Carrera models have evolved, the car has gotten larger, heavier, more sophisticated, and more luxurious. Much of this is understood but has been criticized by the most ardent Porschephiles. The Porsche factory isn't immune to such criticism or feelings and took this opportunity to create a limited-run special edition model that, without being anachronistic, reinterprets many classic or old-school 911 themes into modern form.

The Sport Classic's double-domed roof panel was a bespoke piece for this special edition only, as is the modern spin on the Carrera RS inspired ducktail rear spoiler. (Photo Courtesy Corporate Archives Porsche AG)

Company leadership asked its Porsche Exclusiv division to create just such the thing. It's called the 911 Sport Classic, and the car made its world debut at the Frankfurt Motor Show in 2009 as a 2010 model. Just 250 were built, and they were all sunroof-less, rear-drive-only 991-series coupes. Unfortunately, they were not homologated for sale in the United States. The better news is that it combines a thoughtful and highly legitimate combination of meaningful performance upgrades and freshened retro design touches.

This very special, limited edition lives up to its name: Sport Classic. It's very sporty and leans heavily on modern interpretations of several classic themes and cues. It's a pity that North American enthusiasts couldn't buy them. (Photo Courtesy Corporate Archives Porsche AG)

For such a low volume production model, Porsche went to great lengths, effort, and expense to create unique coachwork that spoke to the terms "sport" and "classic." The roof panel is a special piece (just for this car) with a unique double-domed design. Some might liken it to a variation on Zagato's seminal double-bubble styling touch, but Porsche's domes are wider and flatter than seen on most Zagato models, which nixes any meaningful comparison. It also mitigates any risk of an innocent onlooker calling it a double-bubble design. They are much more clearly raised-dome sections than bubbles.

All Sport Classics wear the Carrera S's wider rear bodywork and fender flares with an increased track of 44 mm (1.73 inches). The lower rear fascia is also a unique piece built to accommodate dual exhaust pipes that were relocated from the center of the fascia just below the license plate, which was common on several Carrera and GT models, to slightly more outboard positions just below the inward dimension of the taillights. Another nostalgic element clearly aimed to recall the iconic Carrera RS 2.7 and 3.0 is a modernized version of the ducktail Bürzel rear wing. The final retro-futuristic-inspired touch was a full set of Fuchs 5-spoke-style alloy 19-inch wheels with black centers and polished rims. To further emphasize the Sport notion of this limited edition 991, the 911 Sport Classic was offered only with the 6-speed manual transmission and PCCB Porsche ceramic composite brakes. The PASM sport suspension calibrations lower the car about 3/4 of an inch over standard Carrera models.

The cabin was also enhanced on many levels. The adaptive sport seats featured a special woven leather pattern for the center cushions, and the dashboard was finished in Espresso Nature leather. Only one exterior color was offered, appropriately named Sport Classic Gray, that featured slightly darker gray contrast stripes across the front hood, roof, and rear deck. It was understated, classy, and very elegant.

The naturally aspirated 3.8L flat six had 402 hp with an estimated 0–60 time of 4.6 seconds and a top speed around 188 mph. It was all yours if you were one of the 250 lucky owners with a factory-suggested retail price of 169,900 at the time (about $180,000 today). All 911 Sport Classics sold out immediately upon announcement and remain highly sought after among 911 aficionados today.

2016 911R

After a long and successful succession of modern-era Speedsters, Spyders, Turbos, RSs, and GTs (2 and 3), Porsche had learned the value of mining its catalog of greatest hits to seek inspiration for new, special edition models to further burnish the brand and create high profit, limited production editions.

Porsche 911Racing began, from a factory standpoint, with the 1967 911R. It weighed less than a standard 911, handled more sharply, and had considerably more power. Old-school analog in every way, it only had a manual transmission and was devoid of needless weight- and cost-adding extras.

It was a great formula in 1967 and seemed like a valid one nearly 50 years later, so Porsche brewed up a new 911R, which was unleashed on the world at the 2016 Geneva Motor Show. Porsche had taken some guff in that a previous-generation GT3 was only offered with the positively outstanding but still largely automated PDK dual-clutch transmission. The message for a new 911R was as clear as it was in 1967: less weight, more power, fewer frills, and a manual transmission only.

Porsche described it as such, "Its 500 hp, 911R 4.0L naturally aspirated flat engine and 6-speed manual sports transmission places the 911R firmly in the tradition of its historic role model: a road-homologated racing car from 1967. Produced as part of a limited production series, the 911R (R for racing) performed in rallies, the Targa Florio, and in world-record runs.

As Tim the Toolman Taylor always said in the **Home Improvement** *TV show, "RRRR." In Porschespeak, this moniker has been employed twice: in 1967 and again in 2016. (Photo Courtesy Corporate Archives Porsche AG)*

Poised like a white tiger ready to strike, the nouveau 911R sits low on its enhanced suspension and center-lock rolling stock. Several colors were offered, but like the original 1967 model, most were white with a choice of red or green stripes. (Photo Courtesy Corporate Archives Porsche AG)

There was no Turbo-like wing for the new-age 911R, as the goal was less weight and aero drag. The engine screen was reconfigured, and the Carrera S's standard power deployable wing rose to the occasion when the speed and conditions warranted a bit more downforce. (Photo Courtesy Corporate Archives Porsche AG)

Here's a look at the 911R's green stripe variant. It's quite the contrast from the RubyStone Red 964 RS sitting behind it. (Photo Courtesy Corporate Archives Porsche AG)

"Like its legendary predecessor, the new 911R relies on systematic lightweight construction, maximum performance, and an unfiltered driving experience. This special limited edition model of 991 has an overall weight of 1,370 kg and is currently the lightest version of the 911. With the high-revving 6-cylinder naturally aspirated engine and manual sports transmission, Porsche is once again displaying its commitment to especially emotional high-performance sports cars. Developed in the motorsport workshop, the 911R extends the spectrum of high-performance naturally aspirated engines alongside the motor racing models 911 GT3 and 911 GT3 RS."

Unlike certain special high-performance and racing Porsches, this race car for the road was homologated for sale in most of Porsche's world markets, including North America. The new 911R was in fact street legal, yet the expectation was that serious owner/drivers would have theirs out on a time-trial track-day event at every opportunity. This very special modern R was optimized and upgraded at nearly every point over and above the standard Carrera and Carrera S model. In fact, from a purpose and specifications standpoint, it was really a GT3 without the pronounced rear wings and PDK transmission.

Porsche further described the engine and its performance potential: "At work in the rear of the 911R is the 6-cylinder flat engine with a displacement of 4 liters, familiar from the 911 GT3 RS. The racing engine delivers 500 hp at 8,500 rpm and generates 460 Nm [338 ft-lbs] torque at 6,250 rpm. From a standing start, the rear-engine car breaks through the 100 km/h [62 mph] barrier in 3.8 seconds. In keeping with the purist character of the vehicle, the 911 with its lightweight design is available exclusively with a 6-speed sports transmission. Short gearshift travel underlines the active driving experience. The forward thrust of the 911R continues to a speed of 323 km/h [200 mph]."

Naturally, the suspension and brakes were upgraded to match the go. According to Porsche, "The specially tuned

Notice the three pedals in the driver's footbox. Learn to use them if you wish to attempt to master the 911R's considerable performance portfolio. The houndstooth seat inserts are a lovely retro touch. (Photo Courtesy Corporate Archives Porsche AG)

standard rear-axle steering guarantees especially direct turn-in characteristics and precise handling while maintaining high stability. The mechanical rear differential lock builds up maximum traction. Ensuring the greatest possible deceleration is the Porsche ceramic composite brake (PCCB) as a standard feature. It measures a generous 410 mm on the front axle and 390 mm on the rear. Ultra high-performance tires of 245 mm at the front and 305 mm at the rear are responsible for contact to the road. They are mounted on forged 20-inch lightweight wheels with central lock in matte aluminum.

"Motorsport development has specially adapted the control systems of the Porsche stability management (PSM) for the 911R. A double-declutch function activated by pressing a button for perfect gearshifts when changing down is also part of the repertoire of the 911R as is the optional single-mass flywheel. The result is a significant improvement in spontaneity

The 911R has lightweight, carbon fiber–shelled sport seats that offer superb support and comfort, along with access ports should you wish to fit roll bar–mounted racing harnesses. The chocolate leather trim is an elegant complement to the otherwise businesslike black cabin. (Photo Courtesy Corporate Archives Porsche AG)

Know your place—in the 911R production run, that is. (Photo Courtesy Corporate Archives Porsche AG)

and high-revving dynamics of the engine. For unrestricted practicality in everyday use, and to protect the carbon composite front spoiler, a lift system can also be ordered. It raises ground clearance of the front axle by approximately 30 mm at the touch of a button."

Even the bodywork went under the weight-saving knife: the front hood and fenders are made of carbon fiber, and the roof is made of magnesium, which substantially reduces the center of gravity. The rear windscreen and rear side windows are lightweight plastic. Additional dietary factors are the reduced insulation in the interior and the omission of a rear bench seat. The seat shells are lightweight carbon fiber, and more weight was saved here and there around the car in places most people wouldn't notice or care about. This was a serious, focused effort to optimize the 911R in every possible category.

Technically, the 911R was offered in two colors, white and silver, with accent stripes in a choice of red or green. However, a paint-to-sample option was also available at considerable extra cost to allow the discerning 911R buyer to somewhat tailor the machine to color-palette taste. We've seen them in black, Lava Orange, and dark metallic blue, and the effect is just as stirring either way.

What's the 911R like to drive?

"It's a car just for a fun day," according to an article in *Car and Driver* magazine. "It's about how good you feel in the car and not how fast you can go."

The 911R is neither buttoned up nor a particularly responsible car. It's not a long-distance tourer, as many versions of the 911 became. It's loud. It vibrates in a way that a standard-issue 911 would never be allowed to do. It comes only with a manual gearbox. It is as close to a purist's 911 as possible this deep into the regulated 21st century and it is closer to Program Director Andreas Preuninger's heart than anything else he has worked on in his 15 years on the job.

From the outset, Porsche was upfront about the fact the new 911R was to be a decidedly limited production model and needed to develop a regimen for sales and distribution, as it was immediately and abundantly clear that demand would far exceed the supply of 991 cars to be produced. The number was chosen in recognition of the car's underlying platform architecture: the Type 991. The cars were first, and thus only, offered to select, loyal, and financially capable buyers for a list price of $185,950. All were spoken for upon the announcement and customer notification.

Car and Driver's Eric Tingwell has a spot-on summary of the price and purchase dynamics.

"You can't have a 911R, not even if you can muster the $185,950 base price," he said. "This purist's 911 is not a new model line. It is a very special edition. It's constructed of steel, carbon fiber, and magnesium, among other less compelling ingredients. Once those elements are combined, the result becomes unobtanium. A grand total of 991 examples of the R were built; a nod to the current 911's generation code.

"Preuninger acknowledged the company could sell at least a few multiples of that number. If the price and limited production were not significant enough barriers to purchasing one, consider that, at least in the United States, the 300 American 918 Spyder owners were given the right of first refusal. Porsche won't say how many 918 owners bought 911Rs. The company will say only that some of the U.S. allotment of Rs were purchased by non-918 owners. This turns the 911R into an investment property as much as an automobile in which to pursue the joy of driving. A 911 with the 500-hp 4.0L naturally aspirated flat six from the GT3 RS track car bolted into its ass, sending all that power through something not available in the GT3s, a 6-speed manual gearbox? Now we're talking."

Needless to say, it wasn't long before this very select market began speculating them. Several new cars with no miles on them traded hands upon delivery for at least a million dollars. As of this writing, the market has settled a bit, and they rarely trade hands for something less than $300,000 to 500,000. A Porsche special edition? Indeed!

2004–2005 Boxster 550 Spyder

From the beginning, this car was the Boxster's mission to riff on, take advantage of, and recall the sporty, racy, open air, lightweight driving appeal of the original 550 Spyders of the 1950s. On the whole, it has accomplished that with varying degrees of success.

The original Spyder was a flyweight, high-revving race car, and given modern requirements for safety, drivability, comfort, and technology. It's no easy task to recreate the feeling of a street-legal retro sports car. Near the end of the original 986 generation of Boxster, Porsche whipped up an attractive special edition model that somewhat deepened the connection between the mid-2000s and the 1950s, so much so that this limited edition model was branded after its namesake. As if by magic, it was perfectly timed to commemorate the 50th anniversary of that 1950s racing classic.

Some say the Boxster has attempted to capture some of the 550 and 718 Spyder's panache its entire 25-year career. It was particularly successful in this first Spyder-edition Boxster. The size, proportions, general Porscheness, and, in this case, color scheme of the 550 Boxster Spyder managed the job credibly in a car that looked much the part and is a joy to drive. (Photo Courtesy Corporate Archives Porsche AG)

42

This 550 Spyder-edition Boxster was based on the step-up 3.2L Boxster S model, rated at 258 hp, which was a big advance on the 2.7L base Boxster powerplant. The special Spyder got a further bump to 264 thanks to a bit of engine tuning and a zoomier sport exhaust, which made it the most powerful 986-gen Boxster produced.

To paraphrase an old saying about Ford Model T color choices, you could have your Boxster 550 Spyder in any color you wish, so long as it was GT Silver, a color shared with the exotic 10-cylinder Carrera GT. The Boxster S wheel spokes were treated to a slightly smokier shade of metallic gray. Two interior color themes were offered: Dark Gray or Cocoa Brown. The special sport seats earned painted composite rear back panels, the ride height was lowered just a bit, Litronic headlights were included as was a sportier short-throw shifter. The dual exhaust system received a unique tailpipe finish, and various parts of the exterior and cabin were splashed with a brushed aluminum finish.

The 550 Spyder design package made the very most of the original-generation Boxster look and platform: a few splashes of aluminum bits here and there, the dark gray centers on the S wheels, and a top color that works with the silver exterior and red/burgundy cabin. (Photo Courtesy Corporate Archives Porsche AG)

Shiny rollover hoops add a racy touch, and the unique two-story exhaust tip adds heft. Later Boxster Spyders became faster and more sophisticated, but the appeal of this package is undeniable. (Photo Courtesy Corporate Archives Porsche AG)

It was a compelling package that faithfully honored some of the ethos and design touches of the original 550 Spyder. Some consider it the ultimate 986-generation Boxster as the first to be called Spyder. Even today, in the shadow of further advancing technology, infotainment, and performance, it's a handsome machine that's a joy to drive. In keeping with the original Spyder first breaking cover in 1953, just 1,953 of these special edition Boxsters were produced.

2016 Boxster Spyder (981)

The previously referenced 986-series Boxster 550 Spyder was well conceived and well received. Yet enthusiast buyers wanted something even more 550 Spyder–like. Never one to miss a golden opportunity to please its customer base and sell a few more cars, Porsche rethought the formula around the updated 981-generation Boxster platform. In this case, it recognized and honored the 718 Spyder, itself an extension and higher performing advance of the original 550 models.

The new Boxster Spyder was unveiled at the New York Auto Show in 2015 and appeared to offer more of what buyers wanted (performance) and less of what they didn't (weight, a fully automated power top, too many accessories, or an automatic transmission). The 718-inspired new-generation Spyder received a substantive remodel. It's most easily recognizable by the double-hump head rest fairing design of the new rear

This is a genuine 718 Spyder, and it's clear where later Boxster Spyders got the humped deck idea. It's a great look then, and it still is.

decklid. While it's true that the original 718 Spyder of the early 1960s only had one head rest fairing, the new car had two, but the effect was convincing and nobody denied the new car's extra hump just because the old car only had one for the driver since it was primarily a race car.

The 981-series Spyder's other immediate visual tell is a much revised and simplified convertible top. No longer a one-touch, power retracting, and automatically self-covering piece, the new top raises and lowers by hand with minimal power assist. Plus, the fabric was thinner and lighter than the standard lined Boxster tops. Some called it vestigial, and others were satisfied that it was simpler and lighter. The top also featured fins or buttresses that visually extended the rear roofline farther back on the deck.

Naturally, the powertrain, suspension, and braking systems all went on a high protein regimen. The new Spyder earned, for the first time in a Boxster, a genuine 911-spec engine with 3.8L and 375 hp. This engine was also shared with the Cayman GT4 performance coupe. One transmission choice was offered or necessary, which was an old-school clutch and stick 6-speed manual transaxle. No Tiptronic automatic or PDK dual clutch was welcome.

The ride height dropped by 20 mm. The springs, bushings, and anti-roll bars were all retuned for a firmer, sportier, flatter-handling persona at the cost of only minimal ride quality. This was the most powerful and quickest Boxster produced to date and capable of 4.5-second 0–60 times.

The 718 Spyder had one hump on the deck, and the new Boxster Spyder had two. In as much as the modern car has two seats, it would have looked odd with just one bubble, so Porsche did an admirable job to make the look work for today. (Photo Courtesy Porsche Cars North America)

It took more than a good bit of mechanical design engineering to get the Spyder's top to disappear so effectively and reduce its weight and complexity. (Photo Courtesy Porsche Cars North America)

It was another great bit of design work to add some fabric buttresses that touch down a bit farther along the back deck, which adds a bit of visual length to the roofline to make the top look less like a football helmet left on top of the car. (Photo Courtesy Porsche Cars North America)

The front and rear fascias are shared with the aforementioned Cayman GT4 Coupe. Many photos of this model tend to show white cars, yet Agate Grey Metallic, Racing Yellow, Carrera White Metallic, Jet Black Metallic, Lime Gold Metallic, Dark Blue Metallic, Carmine Red Metallic, Mahogany Metallic, Rhodium Silver Metallic, Guards Red, Black, GT Silver Metallic, and Sapphire Blue Metallic were other paint choices.

Inside the cabin were lighter weight sport seats and a new and sportier 360-mm-diameter steering wheel rim. There were a smattering of Spyder identifiers here and there, inside and out. To further drive home the message of reduced weight, an audio system and air conditioner weren't included as standard equipment yet remained options.

The car's base MSRP in North America was $83,095, and they sold out upon announcement. Just 2,400 were built for worldwide markets, and only 850 were destined for North America. Until that point, the fastest and best performing Boxster became the most expensive, rarest, and is among the most highly sought after today.

2020–2021 718 Spyder and Cayman GT4

As if to underscore and fully remind everyone of the unimpeachable platform and hardware connection between the open-roofed Boxster and the Cayman Coupe, when Porsche released information about high-performance special edition variants of each, it did so in the same official press release entitled "Pure Fun: The 2020 Porsche 718 Cayman GT4 and 718 Spyder."

Porsche enjoyed considerable success with the two previous-generation Boxster Spyders, so it was only natural to offer another round for the newest and most developed 718 generation of Boxster and Cayman. Porsche took a somewhat calculated risk in developing the new 718-platformed cars based around a new, horizontally-opposed water-cooled

Why do Porsche Spyders always look so great in silver? Because they did in the 1950s. The new 718 Boxster wears the Spyder ethos with perfection. (Photo Courtesy Porsche Cars North America)

The Boxster Spyder and Cayman GT4 are cousins beneath the skin, but it's not fair to call them the same car. One is a closed coupe, and the other is an open-topped roadster, but both pack big power and carve out a meaningful spot in the Porsche lineup. (Photo Courtesy Porsche Cars North America)

Some like that the Boxster's dual exhaust meets in the middle of the lower rear fascia. Others prefer a more outboard style, as on the 718 Spyder. (Photo Courtesy Porsche Cars North America)

Early on, both the 996 Carrera and 986-gen Boxster were criticized for sharing a nearly identical instrument panel, dash, console, and interior treatment. Both are now different and substantially upgraded from those days to very good effect. (Photo Courtesy Porsche Cars North America)

flat-four engine family. Why not, since all 356s and original 550 and 718 Spyders were 4-cylinder powered, so there was a logical connection there. Plus, an engine with fewer cylinders offered potential benefits in terms of meeting emissions standards, as well as corporate average fuel economy (CAFÉ) requirements too.

The only rub is that a certain constituency of the Porsche Faithful wasn't initially thrilled with the idea since they had come to love their creamy, smooth, torque sixes. Plus, the new engines' exhaust sound was a bit more puttery to some ears and was sometimes compared to that of a Subaru.

For these special models, Porsche whipped up something much more familiar in the form of a naturally aspirated 4.0L flat six good for 414 hp and 309 ft-lbs of torque, along with a 6-speed manual transmission. The transmission includes a new AutoBlip feature that handled the rev matching and heel-and-toe downshifting on the driver's computerized behalf.

The 718 Spyder's aggressive design more than delivers on what the 4.0L naturally aspirated flat six delivers. (Photo Courtesy Porsche Cars North America)

True to its new-found, old-school horsepower, the 718 Spyder employs a track-bred Porsche Active Suspension Management (PASM) setup with adaptive dampers, helper springs on the rear axle, and a ride height that is 1.18 inches (30 mm) lower than a standard 718 Boxster or Cayman.

According to a Porsche press release, "It also allows for manual adjustments of camber, toe, ride height, and anti-roll bar settings. The front axle is taken from the 2018 911 GT3, while the rear axle is a specific design for the GT4 and Spyder. The brakes on both models are adopted from the 911 GT3. The standard grey cast-iron rotors measure 380 mm front and rear. The optional Porsche ceramic composite brake (PCCB) system features ceramic composite rotors measuring 410 mm in the front and 390 mm at the rear to provide a weight savings of approximately 50 percent from the cast iron equivalents.

"At the rear, a standard mechanical limited-slip differential with Porsche torque vectoring (PTV) helps maintain optimum traction. The GT4 and Spyder are fitted with specifically designed 20-inch wheels shod in ultra high-performance tires measuring 245/35 ZR 20 at the front and 295/30 ZR 20 at the rear. The wheels as standard on the 718 Spyder feature a silver finish, while the GT4 is equipped with wheels painted in Satin Platinum. Other wheel finishes are optionally available. ABS as well as electronic stability control (ESC) and traction control (TC) have been specifically calibrated for the cars and, as is typical for a GT model, ESC and TC can be switched off in two stages. The 718 Cayman GT4 is capable of lapping the Nürburgring Nordschleife more than 10 seconds faster than its predecessor."

This all makes for a very serious sports car.

The Porsche press release continued, "The 718 Cayman GT4 and 718 Spyder are immediately recognizable as the most potent and track-capable models within their range, and each have their own unique styling elements. Both cars feature a front spoiler lip with recessed model designation, a central air outlet ahead of the front luggage compartment lid that aids downforce and cooling, and tinted taillights. The design of the 718 Spyder is further characterized by a manually operated lightweight fabric top, a rear lid with two dynamic streamliners, and an automatically extending rear spoiler designed specifically for the car.

"A new rear diffuser not only frames the sport exhaust system but also reduces lift on the car. The 718 Cayman GT4 shares this diffuser, which contributes to an increase in downforce of approximately 50 percent compared to the predecessor, in conjunction with the redesigned, manually adjustable rear wing.

"Side air intakes with additional side blades are also specific to the GT4. The interior of both cars underscores their motorsport heritage and driver-focused nature. A GT Sport steering wheel that measures 14.1 inches (360 mm) in diameter is standard and features a top center marker in black on the GT4. The shift lever is 0.78 inch (20 mm) shorter than on standard 718 models to offer a particularly direct and crisp feel when changing gears.

"Standard Sport Seats Plus with raised side bolsters provide a high degree of lateral support. The seat centers are upholstered in Alcantara, as is the steering wheel rim, shift lever, and the lower part of the dashboard. While the 718 Cayman GT4 is decorated with brushed aluminum interior trim, the trim pieces of the 718 Spyder are painted in the exterior color. Other trims are available as options. Also optional on both models are full bucket seats or electrically adjustable 18-way adaptive Sport Seats Plus.

"Air conditioning and the Porsche communication management (PCM) system with Sound Package Plus are fitted as standard. The PCM system can be optionally upgraded with features such as navigation, including Porsche Connect and Apple CarPlay.

"Optionally, the 718 Spyder can be ordered with the Spyder Classic interior package. The package features two-tone leather in Bordeaux Red and Black, extended Alcantara upholstery, GT Silver Metallic interior trim, and a new two-tone fabric top in black and red are

The number 718 was originally fixed to an earlier Porsche Spyder, and it's proper to see it recognized in this model of Boxster. (Photo Courtesy Porsche Cars North America)

reminiscent of historic Porsche racing cars. The 718 Cayman GT4 and the 718 Spyder offer the option of decorative interior stitching in red, silver, or yellow."

The MSRP for the 718 Spyder was $96,300, while the 718 Cayman GT4 retails for $99,200. These prices don't include the $1,350 delivery, processing, and handling fee.

Once again, these models were new leaders in terms of Boxster performance and the most expensive models offered to date. They will be future collectibles to be sure. No production numbers are available, as these were current models still in production as of this writing.

2020 Exclusiv Heritage Design Carrera Targa

In its earliest days as the Special Wishes or custom shop department, what is now called Porsche Exclusiv can design and produce special limited edition production runs, as well as produce a car highly customized to the owner's wants and tastes, which will be covered in Chapter 6.

Besides the previously mentioned 911 Sport Classic, Exclusiv most recently collaborated on a new special edition targa model to commemorate the company's design heritage and the Exclusiv's considerable capability, be it special seat stitching, highly tailored custom paint schemes, or very bespoke builds. This special targa is the Exclusiv Heritage Edition, which artfully blends one of Porsche's latest and greatest models with a beautifully curated and crated tailored look.

The parchment-colored interior is a dramatic contrast to the Heritage Design Edition's rich metallic burgundy paint scheme, although other colors can be chosen. (Photo Courtesy Porsche Cars North America)

It's so quick and easy to open up the 992 Targa's top that you'll want to ride in open air every possible minute. (Photo Courtesy Corporate Archives Porsche AG)

The original Ford Skyliner retractable hardtop of the late 1950s was often lauded for having the "most fun to watch" folding top. Neighbors would come to your house just to see it go through its mechanical ballet to open and close, but we believe Porsche's new targa has taken away that award. (Photo Courtesy Porsche Cars North America)

The new targa profile successfully recalls the look and targa roof-bar style of the original 1960s and 1970s versions without the fussy manually removable and folding roof panel. (Photo Courtesy Porsche Cars North America)

The targa model with a removable central roof section first appeared in production for 1967. The roof option was available on various 911s and 912s. The task to create a folding roof convertible at that time on a rear engine car presented considerable packaging problems. The solution left the front windshield intact and maintained a roll-over bar with integral rear window, along with a folding, pop-out roof section in the middle, to deliver most of the appeal of an open-air sports car without having to re-engineer the 911/912 chassis and body.

It's proven to be extremely popular over the years, having come and gone from the model lineup a time or two, and recently made a reappearance in a new highly engineered and technical completely power-folding top design. The driver no longer needs to stop, pull out a special tool, unseat the roof, fold it, and then store it. In a somewhat complicated ballet of motors, levers, solenoids, and other engineering wizardry, which is highly entertaining to watch, the central top now folds up and disappears at little more than the touch of a button.

The Heritage Design Edition (HDE) is available only based upon the current 992-series architecture. It is numerically coincidental that only 992 examples will be produced. All of them come in all-wheel-drive Carrera 4S form. A total of four exclusive paint colors were offered. However, the most prevalent and often featured hue is Cherry Metallic, which is a deep, rich metallic red bordering on burgundy. It's a rich, elegant color that matches perfectly with the parchment tan and Bordeaux olea leather-trimmed cabin.

Most of the badging is trimmed in gold, which may initially sound like overkill, but ultimately comes off as quite celebratory and is an elegant offset to the Cherry Metallic paintwork. The Porsche crest on the bonnet, wheel centers, steering wheel center, and vehicle key is the same design used in 1963 when the 911 made its worldwide auto show debut. The HDE gets its own model-specific, Exclusiv edition staggered 20/21-inch wheels with black-finished brake calipers. The number gumballs on the doors and the stripe and Porsche lettering along the rocker panels were also design touches intended to invoke and honor the company's racing past.

From a specifications and performance standpoint, the HDE was identical to the Carrera 4S upon which it's based. That means Porsche's S-spec 3.0L twin-turbocharged flat six boiling out 450 hp and backed by the PDK dual-clutch automated manual gearbox. The combination produces a 0–60 time of 3.6 seconds and a top speed of 185 mph.

Watch, fashion, and clothing designer Porsche Design also made its contribution to this special model and produced

Porsche's Exclusiv group is all about the fine details, be it stitching, colors, the world's coolest key fobs, or a Porsche Design mechanical chronograph timepiece perfectly matched to your new Heritage Design Edition Carrera Targa. (Photo Courtesy Porsche Cars North America)

a bespoke chronograph wristwatch that is color and thematically schemed to the HDE.

Like the car, the watch is a limited production piece and offered exclusively to HDE customers. Pricing for the HDE Carrera 4S began at $180,600, not including the watch.

1996/1997/1998 911 GT1

You may believe that carmakers design and develop cars and then decide to race them. This happens in some cases, but more often than not, especially in modern times, carmakers are much more at the whim and discretion of racing sanctioning bodies. Rules and series or classic formulas and specifications come and go and seem to ebb and flow with the tides. Such was the case when Porsche developed the GT1.

There were several evolutions of the racing spec and the Straßenversion (street version). Porsche pretty much had its way with big-game sports car and endurance races during the latter half of the 1970s, the 1980s, and deep into the 1990s with various 935 models and variants, plus the 956 and 962 prototype sports racers. A new set of rules of the mid-1990s begot new classes for World Sports Car machines and Le Mans Prototypes (LMP), plus a variety of production-based GT class specs.

Porsche had already notched a trophy case worth of overall wins, and production-based class wins were of minimal interest, so Porsche went for an all-new, somewhat 911-based prototype to compete for the overall victory. It was called the 911 GT1, and although its general shape and look somewhat resembled a 911 Turbo, it was for all intents and purposes an all-new machine designed specifically for racing.

For a while, Porsche supported independent teams, primarily Joest Racing, by helping the team develop, enter, and run a series of Porsche-powered prototypes. The team enjoyed some success, but nothing was ultimately as satisfying as winning with a car that was entirely developed and built by Porsche, looked like a Porsche, and properly wore a Porsche crest on its nose.

To qualify the new 911 GT1 machine within the class, Porsche was required to produce and make available a certain number of production street versions. In this case, did a street car beget the racing version, or did the race car give necessary birth to a hyper-exotic street machine? In so many words, yes.

So many aftermarket tuners and builders say that they make street-legal race cars, yet none of them can top the Porsche GT1 street version for the Road Legal Race Car Crown. (Photo Courtesy Corporate Archives Porsche AG)

It isn't every day that you see a car developed for the 24 Hours of Le Mans being tested on a public road, unless you happen to be in Stuttgart. (Photo Courtesy Corporate Archives Porsche AG)

Porsche in no way set itself up to dominate a class of one, as Toyota, Nissan, Ferrari, Mercedes-Benz, and others were swimming in the same pond. Noted Porsche author and international journalist Karl Ludvigsen summarized it succinctly.

"Porsche needed a car that was consistent with the look of the 911 Carrera on which it had bet the business," he said. "The racer also had to be homologated as a road car to have a chance of being accepted under GT racing rules . . . It didn't look easy."

Yet, Porsche developed a car that served all masters. The new car was highly carbon fiber intensive and didn't rely on much in the way of steel body or chassis work beyond that needed to claim connection to the street 911, and for safety reasons.

Another major design decision was made at the earliest stages of development. The new GT1 had a true mid-engine placement rather than the 911's engine-aft-of-the-rear-wheels architecture. Additionally, the twin-turbocharged flat six was largely water cooled. It was still a 911 yet different.

It was important that the car was designed, engineered, and built in house. The look resembled the then-current 993 Carrera, and soon evolved to resemble the upcoming 996-era 911s. The layout put the driver and the engine completely between the wheelbase of the car to ensure weight balance that a purely rear-engine design couldn't match.

The engine for the new Super Porsche was a 3.2L unit developed out of the 962 powerplant that used twin turbos and water cooling for the cylinder heads. It was rated at 592 hp and backed by a 6-speed sequential manual racing gearbox. Fueled and ready to race, the 911 GT1 weighed less than 2,500 pounds.

Those are real street-version 911 taillights, but the rest comes straight from the racetrack. (Photo Courtesy Corporate Archives Porsche AG)

Need a near 600-hp prototype class racer for your daily commute? Well, why not? (Photo Courtesy Corporate Archives Porsche AG)

It must have been a big group test day in Stuttgart for the GT1. Notice the trail of factory test and chase cars just behind it. (Photo Courtesy Corporate Archives Porsche AG)

This shot gives you a side-by-side look at both street and track versions of the GT1. The car in the foreground is a slightly earlier version with round headlights and trickier aero bits. This pair was on display at the famous Petersen Automotive Museum in Los Angeles during the Porsche Effect 70th anniversary exhibit celebration.

And what of the street exotic version that needed a fully trimmed interior, road lighting, seating for two, and most everything else you'd expect of a mid-1990s hyper exotic? The engine was detuned for street duty and needed to exhale through a road-legal exhaust system. The engine was recalibrated down to a mere 536 or so hp for street duty, and the cabin was trimmed out for civilian occupants. The sanctioning bodies mandated that at least 25 of the street-legal version must be produced to qualify the 911 GT1 for international sports car competition. Porsche built around 23 of them (production estimates vary), and apparently this was good enough for the scrutineers to demonstrate that the car was real as the GT1 was cleared for competition. Each of the race cars, of which 18 were built, cost around a million bucks a pop, but the Straßenversion was a relative bargain at just under $900,000.

The original configuration of both the GT1 race and road cars looked very much like the frontal aspect of a 993 Turbo, particularly due to its road headlights and lower air-intake fascia. As with everything in racing, much is learned in the early days of any program, and then along came Evo versions of both. The car enjoyed certain success, although it failed to capture overall wins in its first runs at Le Mans. Not to be satisfied with anything less than an unfootnoted victory, Porsche redeveloped the car for 1998.

The same two cars show the differences between the street and track versions of the rear wings, diffusers, and taillight treatments.

The 1997 Straßenversion looks much like a wind-blown drop of mercury and clearly stems from a race car. With equal clarity, it could be nothing but a Porsche. (Photo Courtesy Corporate Archives Porsche AG)

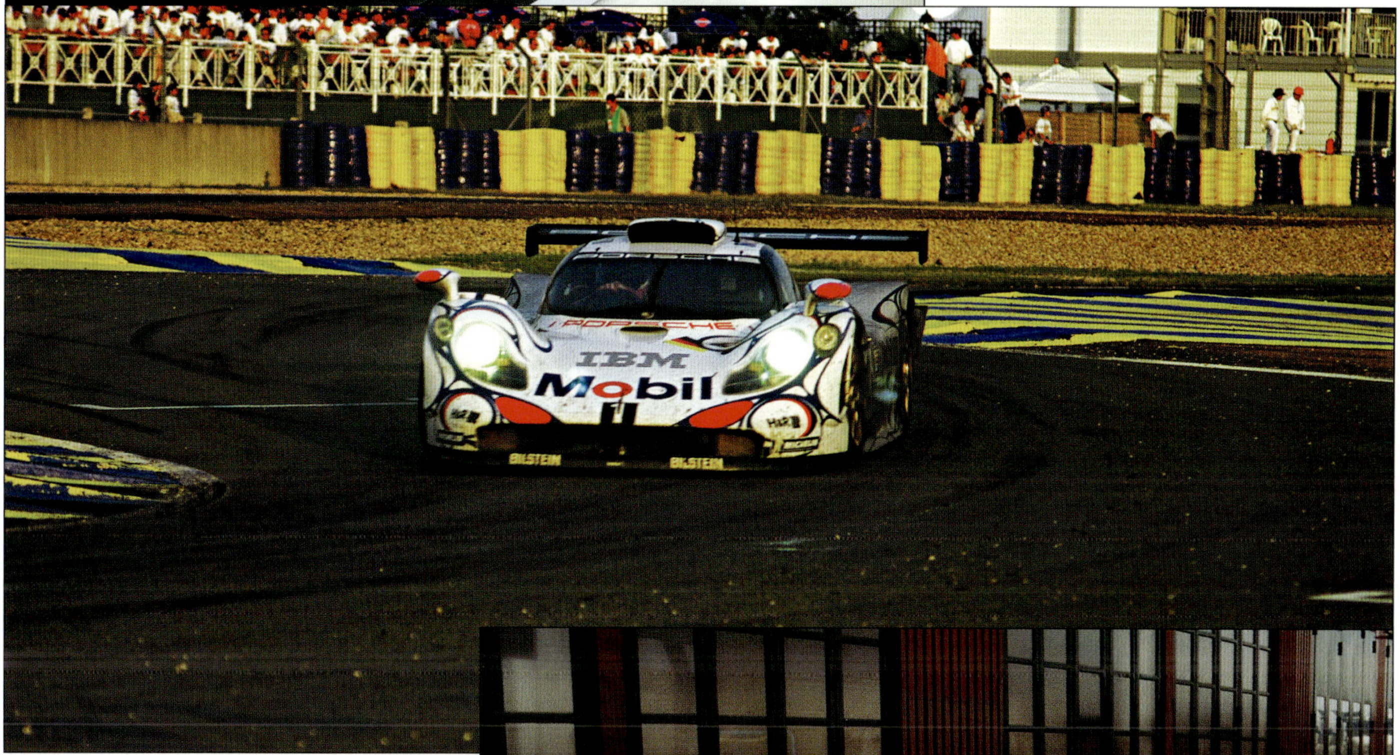

The red number 26 negotiates the curves at Le Mans a few hours before sunset.

Since the GT1-98 was so substantially redesigned over the early-generation GT1s, the street version needed a total rebody job. It didn't matter that it was more attractive or not, as long as the swoopy bodywork made the car faster, which it did. (Photo Courtesy Corporate Archives Porsche AG)

The 1998 24 Hours of Le Mans was the place of reckoning for the substantially updated and redesigned GT1. Here are the two factory team cars at the start of the race on the famous front straight.

At 2 p.m. local time at Le Mans on Sunday of a race weekend with the checkered flag high in the air, the factory GT1-98s fly in formation to take a more than memorable 1-2 finish.

The bodywork was much more radical than the previous GT1, if that's somehow possible, and now reflected the front-end styling of the upcoming water-cooled 996-generation 911. The now-dubbed GT1-98 was ostensibly an all-new car, and only one additional street version needed to be built as proof of concept. The new GT1 was lighter and faster and resembled the pure prototypes it competed against from BMW, Nissan, Toyota, and Mercedes-Benz. Horsepower was now admitted at well over 600.

As both GT1-97s retired at Le Mans that year, hopes and tensions were high as Porsche assembled two dream teams of drivers for the two factory-entered GT1-98s.

Car number 25 was dubbed the yellow car, as it bore bits of yellow trim on its mirrors and nose. Otherwise, it was identically liveried to its twin sister, car number 26, or the red car. Car number 25 was assigned to Jorg Mueller, Uwe Alzen, and Bob Wolleck. The red number 26 was assigned to Laurent Aiello, Stephane Ortelli, and Allan McNish, the future F1 standout for Toyota. All in all, it was an outstanding international cast of standout sports car pilots.

The GT1-98 appeared somewhat outpaced by the Toyotas, Mercedes, and Nissans. However, the exotic new Porsches demonstrated dogged reliability and were squired by a brilliant group of drivers who drove clean and smart to keep the cars together and in good fettle, as the initially fast Toyotas and others dropped out or fell far behind due to reliability and mechanical issues. Finally, at 2 p.m. local time, Porsche brought home a fine 1-2 finish with car number 26 leading its sister number 25 across the line to sweep beneath the checkered flag to earn Porsche its 16th overall win at Le Mans.

And what of the rare street machines? The lone silver GT1-98 street example sits in the Porsche factory museum, and the rest of the two-dozen GT1 road machines populate private collections all over the world. It's doubtful you'll see one running around town on errands to the market or the hardware store. The final value is determined by a transaction between willing buyers and willing sellers, but most estimates put the current number as of this writing at something over $12 million.

A strong case could be made for the GT1 to be the ultimate special edition Porsche. It was both a street car and a race car. The latter was raced by the factory and sold to and raced by privateer teams. The street version is exceedingly rare, but you didn't need to necessarily be a preferred customer with a secret decoder ring to buy one—although it helped. Due to its racing and Le Mans winning pedigree, the fact that it was factory developed and built both as racing and street car, its superlative performance, instant collectability, and the ability to be bought and sold at will, it's hard to argue with it as Porsche's most special of special editions.

2011 911 GT3 RS 4.0

Many Porschephiles cite the 997 generation of 911 as a particular sweet spot in the pantheon of late-model, water-cooled Carrera platforms. It was a clear advance and improvement over the appealing but in some ways flawed 996-generation cars, yet it was smaller, lighter, and a bit less computerized than the later

In either black or white, the RS 4.0 cuts a dashing figure on the racetrack, where it belongs. (Photo Courtesy Corporate Archives Porsche AG)

From this angle, the RS 4.0 looks little different than the 3.8L GT3 RS, but it is. (Photo Courtesy Corporate Archives Porsche AG)

This great shot shows much of the RS 4.0's aero ingenuity. The multi-element rear wing system combines a bit of a ducktail on the engine lid cover, along with the adjustable wing that gets way up into the airstream. At the lower ends of the front fascia, notice the small dive planes that keep the airflow efficient and directed around the fascia. (Photo Courtesy Corporate Archives Porsche AG)

991 generation. Various GT3 and RS models were rousing successes prior to the 997-series cars, and in April 2011, Porsche announced a new GT3 RS that promised to be the best of the breed.

It was certain to be a limited production, special edition machine built pretty much one way, aside from a choice between two colors. The car is was officially named the GT3 RS 4.0, which means it's a member of the GT3 family of premium performance 911s. The "RS" makes it a RennSport model, which is a further definition of premium performance, and the 4.0 tips the car's hand as being a 4.0L GT engine–equipped car and marked the first time Porsche produced a 911 flat-six engine spec exactly double that of

Got motor? The RS 4.0 certainly does. In fact, there's a bespoke spec just for this very special limited edition RS. Props to Porsche for not shrouding the entire engine in plastic or carbon fiber as on some newer models where there's nothing but a couple of cooling fans to see. Everything you see that's carbon fiber is the genuine composite article. (Photo Courtesy Corporate Archives Porsche AG)

The RS 4.0 comes ready to race with lightweight, supportive sport seats and a husky roll-bar structure factory installed. (Photo Courtesy Corporate Archives Porsche AG)

Talk about a driver-focused cockpit. The RS 4.0 includes everything you want and nothing you don't. It's nice that Porsche stuck to a classic RS touch by replacing the normal door handles with the red nylon mesh fabric. It's a retro touch that looks great and saves those few all-important grams. (Photo Courtesy Corporate Archives Porsche AG)

the original 1963/1964/1965's even 2.0L displacement.

True to the somewhat-sacred RS formula that meant a highly tuned, naturally aspirated engine and an old-school manual transmission, this case was a model-specific engine that boiled out 500 hp and a 6-speed stick-and-clutch transaxle. Much of this GT-spec engine drew its inspiration, and a considerable amount of its content, from the 911 GT3 RSR sports racing machine, including a shared racing-spec crankshaft and forged pistons with titanium connecting rods to help the new engine spin to stratospheric levels. In this case it was 8,500 rpm.

"A racing engine like this needs to explode at the top," said the ever-enthusiastic Andreas Preuninger, then project leader for special vehicles at Porsche. "Explode it does, but despite its 8,500-rpm redline, the 4.0 accelerates smoothly and without any hiccups from just above idle. There is so much punch across the rev band that you may often find yourself in a gear higher than you might be in with the 3.8."

Porsche claims 0–60 in 3.8 seconds, 0–120 in fewer than 12, and a redline-limited top speed of 193 mph. Contemporary tests by a variety of media outlets got 0–60 times under 3.5 seconds and 11.6-second quarter-mile times. It's fast by any measure. The engine's carbon-fiber, dual-element air filter housing has a special badge to declare its RS and 4.0 status.

The RS 4.0 is so much more than a standard Carrera with a big motor. Even though this very special edition is an extreme performer, and many will no doubt spend considerable time on the racetrack, it is primarily a street super sports car and packs more than enough creature comforts in combination with its major horsepower injection, a track-worthy but still streetable suspension reinvention, aggressive and aerodynamic design, limited colors, and reduced weight.

Naturally, all of the spring weights were recalibrated just for this model, and the rear suspension lower arms and links are rose-jointed for sharper and more accurate response. The shock absorbers are tuned specifically for the 4.0, as is the Porsche active stability management (PASM) system.

Caster, camber, and all wheel alignment specifications are tuned to this model. The 4.0 wears the wide-hipped, fender-flared bodywork of the 3.8L GT3 RS, along with its

This is a look at the GT3 RS 4.0 in black. It seems, logically enough, that nearly every Porsche magazine in the world put the new RS 4.0 on cover upon this special edition's release.

associated track increase. The lightweight forged alloy wheels are single, center-locking units to show off the rather massive brakes. Cast-iron rotors are standard red brake calipers with ceramic composite drilled and cooled rotors optional, indicated by yellow calipers.

Visually, the car resembles the GT3 RS 3.8 with a few small but notable exceptions. The first is badging and identification decals, and the next are lateral front air deflection vanes, which made their first appearance on a production Porsche. The large, adjustable rear wing mounts on machined aluminum plinths and wears aerodynamic side plates. It all adds up to 82 pounds of downforce on the front end of the car and 348 pounds of downforce aft, which is about 10 percent more total downforce than on the GT3 RS 3.8. The RS 4.0 was offered in white as the primary paint body color, with black as a customer choice option. The striping package combines silver, red, and black graphics.

Equipped as standard with lightweight components such as sport bucket seats, bonnet, and front fenders made of carbon fiber, rear windows, and weight-optimized carpets, the RS 4.0 checks in at about 3,000 pounds with a full tank of fuel. A 6-speed manual transmission is the only transmission offered on this exclusive model, which was limited to just 600 cars. That means a weight-to-power ratio of approximately 6 pounds per horsepower. It's the stuff that race cars are made of, but this one wears license plates and has air conditioning.

The list price in mid-2011 upon the announcement was about $185.950. Naturally, all 600 of them sold out immediately for $1,000 to several hundred thousand dollars over MSRP. As of this writing, they typically trade in the $600,000 range should you find someone willing to sell one.

I've made a case for the GT1 models wearing the ultimate Special Edition Porsche crown. However, if you wish to only focus on street-legal models (the GT1 was primarily a racing car and only enough street versions were produced to satisfy homologation requirements), then a solid case could be made for the GT3 RS 4.0 to legitimately wear that crown, as the one plus ultra Porsche special edition.

CHAPTER 2

ANNIVERSARY EDITIONS AND PORSCHE CLUB SPECIALS

Porsche itself, in search of ways to create special commemorative models, has issued a handful of anniversary editions to celebrate an internal anniversary or perhaps mark the company's relationship with a certain market or Porsche club organization.

Some of these models vary from relatively simple color, equipment, and striping/badging treatments, to more deeply developed models containing those sorts of identifiers plus substantial equipment, hardware, and performance enhancements. Among certain factions of Porschephiles, these specials may be considered more desirable, collectible, and/or valuable. It often comes down to supply, demand, and appeal.

1976/1977 Martini Championship Edition 924

The mid-1970s was a bit of a rainmaker in terms of 924-based special editions. The first among them was the Championship Edition (Martini Racing) 924 of 1976/1977. It was primarily an appearance package with the signature red/blue Martini racing team stripes over a body in white with a model specific interior, though the model also earned front and rear anti-roll bars for some performance gain in the handling. The advertising and marketing of it leaned heavily on several of Porsche's big banger race and championship winners, including

The celebratory Martini 924 was a handsome (if cosmetic-only) edition of Porsche's baseline model. That's not to say it didn't honor the many great racing wins and championships earned by the similarly liveried 935 and 936 racing prototype models that sit behind it in this advertisement.

the championship-winning Martini 935 and 936 prototypes. About 3,000 of the street-bound Martini 924s were produced.

1978 924 Limited Edition

An attractive combination of colors and options, this 924 LE wasn't at all about extra performance per se. A one-year-only special, this limited edition was painted a unique Dolomite Gray Metallic exterior paint with silver and black accent pinstripes. It used the standard 924 powertrain with the 4-speed manual transmission. The automatic was offered as an option, and a 5-speed manual didn't come along until 1979. The only other notable exterior addition was that of front fog lights.

The interior was primarily black with a semi-psychedelic black and white checkerboard square insert fabric called Pasha, which was quite popular in certain 911 models, particularly the 928s. Other than the unique exterior paint color and silver/black pinstripe running along the bone line the entire length of the car, the 924 LE exhibited no badging or other identification to call any attention to its SE nature.

Porsche was particularly proud of the 924's EPA fuel-mileage ratings. The late 1970s was still impacted by the various OPEC oil shortages, and Porsche boasted that its sports car could easily carry you more than 400 highway miles on a tankful of unleaded. While the company couldn't tout the naturally aspirated 924's 110 hp or performance other than the addition of standard anti-roll bars, prowess over that of any of the 911s and many other sports cars, the company stressed the everyday usability, comfort, and enjoyability factor to herald it as the "collector's item that won't collect dust."

Porsche has no record of how many of this LE model were produced or sold, and indications are that it was offered in most of the company's world markets.

Porsche was only a little cheeky when it declared the 924 Limited Edition to be "the collector's item that won't be collecting dust." The LE was a handsome combination of colors and options. It truly was a limited edition, although the paragliders were optional.

Porsche 924 limited edition specifications

Engine Design	4 cylinder in-line, water cooled, cast iron block, aluminum alloy head and oil pan
Bore/Stroke mm (in.)	86.5 (3.41)/84.4 (3.32)
Displacement ccm (cu. in.)	1983 (121.0)
Compression ratio	8.5:1
H.P. SAE net @ RPM	110 @5750
Max. torque ft. lbs. @ RPM	111.3 @ 3500
Fuel requirement	lead-free
Valve Placement	overhead valves
Camshaft	spur belt driven overhead cam
Crankshaft	forged, 5 main bearings
Engine lubrication	pressure lubrication, full flow oil filter
Fuel Supply	electrical fuel pump
Fuel/Air Mixture	Continuous Injection System (CIS)
Electrical system	
Battery	12 volt 63 AMP./h.
Alternator Output	max. 1050 W
Ignition System	breakerless transistor
Drive train	
Clutch	Single disc, dry
Transmission	Standard transmission, 4 forward, 1 reverse, transaxle rear
Final Drive/Ratio	beveled hypoid drive/3.888:1
Drive Axles	double constant velocity joints
Chassis suspension	
Body	unitized construction
Front Suspension	independent coil/shock absorber struts, negative king-pin offset
Rear Suspension	independent trailing—diagonal arm, one torsion bar each
Shock Absorbers	double acting hydraulic shock absorbers, front and rear
Stabilizers	front and rear
Service Brake	dual diagonal circuits, power assist, disc front drums rear
Tires/Wheels	185/70HR-14, tubeless/6J x 14—Pressure cast light alloy
Steering	rack and pinion

Capacities	
Engine	4.5 ltr. (4.75 U.S. qt.)
Transmission	2.6 ltr. (2.75 U.S. qt.)
Fuel tank	62 ltr. (16.4 U.S. gal.)
Dimensions	
Wheel base mm (in.)	2400 (94.5)
Track, front/rear mm (in.)	1418 (55.9)/1372 (54.0)
Length mm (in.)	4320 (170.1)
Width mm (in.)	1685 (66.3)
Height (unladen) mm (in.)	1270 (50.0)
Ground clearance mm (in.)	125 (4.9) at max. load
Turning circle m (ft.)	9.21 (30.2) curb to curb
Performance	
Top speed mph.	120
Acceleration 0-60 mph.	11.5 sec.

Porsche 924 limited edition equipment . . .

• Dolomite Grey Metallic finish • Silver Metallic/Black body sic pinstriping • Pressure-cast alloy wheels • Stabilizer bars • Fog lights • Front seats – silver/black-checkered velour inlays, trimmed with black leatherette • Rear seats – area dividing rear seats covered in silver/black-checkered velour inlays. Seats in black leatherette • Black, leather-covered steering wheel • Special black leatherette boot on shift lever (manual transmission only) • Stereo speakers – two in rear side panels. Additional speaker in dashboard • Manual antenna

Specifications subject to change without notification.

PORSCHE +AUDI

W74-768-5030 3/78 Litho in USA

©1978 Porsche+Audi Division Volkswagen of America, Inc

The company considered the LE special enough to warrant its own unique sales brochure, which was something special we often forget about in this day and age of "we don't have brochures; all the info is online."

Even though this 924 didn't get a performance boost, the package included several features that were normally cost options.

It's an old mantra in the car business: "Don't just sell the steak; sell the sizzle." This brochure spread certainly underscores the attractive young and active couple at whom Porsche squarely aimed the 924 LE.

911 Martini Editions

Martini Racing is somewhat synonymous with Porsche. So many races and championships have been won by Martini-sponsored and/or -entered Porsches that in some minds, Martini Porsche is its own mythical sub-brand, but officially it's not.

Given all the success that Porsche and Martini have shared together, it only makes sense there are Martini-liveried special edition models, but the landscape and variety of them is modestly confusing. British Porsche expert Keith Seume sorted it out.

"If there's ever been a moniker that has resulted in a degree of confusion and the spread of misinformation throughout the UK Porsche scene, it's Martini Turbo. Over the years, the term has been applied to everything from the first factory-built 1976 London Motor Show car to the later 1978 limited edition Martini Championship Edition based on the then-recently introduced 3.3L Turbo and just about any regular 930 bearing the distinctive red and blue racing stripes of the Italian drink company.

"This is that option M42, originally referenced M432, allowed the application of the famous livery to any new 911, coupe, or targa from the humble SC to the mighty Turbo. All such cars have become branded as Martini models and give the impression there are many more examples of the rare breed in existence than there are in reality. We have no way of knowing how many 911s have had the stripes applied, as they were a dealer-fitted option, mostly on Grand Prix White examples, but available whatever the original hue."

However, Seume goes on to explain that "it wasn't until the 1978 model year and the arrival of the second-generation 930 with its larger engine and big 917-sourced brakes that the term was applied to an official model, the aforementioned Martini Championship Edition, that bore the distinctive stripes along with an interior that echoed the original 1976 show car."

In summary, it seems there's no all-encompassing, definitive definition of what constitutes a "real" Martini edition 911 because once the livery can be purchased and installed at the dealer level, the Porsche factory has no way to track or control on what cars this happens or how many were done. I can at least share with you the beautifully restored, authentic Championship Edition 930 Turbo built in mid-1977. Note that it's a right-hand-drive example, as a British-delivered car would logically be. The car wears

You can practically hear the Martini & Rossi TV commercial jingle playing in the background, or that might be the soft whine of the Martini Racing Edition 930 Turbo's KKK turbocharger. This smart livery looked great on the car and had a well-earned reputation. Porsche-built versions, as opposed to those converted or applied by dealers or the aftermarket, are highly sought after and valuable. (Photo Courtesy Andrew Tipping)

The Martini stripe design and colors are virtually identical to those used on the racing 935s and 936s, so the look is good and has credibility. (Photo Courtesy Andrew Tipping)

Some feel the Martini interior was a bit over the top, but so was the 930 Turbo. No one will ever question which racing team these colors represent, although not everyone agrees as to the comfiness of the leather block seat design. (Photo Courtesy Andrew Tipping)

proper 930 Turbo flares, bodywork, 15-inch rolling stock, front spoiler, and whale tail. The red-and-blue-stripe treatment is similar to the Martini team race cars, be they painted primarily white or the sometimes-seen silver.

What really makes this car a dazzler is the highly customized interior treatment. In the case of this car, that means primarily white leather seats, a blue leather dash and instrument panel, red carpeting, and red and blue somewhat blockish leather seat inserts. The look is a bit space age, and the treatment is nicknamed Fuhrmann seats after the famous Porsche engineer and engine designer Ernst Fuhrmann, although there is no confirmation that he conceived or designed them. The purpose behind the unusual seat design, other than its attention-grabbing appearance, was allegedly to reduce body stress on long drives, although Seume mentioned they really aren't all that comfortable.

The Martini 930 received its full measure of 911 Turbo performance from its 3.0L turbocharged flat six with 260 hp at 5,500 rpm, backed by a 4-speed manual transmission (factory installed 5-speeds didn't come along for the 930 until 1989), and a top speed on the strong side of 150 mph.

1979 924 Sebring '79

The year 1979 was particularly successful in professional sports car racing for Porsche. Stuttgart took first and second place at the 24 Hours of Le Mans, a worthwhile first and third at the 24 Hours of Daytona, and an impressive overall win and claimed the top 12 spots in the finishing order at the 12 Hours of Sebring enduro.

The Sebring top dozen was accomplished with big-game racing Porsches from Carrera RSRs to 935s. However, Porsche didn't sell RSRs and 935s as street models in mainline Porsche dealers. To create a model to commemorate this overwhelming run at Sebring, Porsche reached into its bag for its most accessible and least expensive model upon which to base a Sebring '79 special edition car.

Although several versions of the 924 were raced quite successfully, this red Sebring car was decidedly a street and appearance-only machine. All Sebring '79s were red and accented by a yellow and black pinstripe running down the side just below the window line, highlighted by white or black letters on the front fenders that proclaimed "Sebring '79," and

Porsche has won the 12 Hours of Sebring enduro many times, but it positively clobbered the field in 1979. The Sebring '79 924 is just one of many interesting, if primarily cosmetic, special editions Porsche created for its water-cooled, front-engine sports car.

Only 1,292 cars were available, which is an odd number for a limited production car. I've looked, researched, and asked, and no one has been able to confirm why this particular number was chosen.

Porsche went the extra mile to give the Sebring 924 a special interior to go along with its racy red exterior livery. Unfortunately, no more horsepower went along with the deal. Notice that by this time, the 924 used the same flat four-spoke leather steering wheel as the upcoming 911 Carrera 3.2.

The Sebring 924 spec page read much like the standard-issue model.

PORSCHE 924 SEBRING '79 SPECIFICATIONS.

Engine design	4 cylinder in-line, water cooled, cast iron block, aluminum alloy head and oil pan
Bore/Stroke mm (in.)	86.5 (3.41)/84.4 (3.32)
Displacement ccm (cu. in.)	1983 (121.0)
Compression ratio	8.5:1
H.P. SAE net @ RPM	110 @ 5750
Max. torque ft. lbs. @ RPM	111.3 @ 3500
Fuel requirement	Lead-free
Valve placement	Overhead valves
Camshaft	Spur belt driven overhead cam
Crankshaft	Forged, 5 main bearings
Engine lubrication	Pressure lubrication, full flow oil filter
Fuel supply	Electrical fuel pump
Fuel/Air mixture	Continuous Injection System (CIS)
Electrical system	
Battery	12 volt 63 AMP./h.
Alternator output	Max. 1050 W
Ignition system	Breakerless transistor
Drive train	
Clutch	Single disc, dry
Transmission	Standard transmission, 5 forward, 1 reverse, transaxle rear or 3-speed automatic
Final drive	Beveled hypoid drive
Drive axles	Double constant velocity joints

Chassis/Suspension	
Body	Unitized construction
Front suspension	Independent coil/shock absorber struts, negative king-pin offset
Rear suspension	Independent trailing—diagonal arm, one torsion bar each
Shock absorbers	Double acting hydraulic shock absorbers, front and rear
Stabilizers	front and rear
Service brake	Dual diagonal circuits, power assist, disc front, drums rear
Tires/Wheels	185/70HR-14, tubeless/6J x 14—black pressure cast light alloy with polished rims.
Steering	Rack and pinion
Capacities	
Engine	4.5 ltr. (4.75 U.S. qt.)
Transmission	2.6 ltr. (2.75 U.S. qt.)
Fuel tank	62 ltr. (16.4 U.S. gal.)
Dimensions	
Wheel base mm (in.)	2400 (94.5)
Track, front/rear mm (in.)	1418 (55.9)/1372 (54.0)
Length mm (in.)	4320 (170.1)
Width mm (in.)	1685 (66.3)
Height (unladen) mm (in.)	1270 (50.0)
Ground clearance mm (in.)	125 (4.9) at max. load
Turning circle m (ft.)	9.2 (30.2) curb to curb
Performance	
Top speed mph.	120
Acceleration 0-60 mph.	11.2 sec (standard transmission)

PORSCHE
+AUDI
Nothing Even Comes Close.

a white Porsche logotype on the nose that read "924."

The centers of the standard 924 spider-spoke alloy wheels were finished in black with a silver-painted rim and lip surface. Electric batwing exterior mirrors (left and right) were standard as was a removable sunroof. Anti-roll bars front and rear, which were not previously standard on some 924s, were included in the Sebring package, along with a three-speaker stereo system, richer velour carpeting, and a leather-trimmed sport steering wheel.

If the 911 SC deserved a Weissach special edition, so did the 924. It was created in 1981 and was a great look with a specially created paint color and wheels unique to this model.

1981 924 Weissach Limited Edition

Weissach (pronounced Vee-soch) is a smaller principality located near the Porsche factory properties in Germany. In Porsche terms, Weissach's primary claim to fame is as the location of Porsche's engineering facilities, test track, and race shops. Porsche has on occasion called the city's name into play to commemorate certain engineering achievements or special models.

One particularly innovative rear suspension redesign was dubbed the Weissach axle. It was also used to christen another special package of 924-model colors and equipment. The 1981 Weissach Edition 924 is a worthwhile blending of 924 Turbo features and equipment to a naturally aspirated model. By this point in the 924's production life, it had already benefitted from some meaningful updates, including a 5-speed manual transaxle, improvements to the interior, and a wider variety of colors and optional equipment.

The Weissach 924 got a handsome set of ATS-branded basketweave alloy wheels. The car's special paint color is called

Platinum (a warm slightly brownish silver), and it had wider tires and power dual exterior side mirrors. The cabin was treated to upgraded carpeting, a unique upholstery pattern for the seats and door panels, and standard air conditioning.

Unfortunately, there were no meaningful performance upgrades, so the "just enough" 110-hp rating from its 2.0L I-4 remained. Porsche had high hopes for this special edition and declared it to be "a unique 924 that seems to be destined to become a collector's item, for only 400 will be built."

1988 911 Carrera Jubilee Commemorative Edition

This was about the time Porsche became more serious about creating special edition 911s. This one was cooked up by the Special Wishes design team and used the targa platform bodystyle to celebrate the company's 250,000th 911 in 25 years of production. It was based on the second-generation Carrera 3.2 G-series platform that replaced the 911 SC in 1984.

Upgrades for this much-refreshed 911included a larger and substantially updated engine that was increased from 3.0 to 3.2 liters with a 50-states rating of an even 200 hp that only offered a 5-speed manual transmission. About 80 percent of the engine was new as were the computerized engine management and fuel injection systems. The front driving/fog lights were neatly further integrated into the lower front fascia. The new Carrera 3.2 was offered in coupe, targa, and full convertible cabriolet bodystyles. There was no factory Turbo model for 1984.

It wouldn't be a Porsche special edition without a unique exterior body paint color. In this case, it was an elegant shade called Diamond Blue metallic. The spoked portion of the wheel centers were also similarly finished, while the outer rims and wheel lips were polished.

The first special edition Carrera 3.2 was called the Jubilee Wish series and blended an elegant grouping of colors for the exterior, wheel centers, and interior leather. Take your choice of a coupe or targa.

A leather interior finished in a dark blue scheme that was quite complimentary to the unique exterior paint was also included for the Jubilee model. Dr. Ferdinand Porsche's signature is embroidered into the headrest area of the front bucket seats. Other Superior Equipment–level upgrades included power seats, a short-shift gear lever, a stiffer suspension tune, and plusher carpets inside, plus the obligatory badging on the passenger-side instrument panel.

Just 875 cars were produced. They were instant collectibles when new and are highly sought after today.

The 250,000th 911 produced was a cause for celebration and certainly worth a special car. This one was and is.

Herr Porsche himself didn't sign the Jubilee Carrera seats. A computerized sewing machine did so on his behalf.

Other than the colors and the special badge on the dash, this Jubilee edition was pretty standard Carrera 3.2 fare inside, which wasn't a bad thing.

1993–1994 911 30-Year Anniversary Jubilee Edition

In March 1993, Porsche presented the Porsche 911 anniversary edition "30 years 911" at the Geneva Motor Show. Since then, the special 964 has been nicknamed "Jubi" for short. Wearing the Porsche internal code M096, the Jubi 30 is fundamentally a Carrera 4 with the wide turbo body but without wings. This 964 anniversary edition included options with exclusive interior design and numerous customization possibilities. This special model was limited to 911 vehicles that were manufactured in the model years 1993 and 1994. It was sold in a unique dark metallic purple exterior paint color with a decidedly purplish leather trimmed cabin. Not everyone is a fan of this color combination, but it is certainly eye-catching and always starts a conversation.

The Porsche 964 is the successor of the Porsche 911 G-series and came on the market in 1989. The new car was designated a 1989½ model. The 964 was offered with both rear-wheel drive as a Carrera 2 and the all-wheel drive as a Carrera 4. This generation of 911 evolved in many areas compared to the G-series (1984–1989), including power steering and ABS brakes being used for the first time.

The styling was also revised to include a more integrated front and rear safety bumper design. There were new wheel designs, which was a controversial replacement for the long-standing and somewhat traditional Fuchs 5-spoke look.

Smile, Dr. Porsche. The 911's 30th birthday is indeed a happy occasion. (Photo Courtesy Corporate Archives Porsche AG)

Porsche rightly celebrated nearly every worthy anniversary, championship, or other momentous occasion with a special edition. This special and deep purple 964 marked 30 good years for the 911. (Photo Courtesy Corporate Archives Porsche AG)

This 30th anniversary 964 earned a special, slightly modernized 911 badge. (Photo Courtesy Corporate Archives Porsche AG)

To paraphrase Kermit, it's not easy being purple, unless you love purple inside and out. The 30th anniversary Jubilee 964-generation 911 is a striking car that some don't care for but most seem to love. (Photo Courtesy Corporate Archives Porsche AG)

The 3.4L flat six wore racing-derived twin–spark plug heads with more horsepower (250 hp) in naturally aspirated form. Something else new was an automatic transmission called Tiptronic. The 964 was offered in coupe, sunroof coupe, targa, and cabriolet models. Two generations of 911 964 Turbo also returned.

2006 911 Club Coupe

Porsche occasionally goes beyond simply marking its own milestones and anniversaries. In the case of this handsome limited production 997 911 Club Coupe, it's a special commemorative model brewed up to partner with the Porsche Club of America (PCA) to acknowledge the club's 50th anniversary.

Produced only in coupe form, the Club 50 is built around a Carrera S spec and platform. This 2006-only model was limited to just 50 copies. They were available in any color you like as long as it's Azzurro California Metallic, a dreamy blue/green metallic shade intended, or at least named, to recognize the great Pacific Ocean along California's western coastline.

Interior colors varied from Porsche's standard Carrera palette. All models included, by definition, the X51 Power Kit option that juiced the S's 3.8L water-cooled flat six from 355 to a more serious 381 hp. It was a very significant number in that it was a virtual match for the outgoing 996-series GT3 model, although the GT3 is lighter, packs more aero aids, and has a much racier suspension.

However, 381 hp is a solid punch for this luxurious street Carrera S. The package was comprehensive with significant hardware upgrades for the engine, exhaust, and ignition systems. It was all of this while it maintained easy, no-hassle driving manners and a full factory warranty. It wasn't an inexpensive option and ran about $17,000 on top of any other Carrera S, although the X51 group option was standard and built into the price of the Club Coupe.

The 6-speed manual transaxle was the only transmission choice on the Club special. Yet the Club spec included lots of other goodies too, such as the factory optional short-shift kit and Sport Design 19 wheels that are handsome and a bit lighter than on any other factory-offered Carrera S.

Several other options were available on this special model that included but was not limited to carbon ceramic brakes, racier sport seats, the Chrono Sport option group, and a thicker-rimmed, leather-wrapped steering wheel. The Club Coupe was far more than just a few "Limited Edition, 1 of 50" badges here and there.

While it retained a high measure of comfort and civility, it also ranked as a serious performance car: 0–60 in 4.4 seconds, 0–124 mph in 14.9 seconds, and a legitimate top speed of 186 mph. Remember, this is for a naturally aspirated 997-generation model that didn't pack the twin turbochargers of today's Carrera S or Turbo models.

How much for all this speed and beauty? The goods are never cheap. The 911 Club Coupe was listed at $99,911. How clever of them to work the numbers 911 into the MSRP. It's estimated that most of them went out the door at around $110,000. As promised, just 50 were built, and they sold out within minutes of the announcement.

2015 Porsche 911 GTS Club Coupe

If a Porsche factory designed and produced PCA 50th Anniversary special edition seemed like a good idea and an instant sellout, why not go for the Plus-10 and celebrate the Porsche Club of America's 60th birthday with yet another limited edition model? The special edition 911 was based on the

At the time of its release, the PCA 50th anniversary special edition was the most expensive Carrera S you could buy and equally the most powerful. (Photo Courtesy Rich Chenet)

Would it be a special edition Porsche without an identification badge? This was the first PCA Club 50 example produced. (Photo Courtesy Rich Chenet)

This special metallic sky blue was selected to evoke the spirit of California's Pacific Coast Highway 1. It went perfectly with the beige-trimmed cabin. (Photo Courtesy Rich Chenet)

991 Porsche 911 Carrera GTS and was limited to a quantity of 60 units that were all finished in Club Blau. This unique, custom color is best described as a deep vibrant non-metallic purple/cobalt/blue. The car wears Carrera GTS badging as well as Club Coupe identification on the lower portions of the doors. The unique rear wing is patterned after the Carrera RS 2.7's ducktail spoiler and deck. The wheels are unique in that they are a modern take on the classic 5-spoke Fuchs wheels but in a much larger size than the previous 15- and 16-inchers.

The 911 GTS Club Coupe is powered by the same 430-hp 3.8L flat-six engine and 7-speed manual or optional dual-clutch PDK transmission as the standard 911 GTS. This

The Club Coupe and X51 Power Kit equaled the most powerful Carrera model up to this time and earned a front-row seat on* Excellence *magazine's cover for February 2006.

If 50 years was good, of course 60 years was celebrated with another Porsche Club of America Special Edition Carrera. This one was even a little more special based on the GTS model level. The unique Club Blau paint is particularly distinctive. It looks great here on the Porsche factory grounds in Stuttgart. (Photo Courtesy Corporate Archives Porsche AG)

PCA 60 Club Specials are shown by the pair at the PCA Santa Barbara Region concours. (Photo Courtesy Kirk Gerbracht)

rear-wheel-drive Club special edition featured adaptive dampers, a 10-mm-lower ride height, and the wider body from the 911 Carrera 4, although it was only served in 2WD.

The interior upgrades include carbon-fiber trim, Carmine Red seat belts and stitching, a Carmine Red tachometer, unique steering wheel, and "60 years of PCA" details. These included an embossed center console lid, personalized dashboard plaque, and unique door sills.

The Porsche 911 GTS Club Coupe was produced in 2015, and only PCA members were able to purchase one of the 59 cars. The remaining display 911 GTS Club Coupe was won by a PCA member through the car club's online lottery. As you might expect, the cars were sold out upon announcement and are highly sought after and very expensive today.

2021 Boxster 25

For many, it was hard to believe that the Boxster had been around long enough to celebrate its 25th anniversary.

In January 2021, Porsche described the model and occasion thusly: "Porsche Cars North America Inc. (PCNA) is celebrating the 25th anniversary of its Boxster family with a special anniversary model: the 2021 Boxster 25 years. Based on the 718 Boxster GTS 4.0 model and powered by a 394-hp naturally aspirated 4.0L 6-cylinder boxer engine, the special production model is limited to 1,250 units worldwide."

When Porsche revealed the first Boxster concept car at the Detroit Auto Show in 1993, enthusiasts were dazzled at the cars shape, proportions, and detailing. When the production version bowed just a few years later, some of that enthusiasm tapered a bit when they saw the final design and how much the car and the new 996-generation 911 shared in terms from front end and interior design and finish elements. With this 25th anniversary special edition, Porsche worked to recall and recapture some of the colors, textures, look, and feel of that original Boxster concept. The Boxster formula has been a success by any measure and has sold more than 350,000 units since its inception in 1996.

Connections from the original concept to this Boxster 25 edition include splashes of Neodyne-colored trim, which is a copper shade seen here and there on the original show car. The two-tone five-spoke wheels also have a bit of a retro flare to them. Porsche served the 25th anniversary special in GT Silver Metallic, Jet Black Metallic, and Carrera White Metallic to keep the palette simple and elegant. Also, there's plenty of Boxster 25 badging to be seen inside and out.

Staying generally true to the style of the historic original Boxster concept and 718 Spyder race car, the special model

The Boxster family's 25th anniversary photo has the 25-year special edition Boxter front and center. (Photo Courtesy Porsche Cars North America)

It's the Boxster 25 how and where it belongs: top down, on a curvy road, along an ocean. More than just cosmetics, this special edition machine gets unique colors, plenty of 25th year identification, and its own naturally aspirated flat six over and above the turbo fours used in its sibling 718-series Boxsters. (Photo Courtesy Porsche Cars North America)

Over time and generations, the Boxster has gotten a bit beefier and more curvaceous to the pleasure of most buyers. (Photo Courtesy Porsche Cars North America)

The Boxster 25 has a fully loaded cabin in this delicious maroon leather color. It's elegant and sporty. (Photo Courtesy Porsche Cars North America)

This Boxster 25 wears production number 0000. It doesn't mean that it was never built. It's just a special one whipped up for photography and media fleet use. (Photo Courtesy Porsche Cars North America)

You'll never mistake what brand of car this is, what model it is, and what special edition it comes from. (Photo Courtesy Porsche Cars North America)

combines a Bordeaux Red leather interior with a red roadster top made of fabric. The 25th Anniversary cabin gets the full boat upgrade package in brushed aluminum, 14-way electrically adjustable sport seats, door sill trims with Boxster 25 lettering, and the heated GT multifunction sport leather steering wheel. They are all standard equipment on the special edition.

The 4.0L flat-six engine, which is shared with the 2021 718 Boxster GTS 4.0 model, is just the engine most Boxster owners wanted in this 718-series platform architecture, as most of the standard and S versions run turbocharged flat fours. The high-revving 394-hp naturally aspirated powerplant, which is available with either a 6-speed manual transmission or an optional 7-speed Porsche dual-clutch transmission (PDK), really moves this car smartly.

The special edition model reaches a top speed of 182 mph with the manual transmission, and in combination with the PDK gearbox and standard Sport Chrono package, it runs 0–60 mph in 3.8 seconds, which is as fast as several 911 Turbo models of years past. The suspension is also meaningfully tweaked for better handling response and a slightly lower ride height. The new Boxster 25 edition was offered only during the 2021 model year with a base MSRP of $98,600.

2021 Turbo S 20 Years China Anniversary Edition

You might be surprised (or not) to learn that China is among Porsche's most fervent marketplaces. It is in fact now the brand's largest single international market and exceeds Germany and the United States in terms of overall sales. To commemorate its two decades of doing business in China, Porsche created a specially trimmed, limited production Turbo S model exclusively for the Chinese market.

There are no particular performance or specifications upgrades or modifications to this China 20 special edition—not that the near 600 hp Turbo S needs any to begin with. That's aside from a unique non-metallic blue paint scheme that features offset white lettering and racing number bubble 20 graphics and a variety of 20 Years Porsche China badges and identification. Production is strictly limited, and the car was only offered and sold in China.

It may surprise some that China has, in just 20 years, grown to be Porsche's largest international market. They created a special edition Turbo S to mark the occasion. (Photo Courtesy Porsche Cars North America)

The phrase "black and blue" usually refers to a bruise or a particularly rare-cooked steak. In this case it refers to, and looks great on, the China 20 Years special edition. (Photo Courtesy Porsche Cars North America)

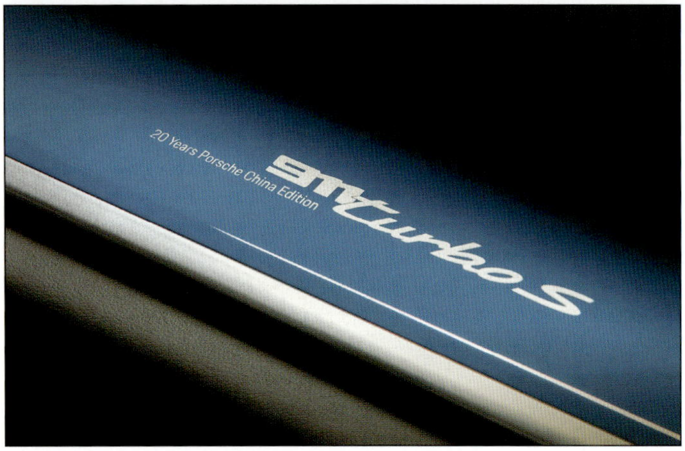

Over time, Porsche has learned and developed many unique ways in which to badge a car. Some are conventional, and others involve newer technologies that are often more elegant than simply stamping out another metal badge and riveting it on the car somewhere. (Photo Courtesy Porsche Cars North America)

Just like today's Indy and Formula 1 cars, Porsche has developed and offers nifty, competition-inspired center-lock wheels for the Turbo S and other top-end models. (Photo Courtesy Porsche Cars North America)

911 50th Anniversary Edition

How does one properly recognize and celebrate the 50th birthday/anniversary of a model so foundational and seminal to its brand that is still successful in its fifth decade? Think about it. The Ferrari 250 GTO, in all its versions, was produced for less than five years. The Jaguar E-Type ran for just 13 years. Certainly, the VW Beetle was produced for more than 50. For a select sports car to evolve constantly and remain an icon, still on the market, and a segment leader after 50 years is something remarkable. Porsche certainly thought so when it came to mark 50 years of the 911 in 2013. No mere tape stripes and badging would do the occasion, nor the car, proper justice.

In 2012 and 2013, Porsche brewed up a special model. It made its world debut at the 2013 Frankfurt International Motor Show to commemorate the 911's first public reveal at the same show in 1963. It was officially named the 911 50th Anniversary Edition, which was quickly nicknamed the 911 50, and produced in numbered and limited quantity for the 2014 model year on the 991.1 platform and chassis architecture.

Its naturally aspirated 3.8L flat six was rated at an even 400 hp, which was the same as the standard production Carrera S

This badge is as self-explanatory as possible. It really has been five decades of the 911.

The lighter of the 911 50's two gray color choices might as well be called ghost gray because it's barely there. In the right light, it looks soft and elegant. (Photo Courtesy Porsche Cars North America)

The darker of the 911 50's two gray color choices is a dead ringer for Steve McQueen's favorite classic Slate Gray. This is the exact 1970 911S McQueen so famously drove in the opening scenes of Le Mans, *his motorsports magnum opus film of 1971.*

What a beautiful sight: rolling green hills, a villa on a mountain top, and a new special edition Porsche. (Photo Courtesy Corporate Archives Porsche AG)

model that year, and could be backed by the customer's choice of the 6-speed manual transaxle or the Porsche Doppelkupplung (PDK) automated dual clutch transmission.

The 911 50 was exclusively built on the wider body work previously offered only on the Carrera 4 all-wheel-drive models. This gave the car curvier fender flares and a wider track, which fit perfectly with the somewhat retro yet freshly designed Fuchs 5-spoke wheels. The wheels measured 20 inches in diameter (both front and rear) and had a 9-inch width in front and 11.5-inch width in the rear. They were wrapped by P245/35R20 tires in the front and P305/30R20 in the rear. The Porsche active suspension management (PASM) system was specifically recalibrated for this model's increased track width.

A zoomier-sounding sport exhaust was fitted standard. Chrome trim strips on the front air inlets, the fins of the engine compartment grille, and the panel between the rear lights emphasize the unique and distinctive appearance of this special edition. The Porsche Dynamic Light System (PDLS) with bi-xenon headlights and dynamic cornering lights was standard.

The 911 50 was only served in three colors: Geyser Gray metallic, Graphite Gray (very similar to Steve McQueen's favorite Slate Gray), and Black. Each car wears two-tone 3D-effect badging on the rear lid with the numbers "911 50," hence the near automatic adoption of the nickname. This logo graphic is repeated in three-color embroidery on the headrest and in two colors as a logo on the tachometer and the alumi-

It's a shame that this generation of 911 doesn't give us more engine to look at, but the important stuff is on the badge, which reads "Carrera 3.8 Exclusive Power Kit."

Another modern rendition on the classic Fuchs 5-spoke wheel was used here on the 911 50 and also the PCA Club 60th Anniversary GTS.

Committed Porsche and hot rod enthusiast Bob Clarke has a particularly wonderful and well-trimmed man cave for his automobilia collection and cars. He parted with two much-beloved hot rods to buy this 911 50.

The 911 50 cabin is all business and leather-lined luxury.

Never miss a good opportunity to badge a special edition automobile, and Porsche didn't on the sill plates of the memorable 911 50.

num door sill plates. It can also be found on the cup holder panel along with the limited edition number of the individual car. There are tributes to the original 911 in the interior as well, such as green labeling on the instruments with white pointer needles and silver caps on the instrument pivot pins, just like 50 years ago.

Another special feature is the center panels on the leather seats, which are designed with a pattern reminiscent of the Pepita tartan of the 1960s. The full leather interior is designed in agate gray or black with contrasting stitching. The 14-way power seats were standard with 18-way adjustable sport seats as an option. The manual gearshift or PDK selector lever matches the decorative panels on the dashboard, doors, and center console and is finished in brushed aluminum.

Porsche quoted a 4.5-second 0–60 time and a top speed of 186 mph. In recognition of the 911's birth year, Porsche strictly limited production of the 911 50th Anniversary Edition to

CHAPTER 3

HOMOLOGATION AND WHEN ROAD CARS BECOME RACE CARS (AND VICE VERSA)

The first three International Race of Champions heat races took place at the late, great Riverside International Raceway. This is Riverside's famous Turn 9, which was a long, right-hand sweeper that leads to the front straight and start/finish line. (Photo Courtesy Corporate Archives Porsche AG)

1963 units worldwide and only in coupe form.

Many of Porsche's most successful racing machines are pure racers through and through. They are designed and built from scratch to be racetrack winners. You can likely name many of them: the somewhat all-conquering 917, 956, and 962. However, so very many stemmed directly from street models, used stock-looking bodies, and built on production-based chassis architecture, especially in Porsche's earlier days before the company was large enough and had the resources to develop from-scratch track attackers.

1951 Gmünd 356SL Coupes

Racing is as essential to Porsche as its cars having wheels and an engine. No event is more fundamental to Porsche's sports car racing lore and legend than the 24 Hours of Le Mans, the twice-around-the-clock enduro that was born in 1923. Some carmakers test the motorsport waters carefully with low-key, somewhat-disguised entries into races that don't immediately give away their intentions. In 1951, that most certainly was not Porsche.

In 1951 and 1952, Porsche had no purpose-built racing models. It had the 356, but the flyweight, high revving, very successful 550 Spyder didn't come along until 1953. Speedsters and 4-cam Carrera engine examples also followed the earliest 356s. Still a fledgling company that produced small capacity sports cars in relatively low volumes, Porsche chose to attempt its splash into big-game racing at Le Mans, which was already by this time the world's largest and most significant venue in sports car racing. Given Porsche's 19 overall victories and countless class wins and podium finishes, it is obvious that the focused efforts on the daylong race through the French countryside have proven correct and more than fruitful.

By 1950, the decision was made to go racing. Ferry Porsche believed it was an inexpensive way of advertising. He felt that journalists writing race reports for magazines and newspapers effectively promoted the cars for free, so it was unnecessary to spend a vast amount of money on advertising. Ferry was quoted as saying, "Money freed from unnecessary advertising can be used to gain valuable racing experience, and the lessons so learned mean that next year's model can be a better car."

The earliest Pre-A 356s built in Gmünd, Austria, were bodied in aluminum, which meant they were lightweight and easy to work with. With the company's move and the estab-

A dapper as usual Ferry Porsche sensed the value in endurance racing and improved the cars to hopefully pick up some positive free public relations exposure along the trail. Notice how many of the men in this photo are wearing hats, coats, and ties. It was a different time. (Photo Courtesy Corporate Archives Porsche AG)

lishment of a more formalized, mechanized production process came a wholesale move to steel bodywork. Some of it was produced by outside contractors, such as Reutter. The steel panels were easier to produce in volume and less expensive, but they were also heavier. The decision to go racing left Porsche with a choice: build a racing model on the new, heavier, steel-body production 356, or do something fresh. They decided to do neither and instead chose to resurrect three existing alloy-bodied Gmünd Coupes for the trip to France.

This may seem to be an odd decision, but there was a method behind the plan, as there usually is with a German engineering-driven company. To begin, there's the case that they were available. Given that they'd been replaced in the production roster by updated models, they were rendered somewhat expendable. The lighter weight alloy coachwork was an automatic bonus, plus it meant they didn't have to pull new cars off the production line for race conversion that would otherwise be sold to generate income. They were judged to be ever so slightly more aerodynamically efficient than the updated for-production steel models. They were rechristened 356SL for "sport licht" or "sport light."

The Porsche brain trust developed a meaningful but straightforward round of modifications to bring the old/new SLs up to racing snuff that included smooth aluminum fairings to enclose the wheel housings that were riveted onto the front and rear fenders. Ancillary driving lights were mounted up front with leather front hood tie-downs. Louvered alloy panels replaced the rear side windows. Inside, lighter weight carpets replaced the stock fabric, and a wooden tool and spare parts box was mounted to the rear package shelf. The radio was binned, although the windshield wipers and washer were retained. A small air intake was cut into the main bodywork just below the lettering on the front hood that housed the horn and also piped a bit of fresh air into the cockpit.

At the time, GT class regulations required a spare wheel and tire be carried aboard and that race cars must run a muffled exhaust system. The 1,086-cc flat-four air-cooled engine, colloquially referred to as an 1100, was street-production rated at just 40 hp, but performance tweaks were allowed in the form of modestly higher compression, a more aggressively profiled camshaft, and bigger carburetors. It was all good for an increase of about 8 hp. Yes, that's an 8.

The new 48-hp race motor, when combined with the SL's weight reduction and aerodynamic measures, meant that Porsche's first factory-developed 356 race car could hit about 100 mph on Le Mans long straights. It's hard to imagine when just 20 years later, the Langheck long-tailed version of the rather almighty 917 pushed 250 mph down those same straights. The engine work was managed by the soon-to-be-legendary Ernst Furhmann, who designed Porsche's first

The 46 Porsche trundles along a straight, where it was soon gobbled up by the much faster and ultimately overall winner Jaguar C-Type. (Photo Courtesy Corporate Archives Porsche AG)

The purpose of the front lid's leather tie-down straps and ancillary driving lights is obvious. The tiny duct cut into the lower front fascia area brings a bit of fresh air into the cabin.

high-performance Carrera 4-cam engine that powered the 550 and 718 Spyders and several 356 Carrera models.

Two of these cars were entered by the Porsche factory for Le Mans on June 23 and 24, 1951: chassis number 063 wearing race number 46 and the car seen in these photos, and chassis 054, which was a virtually identical car wearing race number 47. A third was damaged beyond immediate repair prior to the event and was a non-starter. These were days long before the notion of computerized, laser-cut racing bubbles, numbers, and graphics. The white number bubbles, as were the black numerals, were hand-painted on the nose and doors. The cars were otherwise refreshingly free of other adorning letters, logos, or decals.

Running in the 750- to 1,100-cc sports car class, there was

These louvered aluminum panels replaced the rear window glass, saved a few pounds, and helped exhaust air or moisture from the cabin.

The fully restored engine compartment looks as if it were produced just yesterday. It was the little engine that could and did!

You may wonder why so many race cars at Le Mans carry spare parts and tools aboard. It was simple enough. The track over time has averaged about 8 miles per lap, and the rules are if a car needs emergency repairs trackside, the driver is allowed to make them but with no assistance or parts provided by outsiders. It's better to be prepared.

This humble yet smartly reconfigured Gmünd Coupe led to the Porsche factory's first official class win at Le Mans and began a tradition and relationship with the historic French classic that continues to this day. (Photo Courtesy Corporate Archives Porsche AG)

little to no hope of an outright win against big gunners from Jaguar, Talbot, Aston Martin, and Ferrari. But the goal was to learn and hopefully notch a worthwhile finish in its class. Entering two cars into the field of 70 seemed like reasonable odds, although the number 47 car didn't take the start or run the race due to damage incurred in pre-race practice, so the factory's efforts all fell on the aluminum shoulders of chassis 063.

Driven by Frenchmen Auguste Veuillet and Edmond Mouche, the number 46 car enjoyed a relatively trouble-free race that covered 24,840.65 km at an average of 118.360 kph. Not only was it a respectable in-class placement but it was also good enough to win the class. It credibly finished 20th overall and notched Porsche's first official, factory-backed Le Mans racing effort. Jaguar took its first overall win at Le Mans in an XK 120C at the hands of Brits Peter Walker and Peter Whitehead.

Porsche had done what it set out to do and set the stage for decades of memorable cars, runs, and victories at the famous French circuit. Porsche continued to race the tidy SLs on and off for the rest of 1951, when they were sold into private hands. The number 46 car in these photos was imported into the United States, as were the two sister cars, and ended up in the hands of VW/Porsche East Coast distributor Max Hoffman.

Hoffman then sold the Le Mans class winner to John von Neumann, a West Coast distributor and racer himself. He felt the car would be faster sans its roof, so he somewhat unceremoniously lopped off its entire roofline and painted it red. It was primarily an SCCA competitor from then on and ultimately ended up in the sensitive hands of racer/collector Camron Healy. Healy had one mission: restore number 46 to its factory fresh, original configuration, which included reconstructing the body with its proper coupe coachwork. It was no small task, as no parts existed to do so, and had to be hand-fabricated from scratch.

Rod Emory, in his Outlaw Field of Dreams, marshaled what seemed like a near-impossible restoration of the number 46 Le Mans class-winning Gmünd. He recreated the entire roof structure from scratch with no drawings, plans, or measurements for reference. The job came out perfectly, and the car looks and sits just right. (Photo Courtesy Mel Stone)

For that task, Healy turned to Rod Emory, Mr. 356 Outlaw himself, and Emory Motorsports in the early 2000s. Emory descends from a line of Southern California customizers and hot rodders. His grandfather Neil Emory was the driving force behind Valley Customs, a highly notable force in custom car building in the 1950s.

Rod's business only builds and works on Porsches, so he and his

After considerable measuring, calculating, and guesstimating, the Emory team built a proper wooden form and hammered the new roof structure out of flat sheet aluminum by hand. (Photo Courtesy Emory Motorsports)

No computer laser cut vinyl graphics were used in 1951 or today. The Le Mans Gmünd SL was liveried with paint, a brush, and steady hands and eyes. The look is period perfect. (Photo Courtesy Emory Motorsports)

Fortunately, Team Emory has the tools, skills, and desire to fettle the aluminum bodywork by hand just as the technicians did back at Gmünd in 1948. (Photo Courtesy Emory Motorsports)

minions had the hands, skills, and tools for this sort of reconstructive surgery. It was a monumental effort to document the disassembly and inventory of the car they received. No small amount of computer modeling, buck building, and the rolling and hammering of countless sheets of aluminum was used to get the new bodywork's contours perfect to what it was in 1951. The entire restoration process took on the conservational and preservation

The 46's softly shiny paint glows under natural light. Is it 1951 or 2013? It could be either. (Photo Courtesy Mel Stone)

Team Emory made it a goal to not make the 46's metal finishing work overly perfect. Tight and clean was a must, but an equal goal was to leave in just a bit of the hand-hammered look that was present when the car was originally built many decades ago. (Photo Courtesy Mel Stone)

research and construction efforts that might be seen with any museum-level effort given to the world's most famous paintings, ceramics, furniture, or perhaps a T-Rex skeleton.

The result is breathtaking in its immaculate but not overly shiny appearance and presentation. Just for fun and as a way to reintroduce Porsche number 46 to the world, Healy and Emory entered the car in the prestigious Pebble Beach Concours d'Elegance in 2016. It was a winner in 1951 and a winner again 65 years later when the Pebble Beach judges awarded the conserved, preserved, and sensitively restored Gmünd 356 SL a hard-earned and well-deserved second place in a class against some very heavy hardware.

A street car that becomes race car becomes a show winning piece of history? It would be difficult to find a more legitimate and representative example than this.

Even for a legitimate racing car, the Gmünd Le Mans machine isn't any sort of fast, but it is zippy and feels light on its feet. All the while, that beautifully assembled flat four putters reassuringly along somewhere over your shoulder. (Photo Courtesy Mel Stone)

From Le Mans to Pebble Beach, it is something Ferry Porsche and the SL builders couldn't have imagined in 1951. The car dazzled the crowd with its charm, history, and faithful restoration. It was good enough for a hard-earned and well-deserved second place in class.

The Pebble judges get up close and personal with the Gmünd to appreciate its provenance and high quality but not overdone restoration. In the band of onlookers, Porsche notable Jeff Zwart is second from left.

1967 911R

From 1963 to 1965, after the launch of the 911 and 912, the new platform and design development scene was quiet for a few years until it became clear that the 911 had the chops to be an excellent road racing and rally machine.

The next limited edition was called the 911R and was only produced in 1967. The "R" was for Renn, or Rennin, which indicated a race model. The other big news for 1967 was the introduction of the street-production 911S model. Up until this time, there was essentially a single 911 spec: being powered by a 2.0L version of the new horizontally opposed, air-cooled six that was still internally referred to as the Type 901 engine (take that, Peugeot!) rated at 148 hp. This first 911S engine remained a 2.0L single overhead cam configuration, however it could be hot rodded up to 180 hp primarily via newly configured camshafts and a switch from Solex to Weber carburetors.

The new 911S became the basis for the first factory developed 911Racing model, the 911R. Sold in coupe form only (though by this time the targa top semi-convertible bodystyle had joined the 911/912 lineup), the 911R was stripped of nearly anything that added weight or wasn't needed for motorsport. The 911S was further amped up to 210 hp at a lofty 8,000 rpm via revised camshaft profiles, larger Weber carburetors, and the addition of twin–spark plug heads. Ferdinand Piech, Porsche family member and brilliant development engineer, spearheaded the project. Besides the hotter engine, the other most logical first step was to strip away all non-essentials such as carpeting, sound insulation upholstered door panels, and the headliner.

Quick Vic Elford pedals his 911R through a nighttime rally stage. Who needs course barriers or catch fences? So was the prevailing logic in the late 1960s. (Photo Courtesy Corporate Archives Porsche AG)

The factory engineered and produced thinner, lighter weight metal door skins and front and rear decklids to save important pounds. Some of the standard glass was replaced with plastic Perspex or Plexiglas window material, and the 911's optional lower-front-fascia-mounted fog lights were binned as were the cast-metal intake grilles mounted below the street model's headlights. The rear taillight clusters were replaced with

A gram saved is a gram earned. The 911R was yet another instance of dispensing a cast-pot metal badge in favor of a sticker or decal as a weight-saving measure.

This is the first production 911R, VIN 1, as restored and fettled by Callas RennSport, and on display in the underground vault of the Petersen Automotive Museum in Los Angeles.

All that glitters is gold, and in this case, Ranson Webster's original gold 911R takes pride of place in his fabulous Porsche collection in Nevada.

plastic nacelles and round beehive-style taillamps similar to those used on the earliest 356s, although they were not actually the same pieces. Just 20 of these machines were produced in a variety of factory-offered colors.

Driven by top road racers and rally champs such as Vic Elford, the 911R was highly successful in endurance contests, course racing, and World Rally competition. These uber rare and highly sought-after 911s were hand-built in Stuttgart. Today their individual histories are known and well documented, with values ranging into the multiples of millions of dollars.

A much storied and highly successful 911R was often raced, rallied, and won with Gerard Larrousse behind the wheel. Notice the silver Porsche 904 GTS behind and to the right in this photo.

1970 914/6 GT

Don't think for a minute that "Porsche street cars that became race cars" was restricted to 356 and 911 models. It wasn't difficult to see that Porsche's square-rigged, mid-engine 914 had racetrack potential. A track model wasn't on the agenda when Porsche and Volkswagen joined to create this intended low-cost new

The complete restoration of 911R number 1 included returning it to its original race livery. This shot gives a good look at the model specific taillight nacelles and light fixtures. The change was simple enough. These fixtures weigh a few ounces less than the cast metal pieces found on the stock 911. It's also likely an instant quicker to change a burned-out bulb in these externally mounted lenses. This defined racing 911 look has been replicated and cloned countless times, but the real ones are very rare, with less than 24 original Rs built, including prototypes.

This car looks somewhat like an angry, orange pit bull. Give it some flares and oversized rolling stock in 914/6 GT form, and Porsche's little mid-engine sports car becomes the aggressor. (Media PR Release, Photo Courtesy Petersen Automotive Museum)

There is no 110-hp flat six or mufflers here. A high-protein 2.0L racing engine fortifies the 914/6 GT's stance and suspension upgrades. A tough look and a tough car. (Media PR Release, Photo Courtesy Petersen Automotive Museum)

platform to replace the aging Karmann Ghia in VW's lineup and the 912 as a baseline entry in Porsche's model roster.

Not everyone initially embraced the 914 as a true Porsche due primarily to its Type 411/412–based fuel-injected VW flat-four powerplant. Although once the 914/6 running a true Porsche 6-cylinder 911 engine was confirmed as part of the plan, hardcore Porsche types began to warm up to the 914. Architecturally, the 914 had a lot going for it, primarily for its true mid-engine layout that put the engine forward of the rear wheels and fixed a rear-biased weight problem the 911 had since birth. Plus, the 914 was a pure two-seater, which kept it potentially shorter, lighter, and trimmer than 2+2–based 911s and 912s. The original concept was that the VW-motivated 914/4 would be sold as a Volkswagen, and that the Porsche-powered 914/6 would be sold as a Porsche. That didn't hold, and they were all badged as Porsches in North America, although most other markets' cars wore VW-Porsche badging.

It wasn't minutes before Porsche got busy on a racing version to be called 914/6 GT for the FIA's production-based Grand Touring racing categories. There was no factory-developed version of the 4-cylinder 914. The chassis and front suspension were beefed up, and all the suspension tuning was breathed upon. The 2.0L flat six was seriously cranked up from its street stock 110-hp rating to more like 210. The front decklid, rocker panels, and bumper caps were replaced with lightweight fiberglass pieces, and the fenders wore flares needed to accommodate wider wheels and tires. It also received bigger brakes and a racy, barely muffled dual exhaust system. All in all, it was a car several hundred pounds lighter than a 911. The factory side-window glass and targa-style removable roof panel remained intact.

The 914/6 GT seemed a natural road racer and rally runner, and it proved its mettle in both. One particularly notable finish came early on at the 1970 24 Hours of Le Mans where a 914/6 GT took a well-earned first in class and went home sixth overall. At an original cost of about $11,500, just 16 were factory produced, although many have been privately cloned in tribute since 1970. As of this writing, if a knowledgeable owner will sell one in good condition and the car has any meaningful race history in its provenance, expect to pay around $1 million.

1973/1974 IROC RSR 3.0

Spec racing is a relatively simple concept, although the execution of it on a fair and equal manner can be much more complicated. The primary idea behind the notion is that putting drivers into perfectly matched or highly similar racing cars puts greater emphasis on driver talent and ability with theoretically reduced or diminished variables such as the superiority of one type of car over another and the variances between big- and smaller-budget teams with lesser or greater engineering, car building, or other resources.

Another common thread among spec racing cars and series is that building, preparing, and running cars to a controlled

A pair of freshly built IROC RSR 3.0 Carreras leave Stuttgart on their way to Southern California via Lufthansa Air Cargo for shakedown, testing, and the first IROC heat races at Riverside International Raceway. (Photo Courtesy Corporate Archives Porsche AG)

This charming shot is of factory technicians working on one of the IROC RSRs at the Stuttgart race shop. Perhaps they have just removed the original ducktail spoiler and are test fitting a higher downforce tea tray Bürzel better suited to the series' two high-speed tracks. (Photo Courtesy Corporate Archives Porsche AG)

A dozen of the candy-colored IROC RSR's are finished and ready for the trip to America. The Stuttgart engineering and race shops are seen just behind. It's a most iconic image at a highly historical time and location. (Photo Courtesy Corporate Archives Porsche AG)

specification or formula will reduce overall costs of the competition. The premise behind the original International Race of Champions (IROC) series wasn't so much about reducing costs as it was about reducing variables with the goal of defining or crowning the very best driver(s) from a variety of racing series around the world. It's an age-old round of questions: "Who is better: IndyCar racers or Formula 1 drivers?" "Can the NASCAR guys keep up with sports car racers in identical cars that need to be able to turn left and right?"

The triumvirate of principal partners who dreamed up the IROC series had not only the idea but also the credibility and the juice to be able to assemble and pull it off: 1) the incomparable Roger Penske, Chevrolet dealership owner, former racing car driver, and by 1972, a highly successful racing car builder, team owner and entrant with numerous big-game race wins and championships under his metaphorical belt; 2) sports and event marketing whiz Michael Phelps, who had connections in the sponsorship and television aspects of motorsport; and 3) Les Richter, the retired 11-time All-Pro Los Angeles Rams linebacker and president of Riverside International Raceway at that time.

The formula they cooked up over countless meetings, dinners, and ski trips was a single-make racing series they owned and controlled that pitted a selection of premier drivers from the United States Automobile Club Championship Car (Indy) racing, Formula 1 Grand Prix, NASCAR, and pro level ranks and series from the Sports Car Club of America.

IROC
INTERNATIONAL RACE OF CHAMPIONS

Porsche Weltmeister Rennen

The dream of every motor sports enthusiast will unfold at Riverside International Raceway this weekend when twelve of the greatest drivers in the history of the sport get behind the wheels of identical race cars and go head-to-head in a trio of match races.

The International Race of Champions, hailed by auto racing experts throughout the world as the greatest format ever designed to determine a true driving champion, will be featured along with the 16th running of the Times Grand Prix.

The drivers who will gather here have all attained super stardom in their respective branches of the sport.

Between them they have won an incredible 32 national or international championships, over 250 major professional auto races and have accumulated better than $7 million in prize money.

They have won the Indianapolis 500 six times, the World's Formula One championship twice, the Canadian-American Challenge Cup series five times and the NASCAR Grand National championship seven times.

Their names have been chronicled in the record books over and over:

Bobby Allison, Mark Donohue, Emerson Fittipaldi, George Follmer, A.J. Foyt, Denis Hulme, Gordon Johncock, Roger McCluskey, David Pearson, Richard Petty, Peter Revson, Bobby Unser.

The cars selected for the three races to be run at Riverside (and a fourth at Daytona Beach, Fla. in February) are 1974 Porsche Carrera RSR racing cars, hand-made at the Porsche factory in Suttgart, Germany especially for this series.

The cars retail for $22,500 each and have a horsepower of 320. The only difference in the cars is the color and the lone adjustment the drivers will be allowed to make is to the seat.

The 15 Carreras (three for practice and backup) were shipped to the United States early this month.

To add more intrigue to the format, the drivers must not only switch positions, but also cars, following each race. Thus the winner of Saturday's first race will start last on the grid in the last-place car for the second race. This inversion process will be followed throughout the series. The last placed driver will take over the first place car in the No. 1 grid position.

The Race of Champions is a brainchild of Penske Productions, a company headed by Roger Penske, Les Richter and Mike Phelps.

The spark of controversy set off following the announcement of the series several months ago has

1973 TIMES GRAND PRIX 38 RIVERSIDE RACEWAY

The spectator program at Riverside told the IROC story to attending fans who may not have been familiar with the series' development, drivers, or car of choice.

Much consideration was given as to what sort of cars would suit the two fast yet highly technical road courses imagined for the events. Some options included the small-bore open wheelers like Formula Fords; a Trans-Am-style car that was fast, loud, and made for exciting competition; or sports cars. An important aspect of the car spec decision was a factory that could develop, produce, and maintain the racer fleet. The vehicle aspect was primarily Roger Penske's responsibility, and although his race shops were capable of running a fleet of almost any IROC cars, he and his IROC principal partners felt it was critical from a fairness and transparency standpoint that Penske Racing's engineers, mechanics, and techs strictly

Cool cats indeed, this is the original IROC class of 1973/1974 at Riverside with one of the RSRs. From left to right are George Follmer, David Pearson, Roger McCluskey, Gordon Johncock, Richard Petty, Bobby Unser, Denis Hulme, Emerson Fittipaldi, A.J. Foyt, Mark Donohue, Bobby Allison, and Peter Revson. (Photo Courtesy Corporate Archives Porsche AG)

Porsche supplied this 914 as IROC's official pace car. Even though Dan Gurney wasn't eligible to compete in the IROC series since he was officially retired from professional racing, he found a way to lead the field—even if only on pace and parade laps. At the end of the series, the season champion won this car. (Photo Courtesy Corporate Archives Porsche AG)

The differently colored cars really popped in person. More importantly, they looked great on TV, and the unmuffled, uncatalyzed 3.0L flat sixes sounded glorious. This is Riverside's Turn 7, 7A, and 8 complex. (Photo Courtesy Corporate Archives Porsche AG)

keep their hands off of the cars to eliminate potential suspicion of favoritism should any of Penske's contract drivers be invited to run the series, which was already a distinct likelihood.

The structure of the series was predicated on the running of three heat races at Riverside International Raceway in late October 1973 with a winner-take-all season ender at Daytona International Speedway in February 1974.

The job required a tough, versatile road racer that could be factory built in small quantity and deliver consistent performance among the fleet for a variety of drivers. The plan was for a dozen of the world's top racing champions to compete, which meant a fleet of 15 cars with 12 of them identified to run each race and 3 spares for practice, shakedown, and to replace any given car that was damaged in one of the races. In the name of further equalization of the machines, the cars would be traded among the drivers in between each race via blind draw. Penske Racing was already a Porsche factory team in GT class sports car racing and the SCCA Can-Am series, and the Porsche 911-based Carrera race car quickly became a favorite pick for the IROC-spec racer.

Following the 911's line of evolution, the first factory-developed and produced racing model was the 1967 911R, followed by the ST rally runners a few years later. The formula was more refined with the 1973 Carrera RS 2.7, and a more aggressive development of this car was the Carrera RSR 2.8L machine that boasted more power and bulging fenders with aggressive aerodynamics and rolling stock.

Penske stalwarts Mark Donohue and George Follmer both had experience and success racing Porsches, supported the choice, and participated with Stuttgart in the IROC version's development. The IROC Porsche was very similar to the 2.8L RSR raced by the factory and customer/privateer teams. The primary differences were the use of 5-lug Fuchs wheels instead of the center-lock, single-lug racing wheels run on most RSRs and the step up to a higher compression 3.0L engine aimed at a bit more low-end torque than the higher strung 2.8.

All of the IROC cars were built in the Porsche factory's Weissach/Zuffenhausen race shop from new bodies in white that received additional welded-in structural bracing, a roll cage structure, fire system, racing fuel cell in the front trunk, headers, and an open exhaust. The body was clearly a production-based 911 piece with wider fender flares front and rear, and the use of the Carrera RS 2.7 rear ducktail Bürzel (wing).

The cabin was very production based and included the factory street model's dashboard structure and instrument panel stripped of all racing nonessentials, such as the radio, heater, air conditioning, console, power windows or mirrors, armrests, console, rear fold-down seat, and front passenger seat.

Naturally, a Type 915 5-speed manual transaxle was the only transmission used or needed, and with a rating of 315 hp (although 320 hp is considered a more accurate and often quoted number) and an estimated weight of 1,990 pounds, the IROC Porsche promised spirited performance and close racing.

An important element in the IROC formula was first-class television coverage. For this, Phelps brought in ABC's *Wide World of Sports* as the exclusive broadcast partner. Executive Producer Roone Arledge and his flotilla of racing veteran broadcasters including Jim McKay, Keith Jackson, Chris Economaki, and recently retired three-time F1 champion Jackie Stewart covered and taped the live events for a later rebroadcast.

It is interesting in this day and age of wireless digital cameras and in-car on board camera technology to see the ABC crews wielding large and heavy wire-cabled cameras and wired microphones in the hands of the broadcasters. The cars had to look and sound great on TV, so each was painted a different color with a minimum of sponsorship identification and graphics. The cars were white, black, yellow, beige, and several shades of green, red, and blue. They were quickly nicknamed jellybean and M&M candy colors. All 15 were visually distinct with the driver's name on a black-and-white band on

George Follmer really knew how to pedal a Porsche and won the second heat in the black RSR. Most agreed that the rear anti-roll bar was a bit too stiff. Note the several inches of clear air under the car's right front tire, and the obvious unloading of the right rear as well. (Photo Courtesy Corporate Archives Porsche AG)

This shot summates much of the IROC season 1 story. The incomparable Mark Donohue won two of the three heat races at Riverside and the season ender at Daytona. He announced his retirement at the end of the season and sadly died in an F1 testing crash a few months later. (Photo Courtesy Corporate Archives Porsche AG)

each windshield header and door. The names were changed and covered with a new name band as the cars rotated among drivers and between races.

The chosen champions were a proverbial who's who of international stars: NASCAR standout Bobby Allison, multitalented Mark Donohue, F1 champion Emerson Fittipaldi, Mr. Versatile George Follmer, three-time Indy 500 winner A.J. Foyt, F1 and SCCA Can-Am champ Denis Hulme, United States Auto Club (USAC) star Gordon Johncock, Roger McCluskey, David Pearson, Richard "the King" Petty, Peter Revson, and Bobby Unser. You may wonder why some names are missing. Why not Mario Andretti, Dan Gurney, Jackie Stewart, or 1970/1971 Indy 500 winner Al Unser Sr.? In Andretti and Unser's cases, they were bound by Firestone tire contracts, and IROC was a Goodyear-only series, so that kept them away from that first 1973/1974 season. For Gurney or Stewart, it was simple. The rules required that IROC entrants be full-time, pro-level racers. They had both recently retired, although they were on the scene with Stewart on the ABC broadcast team and Gurney at the wheel of the Porsche 914 pace car.

Naturally, the professional road racers were expected to do well, and they did. Less was expected of the NASCAR and USAC oval racers, but that was a bit of an assumption. Pearson and Allison were both very good road racers, as was Bobby Unser, and they raced and placed well in the series. In the end, two of the three Riverside heat races were won by Donohue, with the other taken by Follmer. The six finalists who qualified for the Daytona season ender were Donohue, Follmer, Foyt, Revson, Unser, and Pearson. Ultimately, Mark Donohue won the day and the championship, after which he retired from racing.

Interestingly, the IROC principles decided they wanted to expand the series' appeal and race on more types of tracks with a bigger variety of drivers participating, so it was decided that the IROC Porsche RSRs would be retired in favor of a new fleet of Camaros, then later a second generation of Camaros, two different models of Dodges, and Pontiac Firebirds.

At the end of IROC season 1, the Porsches were sold off into private hands, which was not difficult to accomplish, as the RSR remained a competitive front-line racer that was still produced and sold new by Porsche. A variety of race teams from the SCCA and IMSA gobbled the cars up post-IROC. Some were raced with moderate and considerable success.

Chassis number 0100 was later owned and raced by notorious drug lord Pablo Escobar. Another was later treated to a slant nose, Flachbau Turbo-Look body, and driven on the street and still powered by its unmuffled 3.0L RSR engine. The yellow chassis number 0016 was owned for a time by serious Porschephile/actor/comedian/producer Jerry Seinfeld. Mark Donohue's white race winner, chassis number 0025, is still owned by Roger Penske. Today, the IROC Porsches are quite valuable and trade hands for multiples of millions of dollars on the rare occasion one is sold.

1981 924 Carrera GT

In spite of its generally tepid performance in its earliest, naturally aspirated forms, the 924 had a lot going for it. To begin, it was the least expensive new Porsche one could buy, and the styling and hatchback practicality appealed to many. It wasn't long before enthusiasts began to really appreciate its great handling balance too. The Turbo model that came along in 1978 certainly gave a glimpse of the 924 platform's performance potential, but the real unlocking of the monster came a few years later.

In the early 1980s, the FIA, the sanctioning body that controlled professional international sports car and endurance racing at the time and largely still does, was fiddling with the rulebooks and opened up competition to production-based, grand touring types of cars instead of the higher performance and more expensive prototype cars. Plus, an amped-up 924 Turbo qualified for IMSA GTO class racing in the U.S. The prototype machines and categories didn't disappear or fade away by any means.

Various 911-based 935s were still highly dominant during this period, but most carmakers that raced in these ranks recognized the value in elevating GT class competition for at least two reasons. One was that GT class cars stemmed from and more closely resembled street-production models, which made motorsports activities more meaningful as a marketing exercise. Another reason was that production-based machines, no

The 924 Carrera GTS had no mere cosmetic makeover. The engine came with much more power, and the suspension was thoroughly retuned. Notice the GTS's blockish rear fender flares, 5-bolt Fuchs wheels, front hood intake scoop, and black rubber spoiler at the trailing edge of the rear window.

The 924 Carrera GTS's frontal aspect was particularly interesting. The intake slots just above the bumper are straight from the street-edition 924 Turbo, you get a good look at the hood scoops and wider fender flares, and the popup headlights gave way to aerodynamically smoother and lighter plastic stationary headlight covers. (Photo Courtesy Kirk Gerbracht)

Ranson Webster's definitive Porsche collection includes this red 924 Carrera GTS and the red Porsche tractor. Talk about an odd couple.

matter how exotically developed or extreme in terms of performance, cost a lot less to develop, engineer, produce, and race than the more exotic prototype machines.

The three special edition 924s previously released by Porsche were primarily cosmetic and equipment packaging exercises. They were nice cars but not high-performance blood boilers. The 924 Turbo demonstrated that the platform had performance potential but something more was needed. That came along for 1981 in the form of the turbocharged 924 Carrera GT. Carrera is of course in recognition of previous high-performance and racing 356s and 911s. The GT acknowledges its place as a production-based grand touring machine, although one is clearly targeted at homologating (approving) this maximum strength 924 for international sports car racing. It was sold as a limited production model in most world markets and never officially imported into the United States, although several have snuck in.

Porsche's approach to add protein to the 924 was relatively straightforward, although that's not to label it as simplistic. There was the standard 924 Carrera GT, plus an edgier 924 Carrera GTS. The Turbo 924 powertrain's tail was twisted tighter in terms of increasing performance. The base 924 engine's output went from 110 hp to 210 courtesy of turbocharging and a host of internal engine mods.

The step-up GTS model was rated at 245 hp. Both were only available with a 5-speed manual transaxle. Body modifications included a hood-mounted intake scoop to provide air to the intercooler, the 924's row of cooling slats in the nosepiece above the front bumper, the 924 Turbo's polyurethane rear wing that wrapped around the larger rear-hatch glass, a set of bolt-on square-shouldered fender flares at the rear, and the use of 911-style five-lug, five-spoke Fuchs forged wheels. All of these modifications added performance function and seriously beefed up the 924's visual persona. Interior mods were relatively minor and included a padded roll bar. The 924's standard rear drum brakes gave way to discs, and the suspension was thoroughly retuned and included standard anti-roll bars, stiffer springs, and beefier shocks. The front bumper and lower front fascias were lighter weight pieces, and the latter allowed better engine cooling.

The GTS version was similar from an overall specification and architectural standpoint, save for the aforenoted power increase and the swap of the 924's standard pop-up headlights for a set of fixed and clear Perspex lens covers. Then, along came an even more racing committed model called the 924 Carrera GTR. The Carrera GT's 2.0L, intercooled, turbocharged I-4 was given more oats in the form of 375 hp, and the car had a serious weight reduction down to a quoted 2,050 pounds.

No matter the model, they're all rare. There were 406 Carrera GTs produced, and 59 of the 924 Carrera GTSs were built. No clear numbers are verifiable as to the GTR racing versions.

Sir Derek Bell and the 924 Carrera GT

Sir Derek Bell is an unquestioned star of Porsche motorsport and racing of any kind. He is also considered one of the kings of Le Mans. This affable Brit has earned a career-defining five overall wins at the great French classic enduro.

Porsche brought a trio of the 924 GTs to run at Le Mans in the 1980 race, even though the car was ultimately considered a 1981 model, and finished a more than credible 6th, 12th, and 13th overall. Bell teamed with another famous Porsche stalwart, Al Holbert, in the number 3 924 Carrera GT for that 13th place overall finish. All three were still running at the end of the race to notch solid finishes. The 6th place entry, car number 4 driven by Jurgen Barth and Manfred Schurti, was the highest-placed GT class finisher and came in ahead of several of the faster prototype machines, including several Porsche 935s.

I asked Sir Derek what he thought of the 924 Carrera GT, and if he was satisfied to be running one at Le Mans in 1980, as opposed to a bigger game prototype-level car that could compete for the overall victory. He replied enthusiastically that the car was "fast, reliable, and easy to drive."

Bell continued, "You know, I had a silver one for the street, which I really liked. Never should have sold that car, and somewhat wish I still had it."

El Supremo Porsche pilot Sir Derek Bell commented how much he enjoyed his personal 924 Carrera GTS. (Photos Courtesy Bill Warner)

This is the 924 Carrera GTSR that Sir Derek Bell drove at Le Mans, where he won handily against many faster cars.

935-19

The biggest challenge in describing this car is deciding where to list it. It's not a street car, although it is based on one. It's very much a race car, although it's not certified for competition in any major professional or other racing series.

This 935-19's Martini livery is unmistakable, as is its startling resemblance to the Moby Dick 935. (Photo Courtesy Corporate Archives Porsche AG)

The 935-19 is a special factory-developed program to recognize, honor, and reprise the overwhelmingly successful 935 racers of the mid and late 1970s and early 1980s. They are where the Flachbau look and models came from, and been there, won

This isn't Moby Dick, but it is an equally or more famous car. It's the Kremer K3 935 that took overall honors at Le Mans in 1979 and is another car that clearly inspired the 935-19.

Exclusive new edition of the Porsche 935

Clubsport race car with 700 hp at the anniversary of 70 Years of Porsche Sports Cars

Weight/dimensions

- Weight: ca. 1,380 kg
- Length: 4,865 mm
- Width: 2,034 mm (incl. side mirrors)
- Total height: 1,359 mm
- Wheelbase: 2,457 mm

Engine

- Water-cooled 6-cylinder aluminium twin-turbo rear-mounted boxer engine and rigid suspension
- 3,800 cc
- ca. 515 kW (700 hp)

Transmission

- 7-speed PDK gearbox with rigid suspension and short throw
- Dual mass flywheel
- Internal pressurised oil lubrication with active oil cooling
- Limited slip differential optimised for racing

Single-seater near-standard non-homologated **race car**

Weight ca. **1,380 kg**

Price: € 701.948 plus VAT

77 units

515 kW (700 hp)

Based on the 911 GT2 RS (991.2)

Tribute to „Moby Dick"

911 GT2 RS: Fuel consumption combined 11.8 l/100 km; CO_2 emissions combined 269 g/km

https://newsroom.porsche.com https://presse.porsche.de

Porsche's own spec sheet for the new-age 935 tells the how, why, and how much about this 700-hp specialty racer. (Photo Courtesy Corporate Archives Porsche AG)

Factory Le Mans Porsche driver Mark Webber, right, pulls the silk off the 935-19 at the Porsche Rennsport Reunion at Laguna Seca Raceway. It's one of those moments the obviously faithful crowd simply couldn't get enough of. (Photo Courtesy Porsche Cars North America)

that at Daytona, Le Mans, Sebring, and several national and international championships. This very special of editions particularly highlights one 935/78 machine nicknamed Moby Dick. Moby wore the most extreme bodywork of all 935s and was liveried in Martini

The transformation from street supercar GT2 RS to 935-19 is remarkable. While the street car's roofline still appears intact, so much of the rest of the bodywork is of new lightweight materials sculpted to save weight and cheat the wind. Even the vent-cooled wheel center covers look straight off of a period 935. (Photo Courtesy Porsche Cars North America)

The racing colors were mostly white, hence the whale reference in the nickname. This car was also among the most aggressive rule-stretching design Porsche ever produced. There isn't a tremendous amount of original 911 left in the car, and it pushed the street car–derived Group 5 sanctioning rules to the limit. You can be sure the scrutineers had fits and heart palpitations when Porsche rolled this machine in for type approval, which it got, but it ultimately proved to be the only such example produced. It ran in just four races and won once.

Moby's maiden voyage took place on May 14, 1978, when it lined up on the grid for the 6 Hours of Silverstone enduro. Jacky Ickx qualified the 935/78 in pole position and ahead of the second-place car, another Porsche 935, by two seconds. The race began under wet conditions, and teammate Jochen Mass drove the car brilliantly under the challenging conditions. By the end of his stint, he was so far ahead that the rest of the field was virtually unaffected by his spray. The Ickx/Mass car never faltered and cruised home seven laps clear of the second-place car. It was Moby Dick's first and only win.

Porsche and Martini had high hopes for Moby at Le Mans in June 1978. Top speeds

This shot clearly shows that the new 935 wasn't born or built in the 1970s or early 1980s. The modern steering wheel and instrument readout are clearly current to today's motorsport spec. The big P for park currently showing on the central readout screen wouldn't indicate anything from a manual transmission. (Photo Courtesy Porsche Cars North America)

There certainly was no PDK gearbox in the 935s days, although many of the contemporary drivers would have likely welcomed it. (Photo Courtesy Porsche Cars North America)

This is a great case of form following function. These front fender vents were on most period 935s to help vent unwanted air pressure from the front wheel-well area to reduce drag and lift. Thus, they are on the new-age 935. (Photo Courtesy Porsche Cars North America)

on the long French track ran as high as 223 mph with Manfred Schurti and Rolf Stommelen on to drive. The car was fast and qualified well, but its race was plagued with a variety of problems and finished 8th overall.

Moby Dick contested two other races in 1978 to bring its career total to four outings. After Le Mans, Jacky Ickx and Manfred Schurti gave Moby Dick its penultimate runs in the 6 Hours of Vallelunga (Italy) enduro on September 3, 1978. Ickx set both the fastest qualifying time and the fastest race lap, but despite holding a comfortable lead, the factory Martini-sponsored 935/78 snapped a fuel injection belt in the last 15 minutes of the race that resulted in an NRF (no results finish).

For its final outing, Moby Dick was entered in the ADAC Norisring Trophy 200 Meilen von Nürnberg on September 17, 1978. In front of a crowd of 90,000 spectators, and in the hands of Jacky Ickx, the Porsche was done after it had completed just 14 laps, not for a lack of speed, but for a lack of stop due to brake failure.

In the eyes of some, a competition history of four races with a single win may not be the stuff that legends are made of, but Moby Dick's place in the pantheon of Porsche motorsport history was truly established and forever made. It's one of those cars the faithful continue to speak of in somewhat hushed tones.

How did Porsche set about to honor and reprise such a legend? As the company no longer produced the air-cooled, 930 Turbo platform on which 935s were based, going that route wasn't a practical solution, nor was delving into the market to buy up 77 of them to form the basis for this limited special edition production run. So, Porsche turned its eyes toward its then-current (2017/2018) ultimate performance-leader model: the rear-wheel-drive, twin-turbocharged GT2 RS. This remarkable machine was nearly as quick as some of the earliest single turbo 935s.

In Porsche's announcement of this extra-special 935 tribute, it added that "because the car isn't homologated [for racing], engineers and designers didn't have to follow the usual rules and thus had freedom in development. The race car's technology for club sport events and private training on racetracks is based on the 911 GT2 RS high-performance sports car. Like its historic predecessor, most of the body has been replaced or supplemented by carbon-fiber composite parts. With its streamlined extended rear [bodywork], the 935

This view demonstrates at least two things: 1) the lightweight carbon fiber and Alcantara, which are special build materials used in crafting the 935-19, and 2) the beefy and nicely finished roll cage structure. (Photo Courtesy Porsche Cars North America)

Jeff Zwart pedals the Road Scholars 935-19 hard up the mountain at Pikes Peak. He narrowly missed an overall win and instead took a well-earned second place in class.

reaches a length of 4.87 meters [19.594 feet] and the width of this exclusive club sport racer measures 2.03 meters [6 feet, 8 inches] wide.

"The spectacular aerodynamics is a completely new development and pays tribute to the Porsche 935/78 Le Mans race car, which fans dubbed Moby Dick due to its elongated shape, massive fairings (flared fenders), and white base color. The distinctive wheel arch air vents on the front fairings, which are also featured on the Porsche 911 GT3 R customer race car, increase downforce at the front axle. Measuring 1,909 mm in width by 400 mm in depth, the rear wing lends aero dynamic balance."

The 18-inch wheels are unique to this model and recall those used on several 935s, so many of them ran steamroller-wide BBS wheels with special aerodynamic center caps designed to flow air through the wheels to cool the brakes. A wide variety of small and large aerodynamic details are adapted from more

Here is another great look at two mesmerizing Martini Porsche 935s then and now. (Photo Courtesy Porsche Cars North America)

recent Porsche race cars, such as the 919 Hybrid LMP1 and current 911RSR. The exposed titanium tailpipes are modeled on the late 1960s 908 racer.

The cockpit is decidedly race car-equipped and -inspired. The carbon-fiber steering wheel and the color instrument display behind it come straight from the 911 GT3R racing model. Naturally, a massive safety and rollover cage dominates the stripped-down cabin. In a nice touch of nostalgia and in a nod to focus on lightness where possible, the shift knob is the laminated balsa wood design similar to that of the 917 and 909 racers and the Carrera GT super sports car. A single racing bucket and six-point harness are standard, with an optional second seat. An air-conditioning system keeps things cool inside while on the track.

Besides the donation of much of its chassis, body, and cabin platforms to the project, the GT2 RS also supplies the powertrain with minimal modifications. That means it's a twin-turbocharged and intercooled 3.8L flat six that is highly similar to the road legal GT2 RS. In emissions-certified and entirely road-legal street trim, that car is rated at 700 hp. Even though it wears a less-restrictive exhaust system in the 935-19 and needn't be concerned with the last nth of emissions efficiency, Porsche maintained the 700-hp output rating.

As with the street bound GT2 RS, the nouveau 935 backs its powerplant with a 7-speed Porsche Doppelkupplung (PDK) transaxle with paddle shifter controls. The system is calibrated and tuned for crisp, lightning-fast up- and down-shifts in this installation. Brakes are in the form of 6-piston alloy calipers out front, and nearly as large 4-piston grabber aft paired with 380- and 355-mm internally vented iron calipers. To provide an extra layer of handling control and safety, the 935 retains the Porsche stability management (PSM) system and ABS. Should the driver have adequate skill and wish to take complete control of these functions manually, PSM and ABS may be switched off by the driver.

The reborn racer weighs 3,042 pounds, which is amazingly spare for the amount of performance and safety hardware it packs. Just 77 were produced at a cost of $701,948, which as of this writing equates to $796,100. Speed always costs money.

The interesting kicker with the 935-19 is that it costs reasonably near $1 million for what is basically a weekend track toy, as it's not race legal in most sanctioned series, nor is its road legal anywhere. These factors make it a training-ground tool for the rich and famous or a museum piece exhibit or garage sculpture for the same demographic.

There is one wild west competition event in which the 935 was ultimately allowed to compete: the Pikes Peak International Hill Climb. In a 935-19 belonging to the Ingram family, of Road Scholars fame and considerably noted Porsche restoration and collection giants, Jeff Zwart, who some consider the ultimate Porsche enthusiast ambassador, made a deal to run his car up the mountain in Colorado in 2020 during the virtually unlimited time-attack competition for supremacy of the 156 corner, 12.42-mile Race to the Clouds.

Zwart, a hill-climb racer of near legendary note, owns several overall and class wins at the Peak. He faced considerable competition from David Donner and David Donohue in equally fast and capable GT RS2 Club Sport machines. David is the son of Mark Donohue, a mostly retired professional and championship sports car racer himself.

In qualifying, Donohue blazed the hill to earn the pole time, although it's not a pure pole position as the cars race up the hill against the clock and not wheel to wheel against each other. In *Panorama* magazine, Zwart commented about his Road Scholars-owned and -sponsored 935-19.

"It's disconcertingly easy to drive," he said. "It generates more g-forces than any car I've ever driven, including my GT3 Turbo."

Zwart was the oldest among the big banger Porsche runners at the event, and while he's vastly experienced and still plenty fast, he admitted that he used this opportunity to re-evaluate his skills, test the limits of the car, and relearn the mountain to incorporate all of these parameters in his approach to a race run.

Donohue didn't complete his run and pulled over mid-course after he brushed the stone embankment wall with his GT2. David Donner took class honors, and Zwart earned a commendable second among the time attack 1 group. Porschemeister Zwart, who has driven 13 Porsches at Pikes Peak, loves the 935 and declared it to be "the best car I've ever driven here." He couldn't imagine that he could have a better car.

A case could certainly be made to say the 935-19 is the most special Porsche special edition of all and ever. Magnus Walker made another observation.

"I get it," he said. "It's a gorgeous car, honoring a run of all conquering and gorgeous race cars, and it's obviously very capable. But with this one, what do you do with it? You can't drive it on the street, there's not a lot of racing you can do with it, and in the end, it's either a museum piece or a very expensive track toy."

CHAPTER 4

LOW-VOLUME PRODUCTION, RESTORATION, BUILD, AND DESIGN SHOPS

RUF Automobile GmbH

RUF Automobile of Pfaffenhausen, Germany, is likely the best known among extreme top-end Porsche specialty and performance concerns. It all began in 1939, when Alois Ruf (pronounced roof) Sr. opened and operated a small, independent automotive and transportation repair shop. Ruf wasn't particularly a Porsche or any other brand of car or truck specialist at the time, but during World War II and immediately postwar, his business was in high demand to get old, worn-out cars back on the road because in most cases, new car production didn't resume until 1946. This is particularly significant for war-torn Germany, where so many automotive and other industrial factories were destroyed by Allied bombing raids.

Estonia and Alois Ruf stand with an anniversary edition RUF CTR. (Photo Courtesy RUF Automobiles)

Ruf continued to operate his mechanics shop and first came into contact with Porsche cars in the early 1960s. Ruf's son, Alois Jr., took over the business in 1974. Even though the RUF Automobile was already involved in the Porsche service, repair, and modifications business by this time, these activities amped up throughout the mid and late 1970s when it was common belief that the 911 models would disappear and be replaced in Porsche's new product lineup with front-engine, water-cooled models such as the 924 and 928.

RUF has long designed and cast its own wheels that are installed on all the new cars that the company builds. They are highly popular as aftermarket add-ons. (Photo Courtesy RUF Automobiles)

RUF began the development and small-volume production of its own highly

RUF CTR Yellowbird number 1 is currently owned by mega enthusiast/collector Bruce Meyer. It is shown on exhibit at the Petersen Automotive Museum's Exotic Cars display in Los Angeles.

CTR stands for racing Group C, Turbo, and RUF.

The Yellowbird's 200-plus-mph prowess has been tested many times, so a competition-level roll cage and harnesses are necessary.

developed, mega-performance, turbocharged Porsche 911–derived machines. Because the company's work was of such high quality and honored the ethos of engineering, design, quality, and performance that Porsche itself subscribed, these activities were accomplished with the Porsche factory's blessing and support. RUF went through the effort and expense to become certified as its own low-volume manufacturer in 1981. Even though the cars were based on Porsches, they were built up and modified from brand new cars and given RUV 17-digit VIN numbers to make RUF Automobile a legitimate original equipment manufacturer (OEM). The company already produced its own line of high-performance alloy wheels and alloy and composite body panels, so this was the next logical step to legitimize itself as a proper carmaker and brand.

It would take the rest of this book to catalog and describe every RUF car or model derivation the company has built in its 40 years as a type-approved OEM carmaker, not to mention customer conversions and individual customs. There's no question that the car and model that really put the company on the global stage is called the CTR, which stands for Group C racing car, T for Porsche Turbo, and R for RUF.

The first production example of this model famously beat all comers in a 1987 *Road & Track* top speed shootout run at Volkswagen's Ehra-Lessien test track in Germany. The roster of competitors was fearsome and included factory OEM top-line exotics and several aftermarket and low-volume production machines and tuners: Porsche's own 959, a Mercedes-Benz AMG Hammer sedan, two independently built hot rod Porsches, and the two Ferraris were a 12-cylinder Testarossa and a twin-turbo F40. Paul Frere and Phil Hill, two world class Le Mans–winning drivers and by then *Road & Track* editorial contributors, were on hand for the driving chores. This company-owned, private test track is more than 10 miles long with one straight that runs for more than 5.4 miles, which is enough for nearly any car to achieve its top speed.

The original RUF CTR was based on the then-new 1989 Porsche Carrera 3.2 Coupe. It was comprehensively redesigned and re-engineered by RUF to include several lightweight body panels and a highly modified twin turbocharged, twin intercooled 3.4L air-cooled flat six backed by the company's own 5-speed manual transaxle. At the time, it was rated somewhat conservatively around 463 hp, but today's estimates place that number at more like 550 to 575. In this era of 707-hp Dodge Challengers and 760-hp Shelby GT500s, 575 hp may not sound like an impressive output number. Remember, this was the late 1980s, and turbocharger and engine management technology weren't what they are today.

Naturally, the car received countless tweaks on its way from a stock street Porsche 911 to RUF CTR. All of the rain gutters and drip rails were neatly cut off and smoothed, and

Even though it was not originally born as a 930 Turbo, the CTR 1 very much looks and earns the part now thanks to lots of lightweight body work, big rolling stock, the big wing out back, and twin turbos under the hood.

This RUF monster is all black leather and mostly business inside, although it does feature air conditioning.

The special intake housing atop the engine draws outside air into the intercoolers and engine compartment. Air is something this car goes through a lot of on its way to over 200 mph.

The CTR is shown down to its bits. The number of special components produced or specified by RUF is why it legitimately wears the right to be considered a full-fledged automaker and legally issues its own VINs. (Photo Courtesy RUF Automobiles)

Big things are always happening or under construction at the RUF factory shops. The orange/red car in the foreground is the current-edition CTR3. It wasn't built up or converted out of an original Porsche. It's designed and built on its own bespoke RUF chassis with an RUF powertrain, bodywork, and VIN. (Photo Courtesy RUF Automobiles),

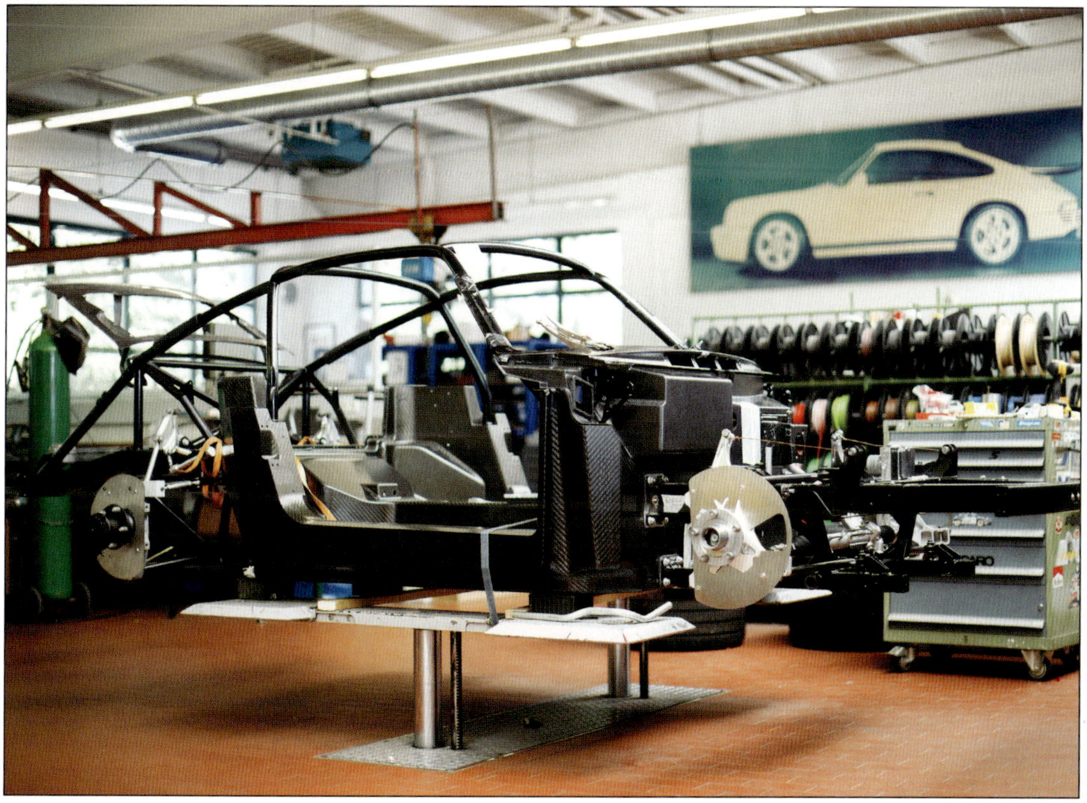

Here's a good look at RUF's bespoke monocoque chassis and roof rails. It's crafted of nearly all composites like a modern race car. This allows RUF the opportunity for tremendous chassis rigidity, weight savings, and the opportunity to place components exactly where it wants. Notice the immaculate factory premises and floor. (Photo Courtesy RUF Automobiles)

There are no mechanized moving assembly lines at RUF. Technician teams install components and work on the car until it's perfect to their standards. (Photo Courtesy RUF Automobiles)

RUF has turned its considerable attentions to the Boxster to give it variations of the RUF power, handling, and styling treatment. This model is called the 3400S. (Photo Courtesy RUF Automobiles)

The RUF SCR, which is a cross between a Carrera 3.2, a 964, and a variety of RUF design cues, is for those who want a powerful, responsive, naturally aspirated large-displacement six sans turbos and such. Note the Carrera RS ducktail-inspired spoiler on the engine cover, the fluted rear bumper that recalls the 959, and RUF's own lightweight body panels and center-lock alloy wheels. (Photo Courtesy RUF Automobiles)

Today's third-generation CTR3 with its evocative design honors 550 Coupes of the past and takes RUF design into the future. The chassis is fully bespoke RUF, as is the powertrain that includes a sequential manual gearbox. If there's ever a machine that legitimately earns the mantle of street legal race car, this is likely it or is among them. (Photo Courtesy RUF Automobiles)

A RUF family photo lines up CTRs, Turbos, and other RUF greatest hits. (Photo Courtesy RUF Automobiles)

The first RUF CTR, which defined and coined the term Yellowbird, leaves its homeland of the Nürburgring and Autobahn to travel to America and its new owner in L.A. after a 2,500-mile round trip of America. Crazy fast yet well-mannered enough for the street, this is one of the cars that forged the RUF legend.

the front and rear fascias were new RUF pieces, although the car wears a factory Porsche rear whale tail–style wing. RUF's own alloy wheels fill the substantially flared lightweight fenders, and the factory installed and not-so-aerodynamic outside mirrors were replaced with small, clamshell-style racing pieces. The car still wears a fully leather trimmed interior and has air conditioning.

Excellence magazine called the screaming yellow CTR number 001 an "obsessive, addictive monster of a 911" that clipped through the quarter mile in just 11.7 seconds and bested all other comers in the top speed test with a top-speed run of 211 mph. The car looked so dazzling in its brilliant yellow paint scheme that it earned the name CTR Yellowbird.

Even though RUF produced 21 original CTRs in colors other than yellow, they are still today colloquially referred to and thought of as Yellowbirds. Frere and Hill both commented how fiercely the car accelerated at the German test track and how generally stable it was at over 200 mph and at V-Max. Today, this first of all CTR Yellowbirds lives in Southern California and belongs to enthusiast/collector Bruce Meyer.

Over the years and decades, RUF continued to evolve as a company and grow its development cycles and product lineup. The CTR lineup has evolved to include a CTR2 Evolution model, a CTR anniversary edition to honor the original that is built on entirely RUF chassis and body architecture, and a CTR3 that rides on a chassis and body architecture platform that is entirely RUF grown and not built from a new production Porsche. Its curvaceous, elegantly aggressive coachwork is the primary design work of Freeman Thomas, formerly of VW, Audi, Porsche, Chrysler, and Ford Advanced Design studios. Its twin turbocharged 3.6L engine is rated at 777 hp in a car lighter than the original Yellowbird. RUF has also produced 964-based models, at least one pure EV prototype, and Boxster-based specials.

The SCR is a machine that combines the most modern high-tech materials and technology in a package that looks like a retro-futurist 911. The overall shape recalls a 964 or Carrera 3.2 combined with a modern stance, detailing, and a ducktail-style rear wing to honor the Carrera RS 2.7. Underneath that classically inspired Bürzel is a 4.0L, naturally aspirated, air-cooled flat six rated at 510 hp, which is the best of old-school 911 and new-school RUF.

Singer Vehicle Design

Let's begin with a few clarifications. There is no such thing as a Singer 911, nor is there officially a Singer Porsche. There is no Mr. Singer who owns or works at Singer Vehicle Design (SVD). However, there are Porsche 911s that have been

This lovely Porsche, reimagined and restored by Singer Vehicle Design, has a decided OEM–quality look about it and is comprised of several greatest-hits design cues from street and racing Porsches past and present. In as much as each SVD build is bespoke to the client, it can spice them up from semi-mild to nearly as wild as you wish. (Photo Courtesy Singer Vehicle Design)

Rob Dickinson's original Brown Bomber is the genesis of today's SVD builds. (Photo Courtesy Singer Vehicle Design)

restored, reimagined, reborn, and optimized by SVD.

Where did the whole Singer thing come from? Rob Dickinson is an affable Brit who was formally educated in design, but like so many young males of his era and nationality, he struck out as a musician with the 1990s alternative rock band Catherine Wheel. In his music days, Dickinson was a guitarist and vocalist, thus he is logically the singer in SVD. Amidst his relatively successful stint as a singer and guitarist, he bought himself a 1969 911.

Dickinson had a vision for how he wanted his Porsche to look, run, sound, and feel. By comparison, it's not so very different from what we've come to think of as the ethos that inspired America's

SVD maintains a good working relationship with the Porsche factory and company by underscoring its place on the horizon as a premier design house, restoration, and custom build brand. (Photo Courtesy Singer Vehicle Design)

Other than the moving assembly lines, the SVD facility is set up very much like an OEM factory. It includes quality-assurance processes and a well-organized parts and inventory department. This is no dark, backwater shop. (Photo Courtesy Singer Vehicle Design)

Each 964 donor car is disassembled about as far as possible and then upgraded, built, and rebuilt from the bare refurbished tub up. (Photo Courtesy Singer Vehicle Design)

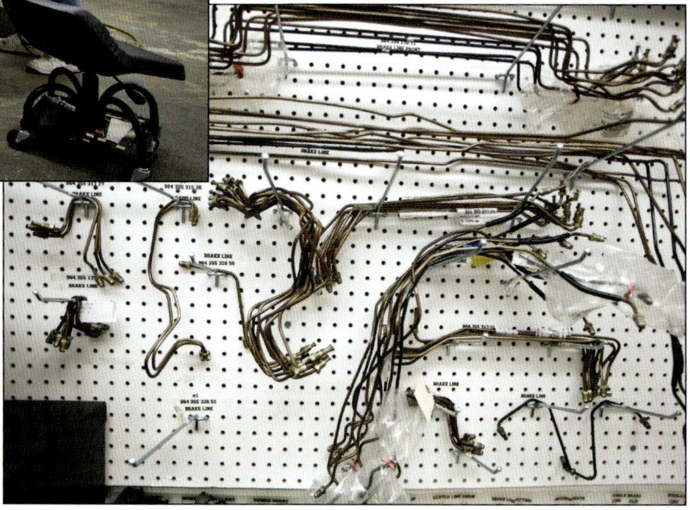

SVD's parts department is inventory controlled much like that of a major car dealership or an automaker factory parts depot. (Photo Courtesy Singer Vehicle Design)

How much quilted Spinneybeck leather is in the trunk of your 911? There will be plenty if you commission an SVD-restored 911. (Photo Courtesy Singer Vehicle Design)

R Gruppe cars. Although, Dickinson's notion was a bit less winged and flared than some of those California hot rods, so he built his car his way. There's a bit of 911R and S/T, and some Carrera RS 2.7 in Dickinson's envisioned blend, but it finished to an altogether more jewel-like level. It long ago garnered the nickname Brown Bomber. People saw it, drove it, loved it, and wanted their own.

Therein was the kernel of an idea born a decade ago: a business named Singer Vehicle Design dedicated to the design, construction, and sale of a series of ultimate 911s. The vision and philosophy behind the look, feel, and specifications of each car SVD builds goes beyond the scope of simply restoring, hot rodding, or recreating any given year or model from the greatest hits list of air-cooled 911s.

"The fact that our work visually recalls the past is more a product of thoughtful consideration of the term 'optimized' than a pre-occupation with nostalgia," Dickinson said. "Sometimes the finest 911 characteristic comes from 1964, and sometimes it's lifted from today's water-cooled models. The company's view is about preserving a moment in time for the owner and capturing a snapshot of the air-cooled period of the Porsche 911. We chose the universally acknowledged finest ingredients and simply poured them into one car."

Dickinson knew that building a few highly customized, bespoke 911s willy-nilly was a short path to bankruptcy. He believed he needed to design and plan the car much like a conventionally produced automobile. That meant he needed a willing and able group of skilled staff and partners to develop and supply the plethora of bespoke, modified, and hand-built parts and components needed. The look and concept he wanted had an unquestioned heritage-inspired aspect about it but were reimagined and optimized at a much higher level than simply building RS 2.7 clones.

Dickinson opines strongly that the 964 chassis is the best basic platform that Porsche ever created as it has all of the proper air-cooled 911 bits built in and benefits from myriad suspension hardware and other development that it picked up along the way. A significant side benefit is that the 964 platform produced from model years 1990 to 1994 (not counting the earliest 964 Carrera 4 models, many of which are dubbed 1989.5 cars) use OBD-I engine management, emissions, and

This relatively early SVD build encompassed a 3.6L engine and a livery inspired by the famous Gulf Blue and Orange color scheme. It's a timeless look for this vibrantly reinvigorated machine. (Photo Courtesy Singer Vehicle Design)

SVD doesn't provide this rather cool Heuer-style clock, but it's a clever aftermarket piece it will install in your car if you wish. (Photo Courtesy Singer Vehicle Design)

This cabin is a combination of metal-finished Porsche interior tub surfaces and acres of lovely Spinneybeck leather. (Photo Courtesy Singer Vehicle Design)

electrical-system architecture. It's much simpler to get all the systems talking to each other and to meet emissions regulations.

The design and concept phase was long and critical because the look, fit, finish, overall weight, and every single surface had to be perfect. Dickinson wanted wider fender flares but nothing that resembled an overstuffed 935. The bumper and fascia treatments needed to utilize the all-important 911 long-hood visuals yet be functional and contemporary.

The only way to get the balance of performance and response Dickinson wanted was to dramatically reduce the car's weight as well as make a serious power infusion, but a stripped-out race car or RS America-style interior wasn't part of the plan. That meant carbon-fiber panels were used for the fenders, hood, and decklid in the name of serious weight reduction.

"We kept the steel door skins in the name of occupant protection," Dickinson said.

The design and clay modeling phase took more than a year to achieve the look, weight savings, structural rigidity, and quality finish that Dickinson sought. He credits development and production partner Aria Group for the car's considerable composite panel work.

It's important to mention the 964 that gives so much of itself in the creation of one of these special cars is, was, and remains a Porsche 911. It's further important at this juncture to clarify that SVD is not a low-volume producer or official OEM in the same sense as RUF. Instead, the company and people comprise a "happiest place on earth" stew of restoration shop, hot rod and mod builder, and the primary consideration as a design entity in SVD.

Current SVD engine installs make clever use of the plenum space in between the cylinder banks as a neat and effective location for the high-flow air-filter housing. Notice that everything in every SVD build is finished to high-tech, concours quality. (Photo Courtesy Singer Vehicle Design)

Every Porsche restored, reimagined, reborn, and otherwise fashioned by SVD is a bespoke job for a very specific, demanding, and financially capable client. A considerable amount of work, modification, and finish comes with the SVD standard, if there is such a thing. Colors and finish choices run a panoramic gamut, and there are a variety of potential options.

There was never a question that the powerplant for Dickinson's ever-so-special 911s would be air cooled and naturally aspirated. Fortunately, the 964 already comes with the ideal 3.6L starting point for just such a Porsche engine. Although in the following years, the company has used turbocharged engines. In the beginning, SVD handed the factory lump to an outfit called Cosworth Engine Technologies that strips the engine to nubbins, punches and drills it out to 3.8 liters, balances, blueprints, and assembles the new long-block to its customary race car levels of quality and tolerance. The original Cosworth-developed spec 3.8 cranked out around 360 hp. While many SVD restored 911s were built with this powertrain, it is no longer offered.

The base engine, if you can use such a term, for an SVD build today is a 4.0L naturally aspirated, single overhead cam flat six developed in concert with Ed Pink Racing Engines. There are ostensibly two versions of the 4.0L: one runs a plenum-style intake system and the other runs with velocity stacks. Both versions are rated at 390 hp. The top naturally aspirated engine offering comes with the multimillion-dollar dynamics and lightweighting study (DLS) spec machine developed with Williams Advanced Engineering. A flat six at 4.0L, it uses special heads that run dual overhead camshafts, four titanium valves per cylinder, and lots of magnesium and other lightweight materials are used to reduce mass. The cold-air intake system is crafted of lightweight carbon fiber, and the exhaust is made of NASA-level Inconel and titanium. This racing engine for the road cranks out 500 hp at a lofty 9,000 revs.

SVD currently offers a choice of two similar but slightly different Porsche/Getrag G50 transmissions: a thoroughly overhauled 5-speed box that came with the 964 or a 993-spec G50 6-speed manual transmission. I asked Dickinson if he has any notion to build a car using the Tiptronic that may come with a given starting point 964. He sneered. One of the several dozen 964s used to create Singer-designed and -restored machines came with a Tiptronic box. It was converted to a 6-speed manual at the customer's request.

As you peruse these photos, you'll notice unprecedented levels of fit, finish, and materials quality. "Besides optimizing and reimagining the Porsche 911's great design and performance, our goal is to finish and assemble this car to jewelry and horological levels," Dickinson said. "We're using at minimum Rolex-quality-level parts and Rolex levels of assembly and finish."

I'm not sure I agree with that. The fit, finish, and detailing level of this astonishing automobile is more like the melding of a Porsche 911, the aforementioned Rolexes, a Prada bag, and a Fabergé egg.

A tour of the interior of any SVD-built 911 will leave you breathless. Every control, surface, and finish have in some way been rethought and optimized in keeping with the Porsche/Rolex/Fabergé ethos. The lightweight carbon-fiber-shelled seats are wrapped in sturdy yet ultra-supple Spinneybeck woven leather imported from Tuscany and highlighted by 16 small aeration rivets like the Ford GT40 in each seat. Smooth,

SVD takes weight savings and advanced vehicle dynamics to the proverbial next level or two by using the dynamics and lightweighting study (DLS). It's a track-focused (although a street-legal 500 hp) naturally aspirated beastie that takes SVD's design and engineering ethos to new places. Just imagine 500 hp at a screaming 9,000-rpm redline. There's carbon fiber and titanium everywhere you look. It's still a Porsche and looks like a Porsche, but it is substantially reimagined by SVD. The flares are obviously a lot beefier, and all the weight savings means the DLS weighs less than 2,200 pounds. (Photo Courtesy Singer Vehicle Design)

Credit Williams Advanced Engineering for the 4-valve, DOHC Porsche engine architecture. The build is as show quality as any other SVD model. (Photo Courtesy Singer Vehicle Design)

supple, and sturdy Spinneybeck leather covers a multitude of other interior surfaces, including the rest of the seat bolsters, backs, bespoke door panels, and floor mats.

The 964's arcane heating, ventilation, and air-conditioning (HVAC) controls are binned in favor of a high-tech electronic control system that manages those functions. An audiophile-level entertainment system has also been developed. One detail that particularly flipped my lid is the clock that was custom re-engineered to resemble a classic Heuer Carrera Chronograph wristwatch. The balance of the instrumentation is visually and mechanically refurbished by a long-standing gauge, clock, and instrument specialist in nearby North Hollywood, California.

The finish and fanatical levels of detail continue underneath. An hour spent looking at the bottom of this car is 60 minutes well invested. The stock suspension architecture is retained, although it received a considerable upgrade courtesy of a Bilstein spa treatment and the fitment of Öhlins Racing aluminum adjustable dampers. Brembo supplies the brakes. The paint on the undercarriage is as smooth and shiny as it is on any of the exterior body panels. This particular car carries, at customer request, a fully Heim-jointed suspension that replaced nearly all the commonly rubber-bushed pieces with spherical rod ends to exorcise any notion of play or slop out of the suspension and further sharpen the steering at the expense of some ride quality over harsh surfaces.

The example we drove was built some years ago and is powered by the original no-longer-produced 3.6L engine. Before twisting the usual key, which still lives in the usual place, let's neaten up a few details we glossed over on the way to 911 heaven.

For example, note that SVD has added an external engine-oil filler like the 1972 911. There's no pure mechanical need for it, but it's a touch the most ardent 911 enthusiasts enjoy, as does Dickinson, so they've added it to these cars. In SVD's interpretation, the cap is fully exposed and not hidden by a flapper door. The cap is a satin-finish milled aluminum piece that clearly says "OIL" to dissuade any misguided gas-pump DJ from accidentally petroling the dry sump.

The unique exterior rearview mirror is super light in spun

aluminum and mounted through the front-quarter-window glass. It's easily at hand for adjustment and perfectly placed for an ideal view rearward. SVD has installed a variety of steering wheels on customer cars, but this one wears the seminal Momo Prototipo piece to complement the certain period look and deepen the connection with legendary Porsches such as the 917. The red-faced tachometer on this car is a particularly racy touch. How about those Fuchs-style modular alloy wheels specially finished just for SVD? Note that the 17-inch wheel and tire sizes were carefully chosen to preserve some semblance of ride quality and a certain period look. At first glance, you may think the motorized decklid wing is a stock piece, but no. It is carefully recrafted entirely of carbon fiber and can be painted the body color or left in its natural weave–look state.

The tires on our tester are Michelin Pilot Sports in 225/45-17 front with 265/40-17s aft.

"We could have gone much more aggressive in the wheel and tire department," Dickinson said. Production Engineer Dorian Valenzuela summarized the notion much more succinctly, "Stuffing crazy 20- or 22-inchers under there would just be wrong."

Agreed.

Is Dickinson's mad plan working? Apparently so. The company has many dozens of builds beneath its belt with a client waiting list to get cars.

What about the ultimate new old-school air-cooled 911s? That's a matter of opinion and taste, but the case could certainly be made for SVD's approach, design efficacy, performance, quality, and result.

Gemballa's designs and body restyling are edgy or extreme to say the least. Some strongly favor it, and others may feel the opposite.

Gemballa

Gemballa was established in Leonberg, Germany, in 1981, and is a tuner, self-declared car refiner, and car builder of primarily Porsches but also Mercedes-Benz, Ferrari, McLaren, and BMW. The company has established itself as a legitimate car producer, is able to produce vehicles with Gemballa GmbH as the manufacturer, and can issue its own VINs. Its highly tuned, and customized Porsches tend to wear evocative-sounding model names, such as Avalanche, Mirage, Mistrale, and Tornado.

In its own mission statement, the company declares itself famous for "the most innovative, unusual, extreme, expensive, and exclusive vehicle conversions." Its styles and designs fall into the "love it or leave it" categories. It's too edgy for some and just right for others. Not content to simply crank away on 911s, the company has worked over exotic 918 Spyder and Carrera GT models as well.

I realize this type of image is hardly popular or relevant these days, but it certainly was in the 1980s, particularly at the big European auto shows. The press release information attached to this Gemballa media photo is too charming to resist. It states, "For many of the over 1 million visitors to the IAA at the Frankfurt Auto Show, the dream automobiles on show are just as much worth the trip as the newest small cars and most economical models. The dream automobiles are often graced on the stands with dream girls. This happy couple was seen at the stand of South German automobile designer Gemballa: a photographic model from Munich and a 300 hp-strong turbo convertible with super-exclusive fittings."

TechArt

TechArt's mission statement is nothing if not clear: "TechArt is the international premium brand for individualization of any Porsche model driven by the highest demands on design excellence, high technology development competence, and our responsible attitude toward emotion and reason."

Established in 1987 in Leonberg (near Stuttgart), Germany, TechArt sells wheel sets, exhaust systems, color-keyed knobs for the dash and instrument panel, shifters, or an entirely bespoke custom-built Porsche. The company is known for very high end and expensive design and fabrication quality. It is one of the few aftermarket organizations that has deeply invested in Porsche's other than 911 models with an extensive lineup of modifications, performance enhancements, and body restyling for the Cayenne and Macan SUVs, Panamera sport sedan, Boxster, and Cayman.

Germany's TechArt is one of the few outside tuning and performance firms that have embraced the entire Porsche lineup from the Boxster and the Taycan to the SUV models.

Strosek builds are also often to the extreme. This 928 has somewhat batwing-hinged doors not quite like that of a Countach, but also somewhat resembles the Mercedes-AMG SLR Coupe. (Photo Courtesy Dirk de Jager)

Strosek 928

Strosek is another Stuttgart-area tuning and custom shop that had its own style of over-the-top Porsche builds. It was founded in 1971 as Studio Auto Mobil Design by transportation designer Vittorio Strosek. From then until 2011/2012, Strosek Gmbh was among the more prolific Porsche customizers and tuners and particularly well known for its highly modified 928s.

Built over many years and in several iterations, Strosek 928s are known for their gull-wing-style door conversions and body modifications, including major revisions to the headlights and entire frontal aspect, wide front and rear flared fenders, more aggressive wings and spoilers, and oversized rolling stock.

In 2011, a fire at the company factory destroyed many body molds and other production fixtures, which essentially put the company under for good. Prior to the fire, Strosek fashioned design concepts based on the Honda S2000 and Nissan 300ZX, plus a number of 911 flat-nose conversions and several custom 944s. After the company closed, Vittorio Strosek rejoined the ranks of independent freelance designers.

Emory Motorsports

Rod Emory was literally and figuratively born into the custom car business, as his grandfather Neil Emory was one of the principal figures of the legendary Valley Custom Shop in Burbank, California. Valley Custom was an old-school shop that built equally old-school custom show cars, lead sleds, and cruisers using heavy-duty handwork and fabrication.

The company employed 1950s-style techniques such as chopping, channeling, and frenching all by hand with metal,

Rod Emory smiles in front of some of his scale-sized toys. The bigger toys are out in the shop.

This computer modeling demonstrates how Emory can modify a 356 chassis to work with factory 964 suspension components to considerably improve handling, offer readily available service parts, and maintain more Porscheness than aftermarket components. (Photo Courtesy Emory Motorsports)

A few of Emory's textbook Outlaw 356 builds neatly blend classic looks and custom touches with a lot of upgraded modern yet primarily Porsche technology. It's a great look, and the cars are a blast to drive. (Photo Courtesy Emory Motorsports)

The Emory Rothsport SOHC flat four in naturally aspirated or turbocharged form is the engine of choice for Emory builds. It offers flexibility and performance far beyond what can be built into the old overhead valver, and it is far less finicky to assemble and maintain than an expensive factory Carrera four-cam engine.

Emory and a couple of his teammates are doing metal fabrication and fitting work old school by hand and with hand tools. There are no automated jigs and presses here. (Photo Courtesy Emory Motorsports)

While the Emory Rothsport Outlaw 4 looks exotic, and it ultimately is, it's based on various Porsche engine architectures, provides modern power supported by up-to-date technology, and fits perfectly within the engine bay of a 356 or 912.

gas welding torches, and lead filler. There were no computerized milling or cutting machines back in those days. Valley's work is not always well known but was comparable to the Barris brothers, Darryl Starbird, and other legends of the time.

Rod chose to pursue his automotive design, customizing, and building pursuits not with the chopped Mercs and Chevys like his grandfather, but instead centralized his passion, skill, and enthusiasm on the Porsche 356.

"It's just such a great design with wonderful shapes, balanced proportions, and great racing models and history," said Rod. "You put 200 hp into one of these cars, firm up the suspension a bit, and give them modern brakes, and they become really fun to drive."

Rod's pursuits have since taken him far beyond basic 356 tuning to include considerable restyling in what's been coined and credited to Emory as the Outlaw 356 aesthetic. Nearly all of Emory's builds involve complete disassembly and reinvention as an Emory Outlaw and include elegant body redesign, highly detailed interiors, modern rolling stock, retrofitted Porsche 964 suspension, and a variety of hot engine options. Although it's not a pure factory restoration shop by design, Emory Motorsports is capable of award-winning restoration work as demonstrated in the 356 Gmünd SL Le Mans Coupe.

While the Emory Motorsports shop has its share of modern high-tech design and fabrication tools, a majority of the work there is still done in an evolved

The fender script on this devilishly black Emory Outlaw says "Special" where one might expect it to say "Speedster." It is, however, special. (Photo Courtesy Emory Motorsports)

Some of Emory's custom Outlaw touches include louvered panels just below the rear window glass, custom aerodynamic exterior rearview mirrors, a serious-looking roll-bar structure inside, and beautiful machined aluminum wheels that ape the look of classic racing wheels of days past. (Photo Courtesy Emory Motorsports)

This 904 Carrera GTS and 930 Turbo aren't Emory builds. They are just eye candy I found hanging out at the shop during my last visit that further demonstrate that these guys live and breathe front-line Porsches.

version of what his grandfather did: hand-shaping metal panels over wooden bucks and anvils, and welding and working the metal by hand to a perfectly shaped and smooth finish. Emory builds are based on all-steel coachwork and largely eschew carbon-fiber and aluminum bodywork. Emory, in concert with Jeff Gamroth of Rothsport Racing, developed an overhead-camshaft flat-four engine as a major step-up option to hot rodding the stock 356's overhead-valve four.

This unique engine was conceptualized as a twin-spark-plug-per-cylinder, 964-series flat six

Like no 356 engine ever built previously, this is the twin-turbocharged Outlaw 4 business end of the Momo Emory 356 RSR. It produces 400 hp from an air-cooled, SOHC flat four of less than 3.0 liters. (Photo Courtesy Emory Motorsports)

Let's call this 356 Carrera meets 935 or angry pit bull meets 356. Emory calls it a 356 RSR. It's his most radical build to date and based on a real yet highly fortified 356 underneath with considerable body mods, a 400-hp twin-turbo Outlaw 4 engine, and Momo wheels, seats, belts, and other accessories. It was built under commission by Momo's Henrique Cisneros around a particular set of 935/956/962 endurance racing wheels that Momo had and Rod Emory just loves. It's the true definition of designing an Outlaw Porsche from the wheels up. (Photo Courtesy Emory Motorsports)

The 356 RSR maintains some of the original cabin architecture that never encompassed the aluminum 935 boost regulator knob that now sticks proud from the dash. Lightweight materials are used throughout the cabin to preserve a racy yet somehow modern 1950s vibe to it. (Photo Courtesy Emory Motorsports)

This handsome bevy of Emory Outlaws is lined up at one of the Los Angeles Luftgekühlt events. The fluted rear engine cover treatment recalls certain 550 racing coupes of the 1950s. It's retro yet custom and modern. (Photo Courtesy Kirk Gerbracht)

redesigned and recast as a four. These engines run from 2.4 to 2.6L, and the SOHC configuration allows breathing, horsepower, and high rev possibilities that far exceed the stock OHV four. Naturally, this bespoke engine family is named Outlaw 4. The engine was designed to be compatible with a number of factory Porsche engine components to create economies of scale and greater ease of service. For those who really want to go wild, Emory and Rothsport can provide single- or twin-turbocharged Outlaw engines that outpower any 356 ever produced by Porsche, and many 911s as well.

Emory's extensive client list includes a number of celebrity enthusiasts. Most have chosen to ideate and collaborate with Emory on their own special, highly bespoke Outlaw.

Glöckler-Porsche Specials

Walter Glöckler was a Frankfurt, Germany, VW car and motorcycle dealer and racer. He saw the makings of a German GT championship series winner in the original Porsche 356 if he could only make it lighter and a bit smaller. He took his proposal to Drs. Porsche and gained approval for a cooperation, as racing was a particular appeal to Ferry.

Glöckler proposed lightweight roadster bodies stripped of all nonessentials and pared down to the minimum possible weight. This was in 1950/1951 just as Porsche began to explore and dabble with the notion of racing its own cars. The initial Glöckler-Porsches were open roadsters, and as dictated by the chassis architecture and rear engine placement, it meant that they strongly resembled various open 356s, particularly Porsche's own 356 America roadster. The cars were by definition quick and ran modified 1.5L engines and weighed little more than 1,000 pounds, although at least one weighed 1,100.

Edgy-looking coupes came along later to be used in longer races and on tracks where better aerodynamics were needed. A small variety of drivers raced the Glöckler cars, including Johnny von Neumann, who achieved considerable success racing Porsches and Ferraris and ultimately became a Porsche distributor.

Mr. Glöckler himself at times raced his cars, as did his brother Helm. Most of the Glöckler production occurred in 1952/1953. The final example, a 1,500-cc coupe, was built in 1954. The curvaceous, ultra-light aluminum coachwork was by Weidenhausen in Germany. A handful of the cars made it to the United States and ran in the SCCA and various hill-climb events.

Information on the seven Glöckler-Porsche generations that were built runs from sketchy to detailed. After tracking down countless magazine articles and race reports, here's a look at the cars in rough chronological order of production.

How handy is it that this Glöckler-Porsche special Spyder is parked next to a stock 356 to allow us to assess its overall design, size, and proportions. This is considered a fourth-generation car and was built in 1953. The location, driver, and onlooker are unknown. (Photo Courtesy Corporate Archives Porsche AG)

This tidy Glöckler-Porsche Spyder was built in 1953. Vestiges of original Porsche design, detail, and proportions certainly remain, but it's obviously an altogether smaller car. It runs a 1.5L engine and weighs only a claimed 1,200 pounds. (Photo Courtesy Corporate Archives Porsche AG)

The lightweight aluminum skin is stretched so tightly over this little Spyder's chassis that it faintly pings when you touch it. Obviously intended and prepped for the track, it's interesting that this car still runs baby Moon–style hubcaps. (Photo Courtesy Corporate Archives Porsche AG)

Max Hoffman is aboard a Glöckler-Porsche in 1951. Note the pair of Jaguar XK-120s, and the 1948 Ford F-1 pickup just behind it. This jewel-like little roadster runs a single-seater-sized racing windscreen, dual mirrors mounted on the cowl, and drilled-out alloy wheels. (Photo Courtesy Corporate Archives Porsche AG)

A lot is going on in this fascinating archival shot. This Glöckler-Porsche began life as a Spyder-bodied car, and a not particularly pretty roof structure was added on either during or after construction. The location is the Grenzlandring, a former high-speed oval racetrack in the Lower Rhine area of Germany near the town of Wegberg, which is located close to Mönchengladbach and the Netherlands town of Roermond. The driver must have done well enough that day given the smiling faces and the wreath on the front of the car. Walter Glöckler is the man standing behind and car and wearing glasses and a camera in the middle of this photo. (Photo Courtesy Corporate Archives Porsche AG)

No. 1: Hanomag/Glöckler

Glöckler's first attempt at car building was in 1948. It was a lightweight, ostensibly homebuilt project based on a tubular-frame chassis that used a variety of mechanical bits from Hanomag. The car's 356 bloodline is fairly clear to spot. Walter Glöckler fielded the car in the 1949 Schauinsland race and won. Not so bad for a first effort.

No. 2: Glöckler-Porsche 1100

The second model from Glöckler's workshop also had a tubular frame. The front axle, transmission, and engine came from Volkswagen. The engine had a displacement of 1,086 cc with cylinder heads from Porsche. The engine's output was given as 48 hp, but when it ran with alcohol fuel, it achieved 62 hp.

The car was designed as an open two-seater, and the aluminum body was somewhat pontoon shaped. A total of two of this 1100 configuration were made. The Glöckler-Porsche 1100 won the German sports car championship in the 1100 class three times in a row: with Walter Glöckler (1950), Hermann Kathrein (1951), and Heinz Brendel (1952).

No. 3: Glöckler-Porsche 1500

Glöckler's third build came about in early 1951. A tubular frame was used again, and the chassis largely corresponded to the 1100 model. A 1.5L 4-cylinder engine from Porsche with pistons from Mahle and a camshaft from Oettinger served as the power unit. Revised in this way, the engine developed up to 85 hp, which was a big step up from the 1100s.

The 1500 was a low-profile two-seat roadster with a rounded hardtop that included a windshield and gull-wing doors that could be attached in a few simple steps and significantly increased top speed. A special feature of the 1500 was the long, tapering rear wheel cutouts. The front headlights of the VW Beetle were installed on the front fenders.

Walter Glöckler raced the 1500 for the first time in the Schauinsland race in August 1951. He won this event and set several speed records on European courses during the year. At the end of 1951, the American car importer Max Hoffman purchased or entered the Glöckler-Porsche 1500 in North American SCCA events. The car ran several sports car races in the USA during 1952.

No. 4: Glöckler-Porsche 1500 with Porsche Chassis

At the beginning of 1952, Walter Glöckler produced another version of the 1500. The body was similar to the one built in 1951. Unlike the previous Glöckler designs, it was built with a shortened Porsche 356 chassis. The engine and drivetrain were fairly straightforward from the 356.

Helm Glöckler won the German sports car championship in the 1.5L class with the number 4. This model was sold to Max Hoffman after several outings in Europe. He campaigned it with different drivers in various American hill climbs and sports car events. The Glöckler-Porsche managed a few second places. This vehicle still exists. It was sold in January 2008 in America for $616,000, and six months later it was shown at the Pebble Beach Concours d'Elegance.

No. 5: Glöckler-Porsche 1100 Roadster

In 1953, Walter Glöckler produced another version of his tubular-frame sports car, which was equipped with a 1.1L 4-cylinder, on behalf of the German racing driver Richard Trenkel. The body was a compact roadster with a narrow windshield; the structure was lower than most previous Glöckler cars. Richard Trenkel won the German sports car championship in 1953 with this vehicle.

No. 6: Glöckler-Porsche 1500 Super

At the beginning of 1953, another version of the tubular-frame roadster was created. It was equipped with a Porsche 1500 Super engine good for 70 hp in street trim and almost 100 hp in racing tune. The car was delivered to the Swiss racing driver Hans Stanek. Unlike the previous Glöckler models, it was painted in the Swiss racing colors of white and red.

In the summer of 1953, the C.H. Weidenhausen carrosserie built two identical bodies on Porsche platforms with Porsche powertrains and a tubular frame very similar to the Glöckler constructions. These vehicles were the first two examples of the Porsche 550, which can be directly traced back to the Glöckler-Porsche from 1953. Some sources consider these cars to be semi-direct forebearers of what became Porsche's own 550 Spyder.

No. 7: Glöckler Coupé

The last Glöckler model was created in 1954. It is a compact coupé with a notchback body, a large panoramic rear window, and concave front wheel cutouts. Some consider it the most handsome of the lot. The new coupé made its debut on the long-distance Liège-Rome-Liège race under Helm Glöckler and Max Nathan. Glöckler soldiered on to finish the event in spite of oil-delivery issues.

After this race, the coupé repeatedly visited the Porsche factory for about six months. At the end of 1954, it was sold to an American customer. A little later, it suffered serious body damage in an accident and was only sparsely repaired. The car was in Los Angeles for a few decades and has been in Germany since 1994. In 2005, the coupé was extensively restored by the Ulrich Weinberg restoration company.

Gunther Werks

Gunther Werks is another high-end, Southern California custom and build shop that takes 911s to the max. Much like Singer Vehicle Design has chosen the 964 as its ideal and only platform for its restored and reimagined 911s, Gunther Werks does its high-quality and high-dollar magic on the 993, the final air-cooled Porsche 911 platform.

Rather than labeling its 993 builds as rebuilt, customized, or reimagined, Gunther labels them as remastered, which is a fair statement considering the amount of work, re-engineering, and upgrading that takes place. These builds are very bespoke, ideated, developed, and finished with the owner's tastes and desires as elemental aspects of the plan. However, it's important to mention that much like the SVD cars, they remain Porsches with Porsche VINs in spite of the considerable level of modifications, replacement carbon-fiber panels, restyling, and oversized engine builds beginning around the 4.0L.

The Gunther Werks mission statement is clear yet lofty: "From the outset, the GW 993 program focused on uncompromised performance and meticulous attention to detail, the kind that Porsche aficionados not only expect but indeed demand. Nothing but the best will suffice. The 993 was the final evo-

Something wicked comes this way, or is it just a fabulous Gunther Werks 911 awaiting its reveal? (Photo Courtesy Gunther Werks)

lution of a story that started right back in 1963 by Ferdinand Porsche himself, and the essence of that car had to remain intact, whilst at the same time every conceivable element of the car had to be improved upon.

"The Porsche community does not take kindly to the molestation of an icon and the last of the breed revered by some as the last real 911. The aim was simple. Take the qualities and performance levels of today's mighty RS models and apply them to the air-cooled 993. Whilst the aim was simple, the execution was far from simple. Bringing the performance to a level that the factory engineers could only have dreamt about 30 years ago, whilst keeping the character of the legendary 993 intact requires a careful balancing act. Utilizing modern-day technology that simply didn't exist in the 1990s, GW started its journey to redefine an icon."

As of this writing, Gunther Werks produces two bodystyles: the coupe and the newly introduced speedster open roadster. The sky is the limit in terms of colors, finishes, interior trim, upholstery, wings, and rolling stock. Every one is custom built,

I was right! The cover comes off on what could only be a flared-fender 993-based Gunther Werks premium build. (Photo Courtesy Gunther Werks)

Gunther Werks derives this curvaceous muscular look by building on the goodness that Porsche gave the 993 with considerable rebody work in carbon fiber. Much like Singer Vehicle Design, Gunther Werks maintains the car as a restored and modified Porsche with a factory VIN and no hint or indication of being a low-volume OEM manufacturer. The design and workmanship is up to premium levels, and most of the cars are bespoke builds to the customer's order. In case you can't read the inscription on the engine, it says 4.0L to hint at the bored and stroked naturally aspirated 4.0L engine that lies below.

and every one is unique. Every one is also expensive. Pricing begins at just below $600,000, and you can drive it higher if you try, but it's doubtful you'll want to, as the company's base build is as nearly custom, bespoke, high performance, and dazzling as you can imagine.

The interior finishes on a Gunther Werks build are done to the highest levels of quality and dominated by leather and carbon fiber in nearly any finish and color livery that the customer may desire. (Photo Courtesy Gunther Werks)

Gunther Werks strips the donor car down about as far as it can go before it's rebuilt with custom carbon-fiber body bits, and everything is restored to as-new condition and quality.

The leather-trimmed engine compartments are spectacular, as is the sound of this heavily fortified, naturally aspirated 4.0L 993 engine. Every component is coated, finished, polished, or plated for maximum visual impact, corrosion resistance, and longevity. (Photo Courtesy Gunther Werks)

As you'd imagine, every inch of the Gunther Werks tiled shop floor is immaculate, and its production processes and quality are measured and evaluated at every turn. Check out the lovely ghostly lead gray finish on this elegant coupe.

The no-longer used or needed jump seat area is fitted with carbon-fiber panels to make a dandy place to mount the fire extinguisher. (Photo Courtesy Gunther Werks)

CHAPTER 5

OTHER NOTABLE PORSCHES

In scouring the world of Porsche for the various specials and special editions that make up the meat and primary purpose of this book, I came across many cars and stories that were interesting and often compelling but may or may not fit neatly within a strict special editions definition or chapter. To not share some of them seemed unfortunate. In the hope that you will find these cars more worthy of learning about, I've included a selection here for your perusal and enjoyment.

Dean Jeffries's Custom 356 Carrera

Dean Jeffries was a member of that exclusive club of primarily Southern California customizers and builders that designed and created cars for television and the movies. They include the Barris brothers, Darryl Starbird, Tom Sparks, and Gene Winfield. Jeffries's more notable works include the original TV series Monkeemobile and another all-time TV favorite, the Black Beauty Chrysler Imperial famously driven by Bruce Lee's Kato character in the *Green Hornet*.

Jeffries is also known famously as an expert pinstriper and has pinstriped countless Indy 500 racers and winners in the 1960s and 1970s. Jeffries also designed and built cars for himself. The most famous among them is the bubble-topped *Manta Ray* show rod of 1963 that was built on a Maserati formula car chassis and powered by a Shelby Cobra Ford V-8.

Jeffries designed and hand-formed the exotic-looking body. The car landed on the cover of *Hot Rod* magazine and took home several top prizes at America's most prestigious rod and custom shows. For a man best known for building and customizing American iron, you may not expect him to have purchased his own 1956 Porsche 356 Carrera with the exotic 130-hp Fuhrmann double-overhead-cam racing version of the air-cooled Porsche flat four.

Some of Jeffries's touches were somewhat conventional and included bobbing the bumpers and entirely reshaping the front headlight nacelles. A pair of high-powered driving lights were faired or frenched into the bodywork just below the reworked headlight treatment. Out back, the 356 benefited from a pair of lead-bonded Mercedes-Benz 300SL gull-wing roof vents and taillights. The rear decklid/engine cover was shorn of all factory badging, although the gold Carrera script badges were retained on the front fenders. Everything on the

Not everyone is a fan of the late Dean Jeffries' 356 Carrera restyle, but it's unusual, interesting, and beautifully crafted. Jeffries designed the modifications and did all the metalwork himself. Unfortunately, it's been shorn of all Porsche badging on the outside but still retains the Carrera script and engine.

Fortunately, through all the years of time and space and owners, the Dean Jeffries 356 retains its original Carrera 4-cam powerplant. Check out the nice detailing and racy machine-turned firewall.

Dean told me personally that he liked the sound of the word Carrera and knew that it meant his 356 had a special engine and connection to racing history, which is why he didn't shave the car of these model badges.

Today, the former Jeffries 356 custom is in pristine condition and very original to the vision of its creator. The more modern silver paint looks plenty sparkly, even without the ground-up fish scales in it.

car was smoothed, tweaked, and relocated to make it one of a kind. The cabin received a considerable makeover, including custom stitching, pleated leather, and a full treatment of somewhat graffiti-style paintwork around the dash and instrument panel. Additional ancillary gauges and instrumentation were also added.

Among his many and considerable talents, Dean Jeffries was an innovative painter. He dreamt up something more than special for his own little Porsche custom, which many consider to be the first notable Outlaw 356. Everyone in the hot rod and custom game experimented with pearlescent paint to give them a bit more spice and glow over conventional metallic finishes. To give his Porsche's single-tone metallic silver paint job some extra sizzle, he blended powdered fish scales into the mix. It's hard to know if the organic material actually gave the paint additional pop or how long the effect lasted, but nearly every magazine article written about the car mentions the paint has a "something extra" about it.

Today, the car survives in private hands and has been repainted with conventional silver metallic paint. Given the extra sparkle in today's modern finishes, it likely resembles what it did when it was first built. One can debate the success or lack thereof in the look of Jeffries's custom touches, but the car is utterly unique in all the world of Porsche and is highly sought after. It was sold at auction for $436,750 in 2018 and was recently listed on the Petrolicious marketplace for over three-quarters of a million dollars.

Janis Joplin's Psychedelic 356 C Cabriolet

We all know of Janis Joplin, the scratchy-voiced rock and rhythm and blues singer who died in 1970 at age 27 from a drug overdose. One of her songs famously featured two iconic brands of German automobiles. Entitled "Mercedes-Benz," she longs for a Mercedes-Benz, even though her friends have Porches. Strangely, Joplin didn't drive a "Mur Say Deez Benz" as she voiced it. Instead, she somewhat famously drove a 1964 Porsche 356 Cabriolet that she purchased for $3,500 in 1968. Licensed in California, she drove it everywhere she went when she wasn't on tour. It was often photographed in front of the famous Troubadour club in Hollywood. Regardless of her celebrity provenance, it was a pretty special car to begin with: a 356 SC powered by the uprated 1600-cc flat four and good for 130 hp.

What really made Joplin's 356 unique in all the world was its psychedelic, some would say "Flower Power," paint

The custom paint mural on Janis Joplin's 356 Cabriolet still looks clear and vivid all these years since it was painted. You can bet that this unusual design was inspired by considerable vision and some recreational pharmaceuticals.

Even the license plate frame tells a story. Otto Zipper was a well-known exotic and import car dealer and sports car racer in Southern California throughout the 1960s and 1970s. He was a common automotive purveyor to Hollywood and the music business, and there's no reason that Joplin didn't buy her car there, prior to its truly far-out art car paint job. It was common to see this car parked on the street all over Hollywood at the time.

scheme. Dubbed "History of the Universe," the hand-painted mural-esque brushed-on custom paint job was the work of her friend and roadie Dave Richards. She reportedly paid Richards $500 for his artistic efforts. This utterly unique Porsche proves that celebrity provenance and an authentic history can combine to create great desirability and value. Joplin's 356 sold at auction in 2015 for a somewhat incredible $1.76 million. As if to add a final measure of tragedy to Joplin's untimely death, she recorded the song "Mercedes-Benz" four days prior to her passing.

Sally Carrera from the Pixar film *Cars*

You can choose to think of a Porsche 996 Carrera as a specific gender, but there's no question that this Sky Metallic Blue Carrera Coupe is female. In fact, she's the friend, and some would say love interest, of Lightning McQueen, the NASCAR-esque lead character of Pixar's 2006 animated film *Cars*.

Voiced by actress Bonnie Hunt, the ever-beguiling Sally never hesitates to put Owen Wilson's Lightning in his place and help him learn a lesson or two. In as much as *Cars* was in the development and production stage prior to when the updated 996 bodywork design was revealed or came to market, Pixar's designers and filmmakers got a sneak peek of the future model since the look needed to be current to the film's 2006 release date.

Perhaps this is what a 996 or any 911 might look like if it were only a two-seater. For its performance as Sally Carrera in Pixar's* Cars*, it lost about eight inches out of the middle, which came out of the rear seat and package shelf area.

Sally was fashioned from design studies, sketches, and digital data. Many of the *Cars* vehicles were built in real life and in full size out of actual cars. This full-sized Sally was modified and customized to wear the body details of the updated 2006 996-generation Carrera. The underlying car was a slightly older, pre-owned 996 red Carrera Coupe, but that was all before movie and TV vehicle customizer and full-scale mechanical shark builder Eddie Paul got to work. The car was retrimmed to be visually identical to the 2006 car that would be Sally and given a light metallic blue paint job, pursed lower intake mouth, and blue-eyed windshield. The custom work was far more than a paint job and a set of eyes. It needed to be shortened to match the design of the car in the film. Paul sectioned 7½-inches out of the car just aft of the front seats and basically nixed the rear 2+2 jump-seat area. The A-pillars also needed to be stretched to make the proportions work and for all the pieces to fit back together.

This car appeared at countless *Cars* movie premieres, events, car shows, and in museum exhibits. What was her sexiest and perhaps most female feature? Look fast in the film or you'll miss it. The 996 Carrera's rear deck wing raises at speed or can be raised manually, and Sally flashes a small lower back tattoo ink at Lightning, to which Lighting replies, "Hey, do I spy a little pinstriping tattoo back there?" An embarrassed Sally backs into a gas station and says, "Ahhhh! You saw that?"

Porsche 911 Junior

You don't have to have a driver's license to appreciate Porsche. In 2015, an enterprising company developed the 911 Junior, which was a fully realized yet pint-sized 911 Cabriolet constructed on

Those who designed and built the Porsche Junior kid's car made a legitimate effort to get some of the critical features to look good, such as the Fuchs-style wheels, overall look, badging, and a genuine 911SC steering wheel.

a kart chassis that was sold through Harrods and Selfridges (London's famous department stores) and through Porsche dealers.

The look is striking upon first glance, as the car appears to be a 50-percent-scale Carrera Turbo Cabriolet, replete with rear whale tail wing and cloth tonneau cover. The headlights are full-sized Porsche units, and the scaled-down wheels are cast to resemble factory Fuchs alloys. The windscreen stands considerably upright, and the Junior is a single seater, but otherwise the proportions and details carry off the illusion. Inside the car features a faux 911 dashboard and employs a full-sized factory 911 SC three-spoke steering wheel. Under the rear engine cover, where you might ordinarily expect a lawn mower engine, resides a smooth Honda 50-cc single-cylinder engine mated to a two-forward-speed transmission plus reverse operated by a manual clutch.

There's no reason not to teach the little tyke how to drive stick at an early age. The gauges are functional, as is the radio. The body was crafted of fiberglass and it seems most were painted red. There are no hard and firm production numbers available, but one number commonly mentioned is approximately 225. They cost about $5,000 in the mid-1980s, but good luck buying a clean one for that now.

The Pre-Panamera 911

Porsche and others have long dallied with four-door versions of existing sports car models long before there were Cayenne SUVs or any notion of the Panamera. One of them is Texas Porsche dealer Dr. William Dick. He apparently didn't see any reason why there shouldn't be a four-door 911, so in 1967, he took a brand-new 911 S from his stock and shipped it to Los Angeles fabricators and race car builders Troutman-Barnes. They worked in Culver City, California's noted race car neighborhood called Thunder Alley.

The Alley was home to Lance Reventlow's Scarab car building and racing team concern and actor/racer James Garner's American International Racing team shop, among others. Carroll Shelby also messed around with cars in this neighborhood. Troutman-Barnes took on the complex task of lengthening the 911s wheelbase, roofline, and overall length by 21 inches. The first unique design feature you'll notice is the suicide doors that meet and latch in the middle B-pillar area. The reason for this was the decision to employ a second set of factory 911 doors in reverse and swapped side for side. The rear door window glass was stripped of the side vent/windwing, while

Look closely at the doors of this quattroporte 911. All four doors are genuine 911 pieces; the rear pair are merely another set of front doors swapped side for side and installed backward. It took the skills of famous fabricators and racers Troutman-Barnes to make it all work.

the windshield, rear-most side windows, and rear window remained stock pieces.

Luxury touches, since this singularly unique Porsche was intended for the doctor's wife, included the addition of power windows that were not yet a factory Porsche option and an interior lavishly upholstered in rich and assuredly expensive tan Lucchese Boot Co. leather stitched by Tony Nancy. Apparently, Mrs. Dick didn't enjoy a manual transmission, so her husband had the car converted to a Sportomatic automated clutch semiautomatic transmission. Custom-installed air conditioning was also included, of course.

No specific dollar amount is ever quoted for this singularly unique custom build, although period articles equate it to slightly more than the cost of a new Rolls-Royce Silver Shadow, which in 1967 was about $10,000, depending upon options at the time. That cost was on top of the base cost of the 911S, so it was give or take $20,000.

Vern Schuppan's 962CR

Australian racing driver Vern Schuppan enjoyed a worthwhile professional career. He competed in Formula 1 for several teams in the early and mid-1970s, raced in the Indianapolis 500 six times with a best finish of third place, and had a variety of Australian and British touring car entries. His most notable motorsport victory on the world stage is likely his 1983 overall victory in the 24 Hours of Le Mans in a Porsche 956. He had famously teamed with American Porschemiesters Hurley Haywood and the late Al Holbert. Schuppan also won the All-Japan Sports Prototype Championship that same year.

Nearly everyone who raced a 956 or its later sibling, the 962, all marveled at how stable, consistent, and relatively easy it was to drive this remarkable successful prototype racer. When Vern Schuppan decided to build his own exotic supercar post-retirement, it's logical that the big Porsche drove his inspiration and the design and makeup of the result. This very personal passion project was dubbed the Schuppan 962C, and along with a slightly different version called the Schuppan 962LM, the cars were developed and built between 1992 and 1994.

Michael Simcoe, General Motors' current global vice president of design, was the principal designer behind the Schuppan 962s, and there was considerable input by the car's namesake racing driver. The looks of both models were unmistakably inspired by the 962 and relied on a Reynard chassis for its foundation. Two similar Porsche engines powered the cars: a 2.65L turbocharged flat six rated at 550 hp and a more powerful 3.3L twin-turbo flat six that cranked out 630. These engines are architecturally similar in specification and overall architecture to the powerplants employed by the actual race cars. The fastest was said to reach 60 mph from a standing start in just 3.5 seconds. Those are remarkable numbers for the early 1990s, and they are only just now being eclipsed by today's best supercars. A 6-speed manual transaxle was the only transmission choice.

Schuppan didn't want the cabin to be a torture chamber, so the interior was fully finished and upholstered and included an audio entertainment system, a data recording system, and even air conditioning. They were frightfully expensive at roughly $1.5 million each and exceedingly rare with only six British-built Schuppan Porsche-inspired supercars ever produced.

The Schuppan's basket-handle rear wing was par for the hyper exotic car course back in the day.

The Schuppan's cabin wasn't lavish or highly detailed, but it certainly was plush compared to a racing 956 or 962. It was fully finished and offered an onboard data system, stereo, and air conditioning.

924 DP Cargo

The poor 924 has far too long been Porsche's undeserved outcast, and if there's a car bodystyle most Americans tend to make fun of, it's the station wagon. The rest of the world tends to take a less dim view of the 924 and certainly of a well-conceived and -executed sport wagon or shooting brake, as they are so often referred to in Europe. The examples are many. Take Volvo's handsome and handy 1800 ES or the Jensen-Healy GT Sportback. Over time, Jaguar, Aston Martin, and Ferrari offered shooting brakes, so why not the front-engine 924? Its chassis is already ideally configured for the Sportback treatment with the powertrain up front and the rear of the chassis already encompassing a yawning rear opening and rear window hatch.

The less-than-conventional Porsche-derived shooting brake in the photos on this page stems from the 1980s. Its design and creation were driven by practicality and economy, but of the financial and not the fuel kind. Certain countries, such as Sweden, tax vehicles as much by bodystyle as other factors. Sports cars are the most heavily taxed, while garden-variety sedans and sport wagons are taxed a bit lower, so a Porsche sport wagon is a brilliant call as the owners enjoy the cache and performance of a Porsche with the practicality and lower tax rates of a Sportback.

DP Motorsport's Ekkehard Zimmermann came up with the idea, and the Cologne-area-based tuner and custom car shop had experience in designing race cars, spoilers, and other sporty body kits. To convert the hatchback 924 for shooting brake duty, he attacked the 924 with a body grinder and cutoff

Load the wagons! The design work and craftsmanship of the DP 924 Cargo looks and works great, and most wouldn't know that a VW wagon donated much of its rear sheet metal to make it happen. (Photo Courtesy Dirk de Jager)

One thing the DP 924 Cargo is not is slow, as this one is built up out of a factory 924 Turbo. It's sporty and handy. (Photo Courtesy Kirk de Jager)

tool to remove most of the upper rear sheet metal aft of the B-pillar, including the big rear window. He could have fabricated all new rear sheet metal from scratch, but that would be more effort than necessary, so he fabricated the design with the rear sheet metal of a Passat wagon and worked with a combination of the VW steel panels and his own fiberglass bits.

Notice the black roof rails aboard the rear half of the deck. They also came from the donor Passat. The VW taillights and other bits are recognizable, yet the job still required considerable restyling and hand-fabrication to make it all work. This car is based on a 924 Turbo and wears 911-style Fuchs wheels. The rear cargo space isn't huge. The idea wasn't to create a van or SUV, but the floor is flat, and the access is excellent. The base 924 Turbo's unmodified 2.0L I-4 remains at 177 hp and is backed by the factory 5-speed manual transmission, which is certainly enough to move the 924 cargo smartly. According to a recent article in *Porsche Panorama* magazine, DP produced a total of eight cargos, three 924 conversions, and five based on 944s. Of the three 924s, this is the only one based on a factory Turbo. It's different and perhaps a little strange to some but also very cool. There's nothing so wrong with a semi-practical sports car.

Roger Penske's IROC Targa

It was primarily due to Roger "the Captain" Penske's prowess as a businessman and his long-standing relationship as a customer and factory-backed championship-winning team with Porsche that the first International Race of Champions season of 1973/1974 was run with Porsche Carrera RSR 3.0s. All 15 of the wonderful multicolored IROC Carrera race cars were coupes, but that didn't stop Porsche's senior management

***The Captain's Chair** is a one-off IROC-powered and -equipped targa built by Porsche for Roger Penske. Besides obvious accoutrements as a fully trimmed interior and two front seats, this car got all of the IROC racing upgrades, save for the more aggressive fender flares and the tea tray rear wing in place of its ducktail Bürzel.*

At least one California owner knew what they had in this special targa, given the Penski license plate.

from putting together a very special IROC-equipped targa for the Captain.

Penske ace development engineer and driver Mark Donohue summed up the car: "It was built with all the right Carrera bits in it, including wide tires and fenders, a special motor, and hill climb gears. He drove it for a while as his personal transportation. I thought it was such a great car that I was even kind of jealous."

About the only thing this car didn't feature was the RSR's wide fender flares. This very special Sunoco Blue IROC Targa had a fully trimmed interior instead of the race cars' largely stripped-down cabin. We can only guess that Mr. Penske would like to have this one back today.

Luftgekühlt LuftAuto Baja 911

Luftgekühlt means air-cooled, and all Porsche 356s and several generations of the 911 and 912 are air- and oil-cooled. Luftgekühlt is also the name of a series of large spectacular events established and promoted by Porsche factory racing driver Patrick Long, business partner Howie Idelson, and a host of other ranking members of the Porsche enthusiast, motorsport, and aftermarket community.

As you might guess, Luftgekühlt events are dedicated and restricted to air-cooled Porsche models. The water-cooled glitterati like GT3s and GT2s need to park outside in the parking lot with the trucks and Priuses. These are massive events and executed at outsized, innovative, and creatively curated locations such as commercial lumber yards and movie studio backlots.

In advance of the 2016 show, the Luftgekühlt brain trust got the idea to create and construct a special car to be raffled off to benefit a charity. Of course, it had to be an air-cooled 911, but what model and what style? Although the 911 wasn't originally conceived for off-road racing or rally competition, specially configured examples over time proved to be extremely competitive and successful in these grueling multi-road-surface contests.

Perhaps the most notable among them was the 959-based Rothman's sponsored 953 and 961 that famously competed in and won the Paris–Dakar rally several times. This tough-looking Porsche was thoroughly modified with a variety of body and chassis protection bars and plates, lots of ancillary lighting, special rolling stock, and a raised stance and ride height for the myriad and often dangerous challenges offered by the punishing African desert terrain.

These famous factory-built and -entered machines have inspired a recent run of Baja-style custom builds that don't quite match the mojo of the rally 953 and 961 but offer credible chops to those who wish to emulate that style and kick up some dust in a 911. Among the first and most interesting of these builds was conceived, designed, sourced, and built by the Luftgekühlt management and a who's who roster of Porsche influencers, racers, and aftermarket providers. The idea was that it would be auctioned off at the 2016 Luftgekühlt event to benefit charity.

Long and Idelson spearheaded the project with major input and involvement from Jeff Zwart. He is a known kingpin in the Porsche enthusiast community as well as an award-winning photographer, cinematographer, and director. Zwart competed many times and won, always at the wheel of a Porsche, at the Pikes Peak Hill Climb, which is perhaps America's original

Luftgekühlt literally means air cooled, and the show's specially created for charity Baja 911 was the subject of this event's watercolor artwork.

Lufti 3 was held at a rather massive industrial complex in L.A. where the Baja was shown and auctioned for charity. It emits a certain 911R vibe but with more modern execution. (Photo Courtesy Kirk Gerbracht)

Not exactly a Paris–Dakar 959, the Lufti Baja 911 legitimately looks the part of a proper off-road-capable rally racer. It also walks the walk with considerable off-road testing and setup by guys who can drive. (Photo Courtesy Emory Motorsports)

Inspiration for today's spate of modern Baja-style-911 builds most certainly came from the factory's highly successful 953 and 959 rally racers. (Photo Courtesy Corporate Archives Porsche AG)

The actual Jacky Ickx Paris–Dakar–winning 959 is replete with African desert dust.

rally-style event. Zwart knows cars, the Porsche market, and can really pedal as a driver. His taste and background made him a perfect inspirational source for developing this very special project car. Zwart also tested, developed, and dialed in the car during and after construction.

They chose and sourced a relatively low-mile 1985 Carrera 3.2 Coupe for the starting point. This gave them an updated late-model 911 from which to work and some all-important components such as the factory's later suspension, other hardware updates, and a fully galvanized body/chassis shell. Emotion Engineering was home base for the majority of the build, and Rod Emory headed up much of the design and fabrication of the rally-style bumpers and underbody skid plates. Benton Performance chimed in with race quality electronics and wiring, and Deus Ex Machina added a variety of details and custom touches. A panoply of aftermarket providers including Pelican Parts, KW Suspension, Pirelli Tires, Recaro, ERP Suspension, WEVO, Rothsport, Tarett Engineering, Swepco, Sachs, and Rennline contributed a smorgasbord of parts, bits, and upgrades.

The car's original Carrera 3.2L engine was disassembled and deeply serviced to a level of something less than an overhaul but far more than an oil change and valve adjustment. All gaskets and seals were replaced, as was every possible fluid along with a major tune-up and fuel injection cleaning and rebalancing. SSi provided headers and a sport exhaust system. A limited slip diff was installed, and all of the engine and transmission mounts were replaced. The suspension received a major redesign and makeover to accomplish the increased ride height while maintaining race levels of body control. The bumpers were bespoke pieces made just for this build, and the custom lighting and grille work, plus a custom roof rack was also mounted on top and came courtesy of Emory.

The cabin got a thorough redo to get it up to competition snuff that included a custom fabricated roll bar, lightweight Recaro sport buckets, RS-style door panels, Schroth competition seatbelt harnesses, and lots of custom touches, such as a bespoke milled rock maple shift knob. It had custom 15-inch wheels with Pirelli P-Zero Rally 195/70-15 tires. The brakes were thoroughly refreshed by PMB, Porterfield, and Goodridge. There are more detail upgrades than there is space to list. It was a piece that not only looked to be in the rally business but proved itself in numerous off-road shakedown runs with Zwart and Long at the wheel.

The very special LuftAuto Baja machine was a standout and crowd favorite even among the many hundreds of great air-cooled Porsches that populated Luftgekühlt 2006. The auction of the LuftAuto machine was low key in presentation. It was a group of folks gathered around the car and RM Sotheby's senior auction manager Ian Kelleher, with Long and Idelson nearby. There was no big stage, flashing lights, hooting and hollering bidder's assistants, or blaring stadium-level public announcement system. Kelleher introduced the car and opened the bidding. I don't recall his opening ask, but it reached $100,000 in an instant.

Bidding proceeded up through the next hundred grand. There was a combination of live bidders in the room and what appeared to be a few phone bidders. The bidding began to slow and flag a bit at the quarter million mark, but the even-voiced Kelleher was persistent and kept going until it was clear that $275,000 was about all there was. He declared the car sold at

This off-road-purposed Baja 911 was made courtesy of Emory Motorsports, Rothsport, and owner Cameron Healy.

Modern Baja 911 builds are at every turn. This one by Russell Built is out of a 964 Carrera 4. It's a decidedly extreme build with a considerable reinvention of the suspension, plus a stout 3.8L Rothsport flat six. Russell Built plans to offer them to customers in a choice of two- and all-wheel-drive versions.

that mark, and it was done. It was a compact, perfectly formed charity auction and donation for a car that didn't cost anywhere near that much to build.

928 Sportwagens

It appears that Porsche at least twice dabbled with extended-length 928s as front-engine, V-8-powered touring sedans or sport wagons. One of them, which most acknowledge as Porsche's first four-door GT, was called the 928 H50 prototype. It rode aboard a noticeably longer wheelbase than standard with much of the car from the B-pillar forward looking much like a factory stock 928.

Just aft of the reshaped front doors are a pair of rear-hinged flipper doors, not unlike those found on many extended-cab pickup trucks. It was a beautifully outfitted machine with the latest low-profile wheels and rolling stock, a rich-looking burgundy paint job, a fully leather-trimmed cabin, and a 320-hp 4.9L V-8. Another two-door 928 with extra seating room and a Sportwagen rear deck treatment was built as a 75th birthday present for Ferry Porsche.

Looking at these wonderful machines, it isn't difficult to understand the inspiration for the current Panamera and Taycan Sport Turismo models.

One of several expanded-use 928 prototypes, this was dubbed the 928 H50. Its wheelbase has obviously been expanded by several inches, and a set of demi flipper doors are fitted in between the front door and the rear section of the passenger compartment. The build job is smooth and up to factory levels of quality and finish, but the proportions come off a bit forced. The idea of a high-performance four-door obviously has merit; it's called a Panamera. (Photo Courtesy Corporate Archives Porsche AG)

Starke Speedster

A number of companies have produced Porsche 356 body kits, re-creations, and turnkey builds for some years, which isn't an all-bad idea, as pristine examples of the originals range from expensive to exceedingly so. In as much as the 356's basic architecture, proportions, and powertrain layout are similar to that of a VW Beetle, it made sense to produce 356-style kits for those who didn't want to put an

This 928 Special built for Ferry Porsche is an extended 928, although this time it has only two doors, and most of the remodeling comes in the form of a Sportback or shooting brake styling treatment of the aft end. It is painted in a very Ferry Porsche appropriate color of dark metallic green.

Were it not for the Starke logos on the nose, most wouldn't guess it to be anything but a customized Porsche Speedster. Starke did a remarkable job of adapting the Speedster's look and proportion to the Boxster platform. You can trim out and finish your Starke Speedster or coupe to look modern custom, period custom, or with a factory stock vibe. (Photo Courtesy Starke)

There is a Boxster underneath this significantly glammed-up Starke redo. With its kit approach, you can build it stock, racy, luxury, or mild, and you still get a car that looks to most like a snazzy Porsche Speedster with the drivability of a modern Boxster. (Photo Courtesy Starke)

A darker, richer interior approach takes on a slightly retro flair with the patterned cloth door panel inserts. (Photo Courtesy Starke)

Rather than build your weekend track toy out of a very expensive original speedster or a fiberglass kit body on a VW chassis, using a Starke-converted Boxster provides a modern suspension, brakes, powertrain, and nearly endless aftermarket parts support. (Photo Courtesy Starke)

expensive classic at risk as an everyday car, weekend runner, or occasional track toy. A hidden benefit of building or buying one of these kit projects is that the owner can personalize, customize, or modify the car to his or her own taste, color choice, and equipment.

Glöckler, Intermeccanica, JPS, Replicar Hellas (RCH), SnakePit, Special Editions (which now produces the previous Beck Speedster model under license), Specialty Auto-Sports, Thunder Ranch, Vintage Speedsters, Seduction, and Zipper are just a few of these companies in North America alone. A deeper online search will surely yield more.

In addition to all of those options, there's now Arizona-based, family-founded and -operated Starke. The Starke Speedster and upcoming Coupe models are different in one major, fundamental way. They're not based on a VW floor plan or powertrain nor built upon a bespoke frame or other chassis. Instead, the Starke cars are substantial rebodies of a Porsche Boxster and retain the Boxster's Porsche-developed and -built chassis, interior, and powertrain. This means the car can have the performance and freeway capability of a modern Porsche and not an old Volkswagen.

The result is somewhat startling. Since the size and general proportions of a Boxster are relatively close to those of a 356 Speedster, the overall effect is convincing to all but the most discerning eyes. The sky is the limit in terms of customizing, color, and rolling-stock choices. Add authentic Porsche-style badging and trim, plus retro wheels and tires, and many people won't know you aren't driving a true classic Porsche Speedster. Any 2005–2012 Boxster will work as the basis for your own Starke Speedster and give you a choice between standard engine spec, Boxster S powertrains and suspension tune, and manual or automatic transmission.

Starke is very transparent about the fact this build takes serious skills and tools, which is likely beyond the average garage tinkerer with the following disclosure: "This is not a do-it-yourself kit. These parts cannot be used to build a speedster by an amateur mechanic or hobbyist. These parts should only be used by a professional custom car builder who can perform metal fabrication, fiberglass work, chassis cutting and modification, subframe design and welding, and custom body work. To build this speedster, you must trim the front and rear unibody of your donor car and design and weld in subframe supports. All of the brackets to attach the body must be fabricated. There are no instructions with these parts. All sales are final with no refunds."

Several levels of Starke conversion component packages are offered in your choice of speedster and upcoming coupe designs at starkespeedster.com.

Polizei

What comes to mind when someone says *police car*? Besides tickets or a night in jail, most think of a black and white Ford Crown Victoria. Believe it or not, since the 1960s, Porsche has occasionally provided the German police with a very special patrol car or two. The car in the top left photo from 1968 is unique in several ways.

This very ceremonial police-spec targa represents the 100,000th Porsche produced. I'm not aware of it being used in any actual pursuit duty, but it must have been fun in parades around Stuttgart. (Photo Courtesy Corporate Archives Porsche AG)

A later 993-series 911 was also tarted up in police trim and appears here at the Porsche Museum. (Photo Courtesy Corporate Archives Porsche AG)

To begin, it is the first 911 Targa to be built for the 1968 model year, and an equally significant milestone is the fact it's the 100,000th Porsche car produced. It's certainly among the very few open-top cop cars you'll see of any brand and in any country. It is painted the traditional-for-Germany white with a black interior. Note the flashing blue light mounted on the targa bar and the rear-facing, engine cover lid-mounted siren speaker. In recognition of the long-ago 100,000 milestone, on July 15, 1996, Ferry Porsche himself presented the 1,000,000th Porsche in proper Polizei livery to the German police.

Spexster

The original Porsche 356 Speedster can be thought of as the 1957 Ford Thunderbird of Porsches. It's the classic model and design that everyone sees and loves through the proverbial rose-tinted glasses. The Speedster's reputation for charm, fun driving, and racing success is well deserved. A variety of people and entities have been trying to recreate or recapture that original magic in a variety of new ways ever since the original left the production scene in the late 1950s. To some extent it includes Porsche itself with cars like the Boxster and other "less is more" concepts that never made production.

In the late 1980s, Paul Deutschman, an industrial designer from Canada, created a 911-based machine called the Spexster. It looked like a roadster with an extremely cut-down windshield, no top, and not so much as a hint of any other windows. The proportions were a bit odd with long doors and an extremely long rear deck section. The front design looked a bit 595-ish. The cabin was strictly for two and had a racy

The Spexster's modern Speedster notion is appealing even if the proportions of this 911-based car come off a bit elongated. Note the innovative dished take on integrated seating.

The Spexster was just strange, interesting, and compelling enough to make* Motor Trend*'s June 1988 cover. There was no chance of Porsche picking up or licensing the design, as the company was already developing its first modern Speedsters at the same time.

dual-cockpit design. The longish nose was intended to balance out the long rear deck proportions. The 911 platform underneath was that of a naturally aspirated Carrera 3.2 with no particular performance modifications. The wheels wore fluted pancake covers similar to those on racing 935s at the time.

The car was shown at the 1988 Toronto Auto Show, perhaps with the intent of limited production. Deutschman and company was a design firm, not a carmaker, and had no plans itself to produce the car. The company instead hoped that another concern, perhaps even Porsche, would buy or license the Spexster concept and produce it themselves. The production reality of this unusual idea ultimately proved to be very limited, as the whole deal never went beyond this single show car.

NRDE Porsches

Norris-Rayburn Design Engineering (NRDE) is owned by Rick Norris and Neal Rayburn and is a Los Angeles, California–based outfit that can be categorized as an early-1980s Porsche modification shop or tuner long before this notion was as commonplace or popular as it is today. NRDE's builds included all manners of performance upgrades, primarily around turbocharging, and a fair bit of body modifications.

NDRE's 911 Targa flat-nose Turbo and uprated 924 showed some imagination and engineering work to make them happen, yet there's no record of how many actually did.

NRDE's 911-based model added an interesting twist that Porsche hadn't yet thought of or offered. At that time, Porsche didn't produce a 930 Turbo Targa or Cabriolet. The factory cars were coupes only. Company principal Neal Rayburn's own 911 was a targa and became the company test bed for its modification designs. Out went the naturally aspirated 3.0L flat six, in went a factory, KKK turbocharged engine, and the Targa Turbo was born. Porsche went on to factory produce this configuration, but this car was likely the first such semi-homebuilt example running around L.A.

Rayburn and company went a step further on his company car and gave it the full Flachbau slant-nose front end conversion, curvaceously flared fenders, hideaway headlights, larger polished Fuchs alloys, and a Turbo whale tail aft.

Porsche later produced a small number of flat-nosed targas and cabriolets with or without the turbocharging, but this unique example was an early representation of these ideas. While so many non-factory Flachbau conversions employed fiberglass fenders, the NRDE build was unusual in that it featured hand-hammered, 18-gauge steel fenders and flares that were unique and certainly expensive. NRDE also filled up the cars with big stereos and alarm systems that were typical of the day, and the suspensions and brakes were upgraded with factory 930 Turbo bits. A turnkey 911 build of this fashion cost around $65,000 at the time, or the full conversion starting with your own 911SC was $25,000.

NRDE also turned its attention to the 924 Turbo. This included a comprehensive performance rebuild of the engine, the addition of water injection to reduce engine detonation, its own round of hand-fabricated flares and spoilers, and wider-than-factory rolling stock. NRDE is long out of business, and no records seem to exist about how many cars they built or converted.

Porsche Tractors

Porsche's own line of tractors doesn't qualify as special editions in the purest sense as they were built in large numbers and in series production for many years. Yet, they certainly are special and a significant element of Porsche's history that many people are somewhat or completely unaware of.

In German, Yiddish, and other languages, to "schlep" something means to carry, haul, or drag it around, which is why Porsche's line of tractors earned the nickname Schleppers. It's a charming moniker, although not an official one. You'll never see a Porsche tractor with a factory-applied badge that says Schlepper. Various models were called Junior, Grosse (large), Master, and Super.

According to the Porsche-Diesel North American Registry (porsche-diesel.com), in keeping with Dr. Ferdinand Porsche's brief of designing tough, simple, affordable "people's

A Porsche Junior diesel tractor takes a bow in front of the Porsche Museum. Thousands were produced, and even though they've been out of production and replaced by newer, more capable, more powerful tractors by other companies, it's said that many of these great Porsche schleppers are still working on small farms around Europe today. (Photo Courtesy Corporate Archives Porsche AG)

This Model 144 with an air-cooled, 4-cylinder diesel engine was among the larger and more powerful Porsche tractor models offered. (Photo Courtesy Corporate Archives Porsche AG)

Ferry and Ferdinand Porsche examine one of their own at a meeting or product presentation. The date and location are unknown. (Photo Courtesy Corporate Archives Porsche AG)

This is proof positive that Porsche tractors can really schlepp. (Photo Courtesy Corporate Archives Porsche AG)

cars" for the German masses, his design firm began working on tractors in the mid-1930s. The most commonly referred to year is 1934. The engines were engineered to be air-cooled diesels, which is important in terms of simplicity and low-end schlepping torque. The earliest production powerplants were single-cylinder engines, yet by the 1950s, there were 1-, 2-, 3-, and 4-cylinder Porsche diesel tractor engines. Interestingly, the first Porsche tractor engines were gasoline powered units. Since Porsche wasn't established as a carmaker in Austria or Germany at the time, Herr Porsche sold and/or licensed his tractor designs to German company Allgaier GmbH and the Austrian company Hofherr Schrantz.

The Porsche-Diesel North American Registry website states, "These two companies used the Porsche engine design and called their tractor Allgaier System Porsche and Hofherr Schrantz System Porsche.

"By 1956, Mannesmann AG decided to get into the tractor business and bought the license for the Porsche diesel engine design and the Allgaier tractor design. They rebuilt and expanded the old Zeppelin factory west of Friedrichshafen on Lake Konstanz to a state-of-the-art manufacturing facility with the most modern machine tool and assembly complex available at that time. Porsche diesel tractors were produced in this facility until the end of 1963 by a division of Mannesmann AG called Porsche-Diesel Motorenbau GmbH. At the end of 1963, an international arrangement was made with Renault to service the Porsche diesel tractors worldwide."

As you might expect of anything designed by Dr. Porsche and company, his tractor was advanced for its day and of

Believe it or not, not all Porsche tractors are red. This green one is the proof, although it does have red wheels. This one also wears Porsche Allgaier badging. (Photo Courtesy Corporate Archives Porsche AG)

The Brumos Museum's Porsche tractor is, as you might expect, absolutely immaculate. It gives a better look at the machine's many pedals and levers that allow it to turn, articulate, and operate tools and implements.

This young lass seems quite pleased to be aboard a Porsche tractor at a Luftgekühlt event in L.A. These machines now seem to be very popular, and no serious Porsche collection is complete without one. (Photo Courtesy Kirk Gerbracht)

A 1954 Allgaier Porsche P312 Kaffeelug (coffee train). This model is a rare gas-engine model built for agricultural applications where farmers did not want diesel fumes near their crops. This model has streamlined aluminum body work. While looking fast (it was not), it was ideal for delicate coffee plantation work in South America.

very high quality. The engineering was simple yet solid with a for-the-time sophisticated hydraulic coupling between the engine and transmissions that intended to make them easier for the farmers to drive. Rear-wheel-drive and four-wheel-drive tractors were produced. Some had very simple controls and instrumentation, and other models had more instruments and gauges than the earliest 356s.

The Porsche-Diesel North America Registry continued, "Between 1956 and 1963 more than 125,000 Porsche diesel tractors were produced. Many of them are still in daily operation on farms and ranches all over the world.

"In this time frame, the American Porsche-Diesel Corporation in Easton, Pennsylvania, sold approximately 1,000 Porsche diesel tractors in North America. Most of the tractors were sold on the East Coast of the U.S. and Canada. A brand-new Junior was about $1,750, and a Super was about $3,600. Very few Standards and Masters were sold due to a problem of them being price competitive with U.S.-made tractors.

"Today, the number of Porsche diesel tractors in North America has increased drastically due to the fact that collecting and restoring Porsche diesel tractors is becoming a unique and affordable hobby. Fully concourse restored Porsche diesel tractors are being traded in the $15,000 to $20,000 range. However, un-restored examples in good running condition usually sell between $5,000 and $6,000."

ElectraMeccanica eRoadster

The original Intermeccanica car building concern was born in 1959, and its original creator was a Hungarian immigrant named Frank Reisner. It was founded in Turin, Italy, which is the home of so many famous Italian design houses and coach builders (Carrozzeria). Initially, the company produced high-performance tuning kits and racing parts for a variety of small-bore sports cars and sedans. It began its life as a carmaker by building and selling Formula Junior racing cars. It's likely that the Buick V-8-powered Apollo is its best-known nameplate. Over its long history, Intermeccanica produced more than a dozen different models, including the Intermeccanica Griffith 600, Murena, and Italia Spyder.

Reisner recognized the magic of the original Porsche 356 Speedster, and in the mid-1970s, he moved to the United States to produce his own re-creation of the iconic 356. Reisner wanted to produce, build, and sell complete turnkey cars, not merely fiberglass body kits to be homebuilt on a VW Beetle chassis as was the fashion at the time. Having worked and produced cars in Italy, Reisner knew the value of getting a vehicle's body proportions, details, and quality just right rather than the odd-looking, close-enough proportions and details of so many inexpensive kit cars.

He called his car the Intermeccanica Speedster because he didn't want to or was able to properly call it a Porsche. Approximately 600 of these cars were produced from 1976 to 1980. Reisner built upon the concept and produced a car patterned after the 1959 356 Convertible D, which was Porsche's car that followed the speedster.

The company evolved over time and moved about the world under a variety of ownership scenarios. The brand and company have recently been recast as Canada-based Electra-Meccanica, which now produces electric cars. Its mainstream model is a single-seat car called the Solo, as in single occupant. It's reinvented the previous Intermeccanica Speedster and Convertible D models into a single electrified Porsche-style car called the eRoadster.

When trimmed out with original-style rolling stock and fittings, most would never know this ElectraMeccanica eRoadster was anything but a real 356 Cabriolet or Convertible, except that it's likely a lot faster. (Photo Courtesy ElectraMeccanica)

As with the original Intermeccanica Speedster, the proportions, detailing, and look is spot-on. Other than the Meccanica badging, it takes an expert to quickly identify that the eRoadster isn't a genuine 356. The chrome trim and detailing are beautiful, and the interior is richly trimmed. This is no home-built kit car. ElectraMeccanica presents the car as a machine with "reliable, powerful performance on a modern chassis and running gear with state-of-the-art EV componentry. The eRoadster comes with air conditioning, heated seats, automatic windows, power locks, and modern infotainment that features bluetooth and USB connectivity with a vintage look."

Given Ferdinand Porsche's early work with electric and hybrid gas/electric transportation, we suspect he would appreciate the design ethos of the company's original 356 combined with a modern, carbon-neutral, electric-powered version of it.

The Apal looks a bit more Porsche-like from the front aspect, with a shallow front nose that is probably pretty good aerodynamically and does a nice job of integrating two sets of ancillary lights.

Porsche "APAL"

What's an Apal, you may ask? It's a fair question in that it's not a name; there was no Mr. Apal involved. Instead, it's an acronym for an industrial process. In this case, it's for lightweight body panel production: application polyester arme de liege. It was originally based in Belgium. Think of it as an early take on composites or a riff on fiberglass. It is believed that approximately 150 of these cars were produced between 1961 and 1965. The lightweight plastic bodies were attached to modified VW Beetle floorpans.

Perhaps 120 were designed as road cars and ran VW engines, and the remaining 25 to 30 were more competition and performance focused and ran a Porsche 1,600-cc engine, transaxle, and brakes with road racing and hill climb events in mind. These versions weighed a flyweight 1,400 pounds. Squint at it just a bit, and you might think it's a cousin or sibling to the 356 Carrera Abarth GTL. Look closely, and you'll see that the finish, detailing, and proportions aren't nearly as tidy as the Italian-designed and -built special Carrera. Unfortunately, no concise records exist as to what they cost at the time, where they were distributed, any sort of race records, or how many remain.

The Apal loosely resembles the general shape and footprint of an Abarth Carrera GTL, yet the Italian Bertone design is much better balanced and resolved. Still, the Apal is sporty and was a moderately successful racer.

Denzel

I promise this has nothing to do with the actor of the same first name. Denzel, emphasis on the "zel," launched as a tiny Austrian carmaker in 1948, around the time as Porsche did similar things in the same country, although Denzel planted its roots in Vienna with Porsche in Gmünd.

It should come as no great surprise that the tiny egg-shaped Denzel initially appeared somewhat similar to what Drs. Porsche were brewing up in Gmünd due to the fact the Denzel roadster also employed a rear-engine platform that ran an air-cooled flat 4-cylinder engine for power. The cars and company were the brainchildren of Wolfgang Denzel. He was taken with the simplicity, light weight, and other engineering benefits of Dr. Porsche's VW beetle.

It wouldn't be fair to claim that one outright copied the other, but the general shape and size of the two cars are remarkably similar, which is somewhat dictated by the rear-engine placement. The Denzel ultimately developed far beyond its original Beetle-inspired roots and underpinnings with its own chassis and aluminum body panels. Denzel hopped up the basic VW engine in 1,300-cc form for more power to nearly double the original VW's 36-hp rating. If the 356 was light, then the Denzel was a flyweight at something like 650 kg (1,430 pounds).

So, is the Denzel a Porsche? No, but the conceptual similarities, general architecture, and design strike an unusual note. It is said that some Denzels ended up powered by Porsche 356 engines, although we've yet to see enough of them in person to be able to verify any numbers. A Porsche did end up racing a Denzel in at least one very early event that I've been able to verify. One of the teardrop-shaped and uber-rare Type 64 streamliners competed in the 1949 Austrian Alpine Rally, which ran for 800 miles along the Katschberg, across the Pötschen Pass, and through the mountains surrounding the Porsche factory. There's no record about which car was faster, but the fact is clear that the Type 64 suffered a mechanical malady and did not finish. The Denzel (identified at the time as a WD for Wolfgang Denzel) Volkswagen kept its little rounded bugeye nose clean to complete the run.

Ultimately something more than just a footnote carmaker, Denzels were manufactured for 7 to 8 years after 5 years of development, and the total output approached 300 units when production ended in 1959. Thus, it earned its own level of success, and its inspiration was undeniable.

The little bug-eyed Denzel has a cute button face and Porsche-style shapes and proportions.

The Denzel roadster is a bit less 356-like from the back, although it's clear where the engine is and what car inspired the Denzel's basic premise.

917 PA Spyder 16-Cylinder

As a front-line prototype racer, versions of the 917 have done it all and won it all, including the 24 Hours of Le Mans, international FIA championships, and the SCCA Can-Am championship twice. They also starred along with Steve McQueen in his motorsports magnum opus film of 1971 titled *Le Mans*. These various 917s all ran horizontally opposed (flat) 12-cylinder engines of varying displacements between 4.5 and 5.0 liters. Many were naturally aspirated and some were turbocharged, but all were 12s.

In the beginning of its efforts in the SCCA Can-Am series in America, the 4.5L 917 with around 560 hp was a bit under-

The need to feed and fire 16 separate cylinders sends fuel injection tubes and spark plug wires every which way atop the engine. Notice the fiberglass fan and injector stacks intended to reduce weight on the stretched, rear-weight-biased 917 roadster. (Photo Courtesy Corporate Archives Porsche AG)

powered compared to the barking 7.0L Chevrolet engines commonly used in the McLaren cars with their 600 or so hp. Prior to developing a serious turbocharging program for the flat 12, Porsche went the "no replacement for displacement" route and experimented with a 6.5L's flat 16-cylinder monster motor that was the largest competition engine Porsche had ever developed at the time and among the most powerful at 755 hp. It spliced 4 more cylinders into the already longish 12 and required a car with a longer wheelbase. The engine itself was 10 inches longer.

Every measure was taken to keep weight increase to a minimum, such as a lightweight fiberglass cooling and intake trumpets, but the longer car weighed more. Even though the chassis was stiffened to accommodate the extra length and weight, it created a less-than-ideal handling attitude but was still fast.

Mark Donohue, a mechanically sensitive and talented development engineer and championship winning–prowess driver, once commented that he could feel that upon starting, one half of the engine fired ever so briefly before the other. Of course, once part of the engine caught, the rest immediately followed. It was a strange occurrence, and credit to the incomparable Donohue for being able to feel and hear it.

Ultimately, Porsche scrubbed the idea of the 16 and developed a turbocharged 4.5L 12-cylinder 917 that weighed less than the 16 and put out at least 100 more hp. Race wins and championships ensued.

914/8 Development Concept

In some cases, the humble mid-engine 914 all too often got sand kicked in its face for having a somewhat standard specification Volkswagen 411/412 flat-four engine. Even the much sportier and decidedly Porsche engine 914/6 took a little heat for only being offered with the base and lowest power rating offered at the time: the 911T engine.

As if to demonstrate what the 914 could really be beyond 914/6 GT and 916 racing homologation models, Porsche dipped into its considerable bag of powertrain tricks and pulled out the powertrain from its highly successful 908 Spyder racing car. The 908 Series III Spyder famously finished second place overall at the 12 Hours of Sebring race with no less than Peter Revson (USAC championship series, Can-Am, Trans-Am, and Formula 1 standout), who teamed with actor/racer Steve McQueen.

The tidy Porsche sports racer was barely beaten by a flying Mario Andretti in a factory 5.0L V-12 Ferrari 512. The McQueen/Revson Solar Racing 908 was powered by a 3.0L flat-eight engine good for about 350 hp in naturally aspirated form.

Porsche's engineering boffins, tired of hearing about the 914's allegedly substandard powertrain offerings, decided to silence the noise creating the 914/8 prototype and mixed the 908's flat eight with the 914's mid-engine, targa-topped body/chassis platform. The result is the handsome beast you see below. Just two were built. The project was headed by 917 development leader and Porsche family member Ferdinand Piech himself. One of the cars' engines was reportedly run in virtually full-race fuel-injected spec and painted orange, while the other was silver, ran carburetors, and was detuned to something around 300 hp. This car was prepared and given to Dr. Ferry Porsche as a 60th anniversary present. Imagine a 300 hp, 8-cylinder 914 likely faster than any production 911 model at the time. Take that, 914 haters!

It's unclear based on his expression if Ferry Porsche (hand on door) is pleased with the driving manners of his 908-powered 914. Note that the roof panel is no longer a removable targa type and is instead a welded-in metal panel painted body color. (Photo Courtesy Corporate Archives Porsche AG)

CHAPTER 6

PORSCHE CUSTOMER EXCLUSIVE: PORSCHE CAN BUILD YOU YOUR OWN SPECIAL EDITION

Imagine you want your new Porsche painted to match your wife or girlfriend's nail-polish color or if you'd like the HVAC vents to be custom wrapped in hand-stitched leather. Perhaps you want your seats upholstered in camouflage canvas.

Porsche has an entire department of talented designers and craft people who can make your automotive dreams come true within reason and depending upon your budget. Born in 1983 as the Sonderwunsch (Special Wish) division, it has since been renamed Porsche Exclusive (or Exclusiv). This innovative group can and will tailor your new Porsche to meet your tastes,

This is just a scrapbook wall's look at some of the myriad of custom touches Porsche's Special Wishes, neé Customer Exlusiv, neé Exclusiv Manufaktur group, can provide its customers who have ideas, will, and funds to execute them on their new Porsche. (Photo Courtesy Corporate Archives Porsche AG)

Many of the Exclusiv builds have been modeled in miniature to document their look and as something to show prospective customers. The ultimate Porsche Matchbox cars? (Photo Courtesy Corporate Archives Porsche AG)

desires, and whims. The primary beauty of working with such an empowered organization within Porsche is that your car is spec'd out, designed, engineered, produced, and finished by the factory under factory auspices. The work is done to OEM quality, and your car's paperwork documents all of the changes, special work, and modifications, which is something that no mere aftermarket tuner can claim.

Sonderwunsch designed and built the factory Flachbau flat-nose 911s; there were 237 cars manufactured in all. The group can produce one car to taste and spec, or small-volume production runs as it did with the Sport Classic model. There are a few limitations as to what Exclusiv can accomplish, primarily in terms of vehicle certification. In other words, you can't specify a vehicle that cannot be certified for emissions, crash, or other safety regulations. For example, they wouldn't be inclined to build a Cayman with a Carrera Turbo S

Leather? There's practically every color and texture you can imagine. The Exclusiv team will leather-wrap your key fob, shift knob, shifter, HVAC vents, or nearly any surface on or in the car you wish in practically any color and texture you can imagine. (Photo Courtesy Corporate Archives Porsche AG)

Just as with leather and special paint colors, you can have contrasting or complementary stitching or piping pretty much as you wish. (Photo Courtesy Corporate Archives Porsche AG)

Exclusiv is the latest name for a great game. Initially called the Special Wishes department, the new moniker gives a better view of Exclusiv's expanded ability for special model runs and not just onesies or twosies. (Photo Courtesy Corporate Archives Porsche AG)

Exclusiv can really go wild on your interior if that's your special wish. Complementing and contrasting elements of a variety of materials can be created between you and your Exclusiv designer. (Photo Courtesy Corporate Archives Porsche AG)

Got leather? Yes. There is all you want and in any color. (Photo Courtesy Corporate Archives Porsche AG)

all-wheel-drive powertrain because that base model doesn't exist in the primary production roster, nor has it been emissions or safety certified for legal customer sale. This unique division has designed and built several special one-offs given to family and board of director members in recognition of birthdays, years of service, and other occasions.

In 2011, Exclusiv and the Porsche Museum developed a special, temporary exhibit that recognized some of the capabilities and great work accomplished by the Special Wish group. These magical dozen machines represent some of the most exclusive and rare 911s ever built. The exhibit was called Unikate Kleinserien, which translates to Unique Small Series. Talk about a greatest hits exhibition.

Another beautiful Heritage Design Edition 992 Targa in colors other than the often-seen burgundy metallic. It looks like this one is about done. (Photo Courtesy Corporate Archives Porsche AG)

Each new car in the Exclusiv studio is protected in every possible way while the final touches are done by hand. (Photo Courtesy Corporate Archives Porsche AG)

A tasty smorgasbord of Exclusiv builds begin with a gold-finished 959 circling clockwise to a red 964 Turbo S Flachbau, a 991 Speedster, the Sport Classic, and the green Turbo S. There's something uber special any which way you look. (Photo Courtesy Corporate Archives Porsche AG)

If a customer wants his 959 finished entirely in gold, Exclusiv will make it so for a price. (Photo Courtesy Corporate Archives Porsche AG)

Unikate Kleinserien literally and appropriately means unique small series. Now a primary specialty of Porsche Exclusiv Manufaktur, the Porsche Museum recently hosted a special exhibit of some of the most interesting examples of the breed. In the foreground is a late-model Speedster, next in back is a Sport Classic, then a customized Turbo S, Dr. Ferry Porsche's 993 Speedster, and an exceptionally rare 964 Turbo S Leichtbau (light build), which is some 400 pounds lighter than an otherwise production 964 Turbo S. (Photo Courtesy Corporate Archives Porsche AG)

The factory only built two 993-series Speedsters: a silver one for mega enthusiast Jerry Seinfeld, and this elegant green example for Dr. Ferry Porsche. (Photo Courtesy Corporate Archives Porsche AG)

Here's another angle at the five utterly unique and special Exclusiv cars described. (Photo Courtesy Corporate Archives Porsche AG)

A 964 Turbo S 3.6 Flachbau is what some consider to be the ultimate factory-produced slant-nosed 911 spec. (Photo Courtesy Corporate Archives Porsche AG)

This is a 993 Turbo S. The green color makes me wonder if it belongs to Ferry Porsche. (Photo Courtesy Corporate Archives Porsche AG)

Okay, now. Just take a breath. (Photo Courtesy Corporate Archives Porsche AG)

2017 911 Turbo S Exclusive Series

The 911 Turbo S Exclusive Series further demonstrates opportune instances where the mainstream model production and the Customer Exclusiv functions can collaborate on moderate-volume special editions for dealer distribution. This car was effectively a commemorative run-out model for the 991 platform in 2017, just as it was about to be replaced by the 992-generation Carreras. This type of build program falls under the category of the newly named Porsche Exclusiv Manufaktur, which is geared to produce more than one-off Special Wishes cars. Expect to see more of this type of activity in the future when Porsche chooses to press the special edition button.

This Exclusive Series was available in the Turbo S Coupe bodystyle or as an uber luxurious wind-in-hair cabriolet version. It received a meaningful power increase, as if it needed one, due to its own specific Power Kit upgrade that took it from the standard 580 hp to 607. The entire car was hand-finished by Porsche Exclusiv Manufaktur to the very highest levels and used extra premium materials, finishes, and interior fitments. It takes a mere 2.9 seconds to go 0–60 mph, and 120 comes up in

There's likely no better way to run out the 991-series production than this Exclusiv Edition Turbo S. All of the colors, finishes, and surfaces are unique to this very special edition. Few were built, and they were very expensive. (Photo Courtesy Corporate Archives Porsche AG)

This is a reminder lest you forget the talented, special hands and minds that designed and built your very exclusive Exclusiv Porsche. (Photo Courtesy Corporate Archives Porsche AG)

The Exclusiv-produced Exclusiv Edition is a wonderful contrast of golds, yellow, black, and carbon fiber neatly synthesized into this one super car. (Photo Courtesy Corporate Archives Porsche AG)

less than 10 seconds. It is fast by any measure.

This limited production Turbo S comes in any color you like as long as its Golden Yellow Metallic. The black-finished 20-inch center-lock alloy wheels were standard, and the Porsche Carbon Ceramic Brake rotor system was standard. PASM and the Sport Chrono package were also standard. Several body components were crafted of genuine carbon fiber, and there were other carbon-fiber finished bits to further distinguish the design. Considerable redesign work was done at the rear of the car to include the Turo Aerokit rear wings, a new rear apron, ram-air scoop, and model-specific, black-finished, stainless-steel exhaust tips.

The cabin was a unique blend of ultra-sporty and high

Now that's a movie-star profile. You can have your Exclusiv Edition Turbo S as a coupe or a cabriolet, although most we've seen appear to have opted for the closed, classic 911 bodystyle. (Photo Courtesy Corporate Archives Porsche AG)

The Exclusive Edition Turbo S cabin is a study in dazzling restraint if that makes sense; a luxurious and racy combination of leather, carbon-fiber, metal, black, gray, and yellow-gold colors. (Photo Courtesy Corporate Archives Porsche AG)

Everything is where it belongs and is driver centric. (Photo Courtesy Corporate Archives Porsche AG)

Why not opt for the Exclusiv-fitted leather and carbon-weave luggage package designed expressly for your car? (Photo Courtesy Corporate Archives Porsche AG)

performance with luxurious comfort that included 18-way adjustable seats covered in two layers of perforated leather. The inside layer was piped with two stripes of Golden Yellow hide, and the seams and Turbo S lettering stitching were also in Golden Yellow threading.

The 991-generation 911 was a massive step forward in the production Carrera's lineage, and this gleaming top of the line limited edition was the perfect way to segue to the 992. There was a special chronograph watch designed and produced only for buyers of this car. Just 500 911 Turbo S Exclusive Series machines were produced for worldwide consumption at an MSRP of $258,500, which didn't include the watch.

Here is more genuine carbon fiber and a further reminder of what you're stepping into or out of. (Photo Courtesy Corporate Archives Porsche AG)

Porsche Design divined a special watch to go with this special Turbo S. (Photo Courtesy Corporate Archives Porsche AG)

CHAPTER 7

INDEPENDENT CONCEPTS AND OTHER IDEAS

Most independent design houses make their daily bread by creating concepts intended for other companies to produce and to solicit business. Some of these concerns have the wherewithal to build an entire car from the ground up, source powertrains and chassis/suspensions from an existing production model, or in some cases, it's nothing more than an electric golf cart motor so it can move under its own power around an auto show floor. Others begin with another firm's car and put their own riff on it with the goal of selling that design to the company that produced the underlying car in the hope they'll like and buy the design and put it into production themselves. Other independent design houses whip up their own take on one particular model with the intent of striking a deal with the underlying manufacturer and produce a small production run of their redressed car.

There are other variations on these themes, but in general, most independents create and build a design for the international auto show circuit to strut their stuff and hopefully sell the design or their talent and capability to a major carmaker.

The Beutler Cabriolet was commissioned by Porsche in 1948 from Beutler in Switzerland. The slightly curved rear fenders are an interesting design touch. This is about as early as the Gmünd-era cars got and is certainly among the earliest open version. (Photo Courtesy Corporate Archives Porsche AG)

Beutler Porsches

Swiss design firm Beutler (pronounced "Boyt-ler") designed and built an impressive run of Porsche concepts and low-volume special models. The first car, produced in 1949, was based on the open 356 roadster. The car was black, and while the redesign touches are largely straightforward, they do change the look of the factory car.

You'd never mistake this for anything other than a Porsche. The majority of the redesign took place at the rear of the car with reshaped rear fenders, deck, and lower fascia. The familiar Porsche beehive taillights are present and accounted for with two of these lights stacked vertically. The engine cover wore a single-louvered vent for engine cooling, and the standard framed split-front windscreen remained. Among the more significant visual changes was the addition of a spun-style full wheel cover. The factory rolling stock at the time was a vented steel wheel that was still in place beneath the new large, polished metal wheel covers that wore a chrome baby Moon-style hubcap. Another major design touch was the deeply inset,

Here, you get a better look at the bodyline that creates the more defined curve of the rear fenders in this Beutler design and build. A smaller, yet similarly curvaceous rump is also seen on the 356 America Roadster that came along a few years later. (Photo Courtesy Corporate Archives Porsche AG)

This is a sales brochure for later Beutler 356B models. While they are unique to this Swiss coachbuilder, they have a more Porsche-like look and detailing. (Photo Courtesy Corporate Archives Porsche AG)

rectangular nacelle for the rear license plate. It is believed that just one of this model was created.

Beutler's follow-up 1956 356 1600 design was a more marked rethink than the company's first effort. In this case, the top, glass, and greenhouse were substantially reworked into a taller, more upright, airy design that incorporated a single-piece windshield. It's arguably not as sporty as the factory's shape, but it is attractive in its own right with a roomier feel from inside.

Unusually, the front end was completely reimagined to include a larger, relatively flat cargo trunk, and a chrome embellished grille and grille opening. It's not something you often see on a rear engine, air-cooled car. Beutler was going for a somewhat more luxurious continental look, so the car was finished in a metallic copper/gold primary color with a creamy off-white top.

Some onlookers commented that the greenhouse resembled a VW Karmann Ghia or a Volvo two-door sedan. The wheel treatment was traditional Porsche with body color–painted wheels, whitewall tires, and the return of a conventional Porsche hubcap. Subsequent owners of this one-off machine perhaps didn't care for the original copper color scheme, as there are photos online of the cars in a light yellow and a very Ferrari-esque red.

The Swiss firm's most adventurous Porsche design based on the more powerful 1600S model came along in 1959/1960 and was a near-total rebody of the then-new 356B. This car also earned a taller, glassier greenhouse with a more upright stance to create room for the rear seats. Beutler's approach was to create more space aft, along with more headroom and increased visibility from all seats. This car also wore a more conventional Porsche-looking nose and front-end design, and perhaps was a bit more squared off. It was painted a proper Porsche silver over a black interior and sported chromed steel wheels and hubcaps. The Beutler Porsche 1600S's more conventionally Porsche look was reputedly mandated by Porsche since some of the previous cars, particularly those with front grilles, didn't offer enough of Porsche's trademark design cues.

All of these cars are as rare as the proverbial hen's teeth with a reported total of only five built. They do on occasion show up at a concours or Porsche Parade event, and there are lots of random photos online, but if you must have a Swiss-styled and -bodied Porsche 356, be prepared to do some digging and financial negotiating to get one.

Kastenhofer 356

Kastenhofer was a Vienna-based coachbuilder known primarily for its construction of Volkswagen Type 2 vans. Perhaps more significantly, it was brought in very early in Porsche's history by Ferdinand and Ferry Porsche to assist with the body building for some of the very earliest Porsche 356s.

The Gmünd factory was very hand-labor intensive and somewhat constricted by the size of its properties and created a relatively slow trickle of production. Thus, other Viennese companies were subcontracted for the work and played a significant role in the birth and early growth of Porsche. These early 356s are considered production models but are somewhat special editions in that they often differed from others in small and significant ways.

The Porsche in these photos date to 1949. The original mid-engine Porsche number 1 was only certified for road use

Here is a Porsche Type 356/2 Cabriolet by Kastenhofer at an unnamed automobile exhibition show in November 1949. (Photo Courtesy Corporate Archives Porsche AG)

The same car is shown with the top now raised. Note the low-mounted accessory driving light, the unadorned baby Moon-style wheel caps, and the frameless split windshield design. (Photo Courtesy Corporate Archives Porsche AG)

The Sauter Porsche hits the track. The date and location are unknown.

and production just the year before, so Kastenhofer-built (and Kiebl, Reutter, Tatra, and others) examples are among the earliest, oldest, rarest, and most sought-after Porsche models. Finding surviving examples today is on the scale of Holy Grail and Hope Diamond-level significance in the company's history. The example in these photos is often referred to as the fifth oldest Porsche.

1951 Porsche 356 Sauter

Porsche clearly had its sights set on motorsport, but in the early 1950s, it didn't produce a comprehensive lineup of racing machines like it did much later in its history. This super lightweight alloy-bodied version of the pre-A 356 was developed as a joint venture between Porsche and Heinrich Sauter, a European industrialist and racer. Sauter and fabricator Hanz Klenk collaborated with the company to create this handsome, lightweight, open 356 that featured modestly recontoured body work, including the notable conversion to rear-hinged suicide-opening doors. The original 1.5L flat-four engine was uprated to a then-impressive 55 hp to give the car an estimated top speed of 115 mph. It proved to be a successful formula, as the compact Porsche competed in seven sports car races in 1952 and won six of them. It is purported they thought of producing more of them, but this race-winning 356 special remained a one-off.

This is the lone Sauter 356 build and extant. It was light, clearly intended for racing, and featured unusual rear-hinged suicide doors.

This view shows the rear-hinged doors opened, which some felt allowed the driver to get situated into the car faster in the event of a running start. (Photo Courtesy Petersen Automotive Museum)

The lithe Sauter 356 also somewhat resembles the 356 America Roadster that soon followed it. (Photo Courtesy Petersen Automotive Museum)

Porsche Abarth 356B Carrera GTL

Vienna-born car designer, racing driver, race team entrant, and performance tuner Carlo Abarth (1908–1979) is most often connected with Fiat and primarily other Italian brands. He had a hand in the design and development of many vehicles, including bicycles and motorcycles, across many significant marques throughout his life and career. It has long been said that anything Abarth put his mind to and hands on went faster. One brand he's not often associated with is Porsche.

As strange as the pairing seemed, upon further look, it's clear that Porsche and Abarth had certain things in common and much to offer each other. Abarth's cars were generally very light and successful on the racetrack. By the late 1950s, Porsche's motorsport success was significant but far less developed than it is today. The street versions of the 356, wonderful cars that they are, were relatively heavy, constructed mostly of steel chassis and bodywork, and not terribly aerodynamic. Although in Carrera form, the 356's double overhead camshaft, dry sump, oiled flat four was a high-revving gem of a motor.

Porsche had the Carrera-powered lightweight 550 Spyder and its derivations, but it was exotic, expensive, and most often seen as an open roadster. Abarth tuned these engines for even more power and had the bandwidth to design and produce a lightweight Porsche coupe racer that incorporated the wonderful Carrera engine. Carlo and company had experience building limited runs of special cars, so Abarth was a logical choice as an ideal sub-vendor to create and produce a short run of 356-based, Carrera four-cammer-powered coupes called the Porsche Abarth 356B Carrera GTL (Grand Touring Lightweight).

For the design, Abarth engaged one of the very best that Italy had to offer: Franco Scaglione. He was most active from the 1950s through the 1970s and worked with Bertone, Zagato, and others during an illustrious career run of dazzling seminal concept and production hardware. Scaglione is perhaps best known for the three aerodynamic Alfa Romeo concepts he conceived called Berlina Aerodinamica Tecnica (BAT). There were three cars (BAT 5, 7, and 9) built from 1953 to 1955. All were coupes and are considered by many to be among the greatest concept cars ever designed and built. He also created important designs for Stanguellini, Jaguar, and Aston Martin. In other words, Scaglione more than had the chops to do wonders for what became the racing 356 Carrera.

The look he came up with still demonstrates recognizable Porsche DNA, but the proportions and detailing are different. Although the chassis is relatively stock, the Abarth Porsche's nose and frontal aspect are much lower, slimmer, and more aerodynamic with no bumpers and a set of high-powered driving lights that neatly frenched into the front fascia.

Abarth's body was smaller than the Reutter-bodied 356 in every dimension and reduced the coefficient of drag (Cd) from 0.398 to 0.365. The window lines are different, and the rear roof and deck section are more streamlined. There are many cooling gills and louvers found aft to keep the Carrera motor cool under the fire of competition. Because it was comprised of all-aluminum body panels, the Abarth GTL was approximately 160 pounds lighter than a standard 356 Coupe.

The first prototypes were finished in early 1960. The agreement between Porsche and Abarth was for 20 GTLs. There is some evidence that the original plan was for Turin's

The fact that the Abarth Carrera GTL looks like both an Italian sports car and a Porsche is tribute to the genius of designer Scaglione. The shallower nose provided somewhat improved aero, as did the smooth roof and deck. Besides, it's just beautiful.

Obviously, lots of cooling is going on back there given all the louvers and the pop-up vent to catch a little airflow off the roofline.

This fabulous Abarth Carrera belongs to the man in the chair back there, Porsche enthusiast/collector/racer extraordinaire Ranson Webster. He likes this car so well that he has two of them. The engine below his desk is made of an unobtainium spare 8-cylinder Porsche F1 engine because he has one of those too.

This Abarth Carrera nicely shows off the curvy fender line punched into the GTL's wonderful, lightweight Italian aluminum skin. (Photo Courtesy Kirk Gerbracht)

Carrozzeria Zagato to produce the cars, but in the end, for reasons not abundantly clear, the job was done by Carrozzeria Motto in Turin. The quality-insistent Porsche was apparently less than enthralled with Motto's somewhat casual approach to construction and metal finishing, but these were race cars, so the fine details weren't as critical. The point is that the cars were light, aerodynamically better than the 356s, and fast.

The first two prototypes were immediately pressed into service in two of the most difficult endurance contests: the Targa Florio and the 24 Hours of Le Mans. Paul Ernst Strahle had a superb run in the 1960 Targa and won the GT class and finished an impressive 6th overall. Porsche stalwarts Herbert Linge and Hans Joachim Walter finished 10th overall and first in class at Le Mans the same year. The car was reportedly good for nearly 140 mph top speed down the Mulsanne Straight, and Porsche listed as the official entrant.

In 1961, Porsche introduced a stronger version of its Carrera engine called the 692/3a. It featured wider main bearings to allow higher RPM. The top end was also changed with more aggressive intake camshaft profiles. Carburetion reverted back to Solex pieces with a larger 44PII-4 unit. This provided about 165 hp when used with the unmuffled Sebring sports exhaust. Talk about a giant killer. It's even more impressive when you consider the weight-to-power ratio of 165 hp in a car weighing just less than 1,800 pounds.

The cars also ran and did well stateside, including good runs at the 12 Hours of Sebring and the 24 Hours of Daytona. Today, these rare Italian-bodied Porsches are highly sought after by vintage racers and Porsche collectors of all stripes. Among some of the primary legends that raced them in the day include Stirling Moss, Graham Hill, and Jo Bonnier.

356 Zagato Coupe

Various carmakers, particularly British ones, have recently produced a variety of factory-built, factory-approved, Second Sanction continuation examples of some of their most iconic, rare, and valuable models. Aston Martin was among the first to cut loose with a modern production run of its rare and expensive DB4GT/Zagato Coupe of 1960 to 1963. The achingly beautiful original was designed by Ercole Spada, and just 25 were originally produced. It is believed that just 6 Sanction II and Sanction III cars were built. Jaguar soon followed with a reissue of its own XK-SS, a late production street version of its seminal D-Type racer of the mid-to-late 1950s. Bentley more recently jumped on the continuation bandwagon with a run of certain blower models from the 1920s.

Zagato is among Italy's and the world's best-known and most storied design houses and coachbuilders. The company's current head is Dr. Andrea Zagato, whose grandfather founded the company in 1919. He is a very thoughtful man and didn't see the value in stamping out volumes of new production versions of past company greats.

Noted author and journalist Axel Catton said, "In almost 100 years, Zagato has designed and built roughly 400 different car models; some very well-known ones, others less so. Not all of them have survived. That's why we decided a few years ago to re-create some select models that have been essential for our brand's development throughout its history. These cars were important for the design development of our company and are definitely lost to the world, which means there are no surviving original examples left."

Look at an Emory Motorsports-redesigned 356 Outlaw Porsche. The resemblance to this tidy curvy little Italian jewel of a machine is striking, although Emory had no knowledge of this car when he built his. Great minds so often think alike. Maybe there's a little Cayman Coupe going on here too. (Photo Courtesy Zagato)

This single drawing had been hidden away in the Zagato studio for decades and proved to be the inspiration, or at least the design direction, for building a small run of 356 Zagato Coupes. (Photo Courtesy Zagato)

The Porsche 356 Zagato Coupe that nearly ended with a decades-old design rendering is finally born and sees the light of day. (Photo Courtesy Zagato)

Every design detail of this Fabergé egg of a car is simple and elegant. Check out the semi-Cayman-esque rear side window. (Photo Courtesy Zagato)

Simple lightweight door cards and minimal carpeting are featured along with dainty and beautifully chromed door and window handles. (Photo Courtesy Zagato)

The cabin is spare and unadorned, which is quite proper for a light and lithe sport coupe or racing car. (Photo Courtesy Zagato)

Bumpers? Don't confuse me with bumpers! (Photo Courtesy Zagato)

This ensures that there can never be any confusion between the original and the re-creation. Rather than call these cars Sanction II or Second Sanction, they've been nicknamed Sanction Lost.

The story of the lithe, curvaceous Sanction Lost 356 Coupe in these photos began with a French racing driver named Claude Storez, who went to Zagato in the 1950s to design and craft a lightweight sports racer built on his 356 Speedster. The car was designed and built by Zagato and indeed lighter than a standard steel-bodied 356 and quite beautiful. Storez entered his car in the 1959 Tour de France auto race, but sadly neither car nor driver made the show. In February of that year, Storez was killed in a tragic accident while competing in a rally in Reims, France, and his fabulous custom-designed and -built 356 was totaled.

When contemplating the production of certain Sanction Lost models, it was discovered that in addition to Storez's open-topped 356s, a coupe version had also been ideated and sketched out by Zagato's designers. The drawing is dated September 11, 1959, but the car was never built. It took a considerable amount of scanning, digitizing, and computer-aided design work to make the original photos of Storez's speedster and the drawing of this mythical Zagato 356 Coupe into something that could be developed and built. Porsche also assisted in the process.

The result of this deeply involved labor of love is the elegant machine you see in these photos. The curvaceous coachwork is hand-rendered in aluminum and rides aboard a conventional 356 chassis platform. It was decided that just 9 cars would be built, and one of the Storez speedster's would also be constructed at the same time.

Besides its fabulous lines and perfectly balanced proportions, what immediately strikes you is how clean and simple it looks. There are handsome chromed window frames, Porsche lettering on the nose, and discrete rectangular Zagato badges in the middle lower section of the door panel. There's a daintier, simpler 356-esque chrome spear running down the front trunk. The headlights are enclosed with aerodynamic Perspex covers, and there's a pair of small horn grilles and running lights just below what would be the bumper line if the car had bumpers.

The interior is equally and elegantly simple with a clean metal dash that housed just enough instrumentation. The seats appear to be a cross between Speedster and 550 Spyder chairs

An unimaginably perfectly balance profile. This is the kind of stuff that the Italians nearly always get right. (Photo Courtesy Zagato)

Here is a compelling auto-show image with the Zagato-redefined Carrera GT next to a Zagato Aston Martin.

This is a recently built Sanction Lost replica of Storez's original Spyder. (Photo Courtesy Zagato)

with everything neatly wrapped in leather. A polished aluminum spoke, wooden Nardi steering wheel controls the tiller. The car runs a virtually new 1,600-cc Speedster powertrain. Dimensionally, it's 5.4 inches shorter than a 356 B Coupe and 5 inches shorter overall. Since the car is based on an actual production Porsche and not assigned a VIN as a Zagato or a special build, it can be licensed and registered as a 356, although I'd suggest insuring it for more.

Just 9 were hand-built in Milan at a cost of about $450,000. Expect to pay as much as 10 times that amount to acquire one of these rare Sanction Lost machines today.

Zagato not only worked some magic on Spyders and 356s but he also put its metaphoric pencil to paper on the big V-10 Carrera GT. Most of the redesign took place in the engine cover and rear wing areas.

Bertone 911 Roadster

When introduced, the Porsche 901/911 was only designed, built, and debuted in closed coupe form. The targa and cabriolet models all came sometime later, perhaps for little other reason than managing the proportions of rear- and mid-engine open cars can be challenging and yield some less-than-ideal results. Although, Porsche clearly made it work on several generations of Porsche 356 Cabriolets, Convertibles, and Speedsters. The 911 was an all-new car and a largely new idea, so the coupe was the natural place to begin. That doesn't mean that creative independents couldn't or wouldn't give an open 911 job a try.

One such creative independent was Italy's Bertone, whose catalog was littered with a wide variety of open cars, from elegant luxurious cabriolets to spare sporty roadsters. In 1966, this Milan, Italy, design house and coachbuilder took a good hard swing at the 911 and came up with a balanced and aesthetically pleasing open roadster version of Porsche's new sports car. Porsche dealer, importer, and racing driver Johnny Von Neumann also had a hand in pushing this project forward. The body was entirely new and contained few if any immediately noticeable Porsche design cues short of the instrument panel and exterior badges.

The tidy roadster was a pure two-seater and featured quad headlamps up front with hideaway fluted grilles that closed to disguise the headlight lenses. Standard Porsche wheels were binned in favor of Italian Campagnolo alloys. The bumpers were slim, chromed, wraparound blade-like pieces that fit the bodywork nicely. Out back was Porsche's standard 2.0L flat six with a manual transaxle. The rear deck line boasted a raised area that helped the car look as if it were moving forward via a small visual rake in the coachwork and more easily distinguish the rear from the lower-nosed front of the car. It was a great visual touch with nicely balanced proportions.

La Dolce Vita meets 911. This edgily elegant roadster could only be Italian, but not a Fiat, Alfa, or De Tomaso. Instead, it's a 911-based concept by Bertone. There never was any real chance of Porsche picking up the design, as it already had the open-topped targa program underway.

Note the unusual vented headlight covers that retract, and the 1960s-era black-and-gold California license plates, that indicate the car either spent some time in the Golden State or was headed there. It's a cool piece.

The rear detailing in terms of taillights and lower exhaust fascia are decidedly attractive and Italian. In fact, the whole car was quite handsome and looked great in all-black paintwork. It was a solid effort that resulted in no future as Porsche had already began design and development work on the 911 and 912 Targa models. To have licensed this open design from Bertone made no particular sense, which left the Bertone 911 as a desirable yet somewhat lonely orphan. Still, this single example was a showstopper during its international reveal at the 1966 Geneva Motor Show.

1994 Bertone Karisma Gull-Wing 911 Concept

You can love this 993-platformed 911 Italian concept car or not. It makes rather brilliant use of the 911's rear-engine chassis architecture to create plenty of legroom inside and short overhangs front and rear. It seems that nearly every independent transportation designer tries a gull-wing approach now and again. It may or may not be pretty, but the idea certainly improves passenger access to the cabin.

The Karisma retained a bit of a Porsche familial look. Perhaps they hoped that Porsche would pick up on the idea and license the design for production. It isn't as far fetched as it might sound being that this concept study was shown prior to the Cayenne, Cayman, and Panamera models. Inside the

Everyone needs to try gull-winged concept cars, as did Bertone with this reinvention of the Porsche 993-generation 911. It's an interesting look that may or may not be pretty, but it's one that certainly opened up the passenger compartment.

dashboard areas and instrument panel was a wood-trimmed rework of the standard 911 hardware. Attractive? Maybe. Innovative? Certainly. Destined for your neighborhood Porsche dealer? It didn't happen because Porsche had its own ideas about upcoming SUVs and multi-passenger sedans.

Albrecht von Goertz Porsche 914/6

Herr Goertz (1914–2006) is a name not often recognized in the annals of automotive design history, but he should be because his fingerprints are found all over at least three landmark sports car designs. His original and magnum opus is the elegant and fabulous BMW 507 of 1956 to 1959. It was a style setter at the time and remains so today. He also did some early thematic work on what became the Datsun 240Z and had a hand in the MGB-like Fairlady/1500/2000 roadster. Before that, he was involved in the genesis of the exotic Toyota 2000GT.

In 1970, he took a shot at a sport-wagon version of Porsche's new mid-engine 914. Sport wagons have ebbed and flowed in terms of popularity over time and generally find greater favor in Europe than in North America. More familiar examples include the Jensen-Healey GT, BMW Z3 Coupe, and the Volvo 1800ES.

Goertz's 914/6 sport wagon did away with the 914's removable roof panel and flat rear trunk and added an extended roof panel with a rear hatch. An additional small, vertical window pane was added aft of the standard door window line. The 914's window glass garnered somewhat heavy-looking window frames in this daring, if not exactly beautiful, concept. It appears that the 914's factory doors were retained, including its dished door handle. Porsche Fuchs alloy wheels were also employed. The 914/6's 2.0L flat-six powertrain remained. Like the 914, Goertz's concept employs de rigueur for the time hideaway headlights, although in a much pointier visage than the stock 914's profile.

There is no indication that this unusual 914 concept was ever under consideration for any sort of licensing or limited production deal. Perhaps the idea was wrong, the look didn't appeal, or Porsche's managers didn't feel such a model was necessary. Indeed, the brand's 924 and 928 hatchbacks and SUV models all came many years, and in some cases, decades into the future.

Most would call Goertz's take on the 914/6 daring or unusual before handsome or beautiful, but it was an idea. (Photo Courtesy Corporate Archives Porsche AG)

Pininfarina 911 B17 Concept

Over time, several Italian design houses have spun their own takes on various Porsche models. In 1969, Porsche purportedly commissioned Italian specialist Carrozzeria Pininfarina to design a more practical 911 body profile. Pininfarina began with a very standard 911 Coupe and stretched the wheelbase a notable eight inches to allow for more rear legroom in the floorpan. Creating adequate headroom and access/egress necessitated some more radical surgery to the 911's roof and glass lines. The results are certainly more practical and create an open, airy greenhouse, but the story goes that Porsche management understandably didn't like the proportions of the

Pininfarina, known for its elegant designs and sense of proportion, met the brief of designing a 911 alternative with more rear legroom and headroom, but the B-17's look and proportions were off, and it never went further than this stillborn concept car.

result, so the idea, and this particular execution of it, went no further. The Pininfarina B17 remains an interesting one-off.

Italdesign Porsche Tapiro Concept

It's doubtful that any designer or design house has done more seminal mid-engine automotive designs than the incomparable Giorgetto Giugiaro and his son Fabrizio's Italdesign Giugiaro. Although, Pininfarina has created many remarkable mid-motored Ferraris. Then there's the Murray/Stevens McLaren F1, plus many edgy, exotic Lamborghinis by a variety of designers that the house Giugiaros built. They built more amidships earlier, and in so many instances, they did it better than anyone else. Among Giorgetto's earlier greats are the DeTomaso Mangusta that he built while at Ghia. It was a car that lacked great chassis engineering but remains an absolute stunner in terms of exotic proportion, design, and detailing. Later came the Maserati Bora and Merak, the Lotus Esprit, the DeLorean, and the still-fabulous Maserati Boomerang.

From the 1950s to 1970s, after a design study or concept car dream machine had spent a year or so as a turntable toy that worked the international auto show circuit, it was often sold off into private hands to help pay for building next year's new concept. This was especially the case for smaller independent design firms.

Among Giugiaro's design projects for the 1970 auto show season was the Italdesign Porsche Tapiro, which was a crisply folded, mid-engine gull-wing-doored (for both the passenger compartment and the engine bay) exotic coupe based on a Porsche 914/6. Although it was a unique and generally fresh design, Giugiaro's notable handprints are all over it. It also has shadings of the Mangusta and what became the Esprit, DeLorean, and Bora in some of its shapes, proportion, and surface detail. It was painted the prototypical metallic silver

The 914/6–based Italdesign Tapiro concept exhibits many of the great Giugiaro's mid-engine exotic classic design clues synthesized in a new way and in a slightly smaller package than some others. The door-stop nose is an obvious 1970s cue. (Photo Courtesy Italdesign)

If you like gull-wing-style doors, why not four of them like the Tapiro? There was one pair over the engine compartment and another set for the passenger cabin. (Photo Courtesy Italdesign)

and had a warm butterscotch leather-lined cabin.

Power came courtesy of Porsche's S-spec 2.4L flat six that was purportedly good for 220 hp and backed by a 5-speed transaxle that culminated in a reported top speed of about 150 mph. It may have seemed somewhat unusual then or now to see an obviously Italianate exotic doorstop wearing Porsche's chromed logo letters on the nose. The Porsche Tapiro was introduced to the world at the 1970 Turin Auto Show in Italy. The car subsequently made its U.S. debut at the fifth-annual Los Angeles Imported Automobile and Sports Car Show in 1971.

It was likely obvious from the beginning that Porsche had no plans or intention of licensing to produce the design from Italdesign, so in 1972 the one-off Tapiro was sold after it completed its rounds during the 1970 and 1971 auto show cycles. This is where the story becomes slightly murky.

The car was sold to a major Spanish industrialist. In the early 1970s, politically motivated executive and royalty

The Tapiro takes flight! The simple chrome blade bumper is a very Italian design touch. The blocky chrome Porsche lettering is clean, and the graphics are quite similar to the lettering scene on the lower portion of the engine cover of several 911 models. (Photo Courtesy Italdesign)

You might recognize a bit of Maserati Bora in the Tapiro's profile or glassed-over engine covers. It makes sense as both flowed from the pen of the same brilliant designer. (Photo Courtesy Italdesign)

Father and son Giugiaro contemplate the firebombed and now lawn sculpture Tapiro in the Italdesign courtyard. It's a bit amazing how much of the car is intact considering the explosion, ensuing fire, and subsequent water damage. (Photo Courtesy Italdesign)

kidnappings, murders, and car bombings were unfortunately common occurrences. It is purported that a group of social activists who strongly objected to the Tapiro owner's trade and labor relations policies set out to make their displeasure clear in the most dramatic of ways: they planted a bomb beneath the car. It is unclear if the group intended to simply destroy the car or the owner with it. The former is what happened, and the ensuing explosion caused essentially irreparable fire damage. News reports of the day mention no injuries.

Naturally, the bomb blast and fire caused the metal warpage and paint bubbling, the water caused the rust, and this is what's left. It could be restored, but at much effort and a large cost. For the moment, the Giugiaros feel its current state tells a more interesting story. (Photo Courtesy Italdesign)

What a shame, and what a waste. Some years later, the Giugiaros reacquired the badly burned but not entirely destroyed body/chassis. In recognition of its short but somewhat ominous life, they mounted what was left of the Tapiro to a large plinth structure and displayed it lawn sculpture–style in the front garden of the Italdesign headquarters in Turin, Italy.

Three of the wheels remain attached, and remarkably two of them still wear the original tires that appear generally undamaged. The engine is long gone, but the transaxle remains intact and in situ. Vestiges of the front bulkhead and steering column remain. The Tapiro's shape is still largely well defined, although the glass from all four gull-wing window openings is missing. As the car now lives outside full time, all of the sections of the car where the paint was burned away have significantly rusted.

It is possible that the Tapiro could be restored, although it would be a Herculean and brutally expensive undertaking given the warp damage from the fire and the onset of serious rust over the ensuing years. Anything can be restored, but in this case, it is doubtful that it should be. The Giugiaros are quite proud of the statement it makes just as it is. Beautiful and thought provoking, the Tapiro is a testament to be careful how you run your business and where you park.

The flat-six engine is long gone as well as much of the luggage area floor and the passenger-side rear shock tower, but most of the transaxle remains.

CHAPTER 8

BEHIND THE CURTAIN: PORSCHE UNSEEN

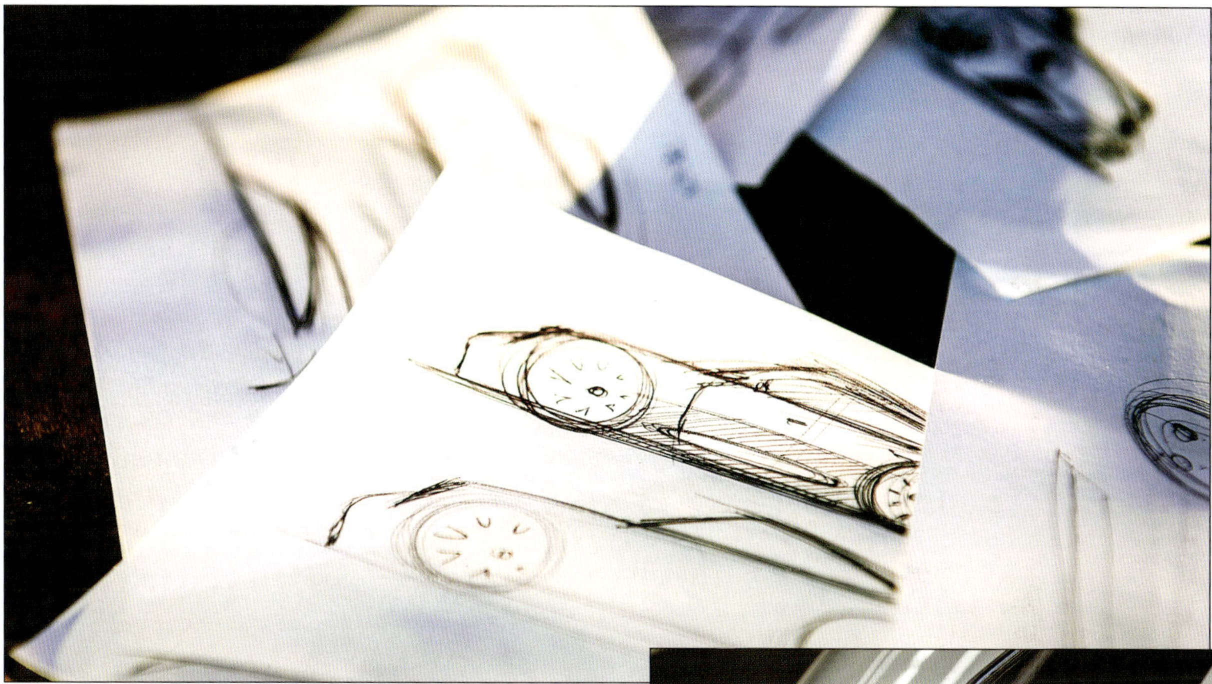

Even though computer-aided design (CAD) is the backbone of bringing an automotive design to reality today, the initial shapes and ideation still take place and are drawn by hand with pen, pencil, markers, and paper. (Photo Courtesy Corporate Archives Porsche AG)

Major factors in Porsche's long-term global success are that it is both an engineering-driven and a design-driven concern. When these functions, departments, and philosophies work together, magical results can be attained no matter if the product is a fine timepiece, a hair dryer, or an automobile.

The original Dr. Porsche was primarily an engineer, but obviously he was deeply aware of and driven by mechanical and aesthetic design. The first Porsche automobiles were built to his

The Porsche logotype has taken many forms over the decades. Here, the familiar block lettering is found at the trailing edge of the 919 Street concept model's roofline. (Photo Courtesy Corporate Archives Porsche AG)

Another Porsche race car for the street? This fabulous design concept model certainly looks the part, but Porsche insists it is not a thinly veiled production exotic under development. (Photo Courtesy Corporate Archives Porsche AG)

Proving you can build anything out of Lego, Porsche has made some good fun out of modeling the real 919 hybrid racing car (left) in the tiny plastic blocks for its non-running and non-driving Lego version (right). Kids of all ages would want this in their toy box.

The most substantive difference between a real 919 racer and this street-concept model, besides the lack of stickers and numbers, is that it doesn't wear the race car's rather massive rear wing or an engine, electronics, or interior. One can only wonder what design treasure lies beneath the car covers on the right side of this photo. (Photo Courtesy Corporate Archives Porsche AG)

The 919 Street concept's rear winglets contain the words "Le Mans Paket," so there's no question as to which Le Mans-winning race car this idea came from. (Photo Courtesy Corporate Archives Porsche AG)

If a running 919 Street concept were ever built using the race car's 900-hp V-4 hybrid powertrain, this is the look most drivers would see as it motored away from them on the Autobahn. (Photo Courtesy Corporate Archives Porsche AG)

The lettering at the top of the 919 Street's dazzling and high-tech light cluster reads "Porsche Laser Lights." We're all familiar with LEDs, but laser headlights aren't yet a thing. Although, they may be a glimpse of some future tech under ideation and development. (Photo Courtesy Corporate Archives Porsche AG)

vision of a compact, rear-engine sports car with an air-cooled engine, and this somewhat dictated the basic proportions that followed this footprint. He and son Ferry and Erwin Komenda shaped the first Porsches around this architecture.

Porsche has always managed its design functions in house. There have been many talented designers and design managers who have worked there and shaped the look of the company's products, but rarely has Porsche gone too far outside of its doors and gates for external assistance or participation. In the earliest days, Drs. Ferdinand and Ferry Porsche and Erwin Komenda were the primary arbiters of the brand's design language. Beginning in the late 1950s, the function was formalized into a focused and specifically tasked design studio/department. It had several notable designers on staff over the decades, and four notable leaders: Ferdinand Alexander "Butzi" Porsche (1957–1972) for the 901/911 and 904 models; Anatole "Tony" Lapine (1969–1988) for the 924, 944, 928, and G Series (911SC and Carrera 3.2); Harm Lagaay (1989–2004) for the Panamericana, 989, Boxster, Carrera GT, Cayenne, 993, and 996; and Michael Mauer (2004–current) for the Panamera, 918 Spyder, 992, Macan, Taycan, and several model revisions and updates. In addition to these highly credentialed and renowned design chiefs, hundreds of versatile and talented designers have worked their entire careers or cycled through the Porsche Design Studio to create the cars we know and love.

Porsche intentionally has a single design studio, which has been located in nearby Weissach since 1972. Instead of opening advanced design studios in the distant metropolises of North

America and Asia, Porsche's designers come from all over the world to Weissach to create the latest production sports cars and automotive visions at the heart of the brand. More than 120 designers and experts for interior, exterior, colors, materials, model builders, modelers, and study engineers work in the Porsche Design Studio.

The design studio is on a journey of the mind into the future of mobility.

Michael Mauer said the following about the design process: "When it comes to the visions we develop, it is not about bringing every car onto the road. Instead, it is more a question of establishing creative space and a relationship with the future.

"There are two possibilities for continuing to develop as a brand: either you improve your products from the present, that is to say step-by-step (it is difficult to be really innovative in this process), or you give free rein to your creativity. The idea is to let your thoughts jump to the day after tomorrow, and to then move back from there to tomorrow. Based on this idea, Porsche develops the product and brand identity that characterizes and secures the appearance of all models in the long term. The design language for future models developed from the long-term vision. In this process, the higher-level goal is to combine the Porsche design DNA with state-of-the-art vehicle engineering. On the one hand, this secures the innovative capability of future Porsche models. On the other, it provides an evolutionary reference to the rich history of Porsche."

All this leads to a remarkably interesting and somewhat historic reveal of a group of design models named Porsche Unseen. Under this title, Porsche for the first time recently published design studies from 2005 to 2019, which have until now been kept under lock and key. The company revealed spectacular visions of several different cars. The early studies cover the segments and are nicknamed spin-offs, little rebels, hyper cars, and what's next?

In this way, Porsche offers an exclusive insight into its design process from the very first drawing to the finished model ready for series production.

"People all over the world love the timeless and innovative design of our sports cars," said Oliver Blume, chairman of the executive board at Porsche AG. "Visionary concept studies are the foundation of this success. They provide the pool of ideas for the Porsche design of tomorrow and combine our strong tradition with trailblazing future technologies."

A selection of these studies will also be on display for fans to admire in person at the Porsche Museum.

Porsche 919 Street

The 2017 Porsche 919 Street (1:1 clay model) was developed on the basis of the technology and design used in the racing Porsche 919 Hybrid and promised to make the exhilarating driving experience of the LMP1 race car available to amateur drivers. The carbon monocoque and powerful 900 PS hybrid racing drivetrain that helped the Porsche 919 to achieve numerous victories at Le Mans are under the outer shell. The dimensions and wheelbase were the same as on the race car.

The James Dean Spyder cues are unmistakable in this edgily handsome Spyder concept model: the numbering, winged-horse fuel company logo, red trim, and silver paint. Check out the deeply cut down windscreen, and the modern, high-tech roll bar. (Photo Courtesy Corporate Archives Porsche AG)

Upon the release and publication of this concept model's existence, magazines and online sources around the world immediately began to speculate that it was really a hidden in plain sight version of a future Porsche hyper car that followed in the footsteps of the GT1, the Carrera GT, and the 918 Spyder.

Porsche has clearly and forcibly denied this speculation. The company does not dispute that a future model is possible but has confirmed that this 919 Street design study is not it, which in a way is unfortunate as a road going version of a Le Mans–winning prototype racer is compelling to say the least.

The late, great Dean's Spyder wore race number 131 on that fateful day in 1955. (Photo Courtesy Corporate Archives Porsche AG)

This concept Spyder is about the same general size and proportion as the current Boxster. Porsche could produce this look and package if it wants to, yet to date there is no indication that it will or has any such plans. (Photo Courtesy Corporate Archives Porsche AG)

Porsche Vision Spyder

With its Spartan, purist cockpit, the characteristic radiator grilles over the mid-engine, red graphic elements, and the suggested fins at the rear, the compact 2019 Porsche Vision Spyder (1:1 hard model) clearly calls to mind the Porsche 550–1500 RS Spyder from 1954. The study was intended to further develop the design identity of Porsche and provide a pool of ideas for future details, such as the ultra-modern roll bar.

The little rebel reference is a clear homage to the Porsche 550 Spyder owned by racer/actor James Dean and the car in which he died in a road accident near Cholame, California, on September 30, 1955. Dean's legend continues to live large as an actor whose career was never fully realized, as a man who died far too young at the age of 24, and as a capable Porsche road racer.

Dean's Spyder actually wore the nickname *Little Bastard* painted on the tail by Los Angeles–based vehicle customizer, pinstriper, and TV/movie car builder Dean Jeffries. Rather than use the bastard reference on its design study, Porsche chose a safer route and instead recognized one of Dean's greatest films, *Rebel Without a Cause*.

Little rebel indeed or a little something best not said. (Photo Courtesy Corporate Archives Porsche AG)

Porsche photographed the Spyder sans numbers and other ornamentation to clearly and cleanly present the overall shapes, surface details, and proportions. (Photo Courtesy Corporate Archives Porsche AG)

Porsche's electric-powered people mover concept looks fresh and inviting to us. How fun would it be to see it done up in racing team support vehicle livery or as an early-1970s American surfer van? (Photo Courtesy Corporate Archives Porsche AG)

With window lines like nothing else, this is no 1960s Volkswagen Type 2 van. The Renndienst concept's look is decidedly modern, and the stance gives the impression of a stout, well-balanced vehicle with the door hinges and openings neatly sculpted into the body panels. (Photo Courtesy Corporate Archives Porsche AG)

There's no sputtering flat four back here. A powerful, high-tech pure electric powertrain fits neatly beneath the floor panels. Porsche has never before produced such a product, but this is a clear indication that it certainly could. (Photo Courtesy Corporate Archives Porsche AG)

One of hot rodding's longest-serving notions is that stance is everything. The Renndienst's wheels are stretched toward all four corners to increase the wheelbase, improve the ride, allow for more interior room, and add visual stability. (Photo Courtesy Corporate Archives Porsche AG)

Porsche Vision Renndienst

The 2018 Porsche vision Renndienst (1:1 hard model) is Porsche's free and modern interpretation of a family-friendly space concept for up to six people. The design team created a futuristic space shuttle with exciting proportions. The Volkswagen Type 2 van reference is no accident. Although Porsche has never in its history produced a van-type model, many over time were used around the Porsche factory and by a myriad of racing teams and racing support functions.

After all, who doesn't love a VW surfer van?

The study shows how the Porsche design DNA with its characteristic surface modelling can be transferred to an unknown vehicle segment for the brand. In the interior, passengers find a comfortable and modular travel cabin. The driver sits in a central driver's seat. The all-electric drive technology is located in the underbody. As a result, passengers enjoyed an unexpectedly generous space and travel experience combined with Porsche-like flair.

All of these concepts' design language are unmistakably Porsche in their styling ethos and represent themes and flavors that may show up in future production models because they demonstrate themes, shapes, and flavors that are in the designers' minds and eyes. It's fair to say that certain ideas, themes, details, and much more stand a reasonable chance of influencing Porsches to come.

This comparison is just a little too obvious and too much fun, but it can't and should not be avoided. Just imagine the pits and paddock at Le Mans flooded by these little guys running people and parts around the track. (Photo Courtesy Corporate Archives Porsche AG)

EPILOGUE

THE PORSCHE MUSEUM IN STUTTGART

Stuttgart, Germany, has been Porsche's literal and metaphorical home since the Porsche family moved the business from Austria to Germany shortly after the first Porsche cars were built by hand in Porsches' workshops. Next to Munich, Porsche is very much the spiritual and employment epicenter of the Stuttgart/Weissach areas. Porsche's business headquarters, its engineering, design, motorsport, and production functions and factories are there, along with a large, elegant, and modern Porsche dealership, and a landmark, avant-garde, and generally breathtaking factory museum.

The company described it as such, "In 2004, the decision was made to build our spectacular building in Stuttgart-Zuffenhausen. With the Porsche Museum, the Viennese architectural office Delugan Meissl created a space that gives architectural expression to the company's self-confident attitude and high standards, while at the same time conveys the dynamism of the Porsche brand. Since 2009, the

The official Porsche Museum's dramatic avant-garde design could also pass for a large interstellar cruise ship from Star Wars. *The building floats dramatically above ground level and allows for much natural light inside. (Photo Courtesy Corporate Archives Porsche AG)*

Many of the views from inside the museum galleries are open plan, and look out, up, or down upon multiple floors of exhibit space and vehicles. It's very innovative and highly artful. Here, the outer ring of cars are production models, while the four silver machines are all race cars. (Photo Courtesy Corporate Archives Porsche AG)

Christophorus, the museum's luxurious 5-star steakhouse, is elegant and welcoming. It's the perfect place to unwind after a day of touring the Porsche factory, dealership, and museum. (Photo Courtesy Corporate Archives Porsche AG)

Museum collection vehicle storage is an art form at Porsche. The glass-walled storage stacks give visitors a look at more vehicles on top of those in the more traditional exhibit spaces, plus a glimpse into the museum workshop.

museum has been a meeting place for employees, lovers of design, and Porsche enthusiasts from all over the world."

Depending upon the exhibits currently in place, the museum floors usually contain around 100 different vehicles from the rarest models to factory design studies, popular production vehicles, and racing cars. The property also houses the company's in-house collection, motorsport quality workshops, vehicle storage, models, motorsport trophies and awards, meeting rooms, a world-class steakhouse called Christophorus, and a snack shop called Boxenstop that translates to "pit stop."

The museum maintains regular hours, offers guided and self-guided tours, and is fully open to the public. Ticket prices are reasonable, and the museum often offers special programs for kids and commemorates certain events in the Porschesphere.

The Porsche Museum
From Germany: +49 (0) 800 356-0911
From abroad: +49 (0) 711 911-20911
Email: info.museum@porsche.de
Website: porsche.com/international/aboutporsche/porschemuseum/

Cars are art. In this case, it's a sculpture made up of several Porsche 956 endurance racer body panels. The 956 and 962 prototype racers are handily among the most successful in Porsche history, and for many years, they dominated at places such as Sebring, Daytona, and Le Mans. (Photo Courtesy Corporate Archives Porsche AG)

This is just a small smattering of Porsche's collection of racing trophies garnered over its 70-plus-year history. This is no mere bookshelf display of them, either. (Photo Courtesy Corporate Archives Porsche AG)

It's doubtful any Porsche would enjoy fine-tuning more than at the museum's hospital immaculate workshop and restoration areas. These techs are factory certified and qualified to work on any vehicle wearing a Porsche badge. (Photo Courtesy Corporate Archives Porsche AG)

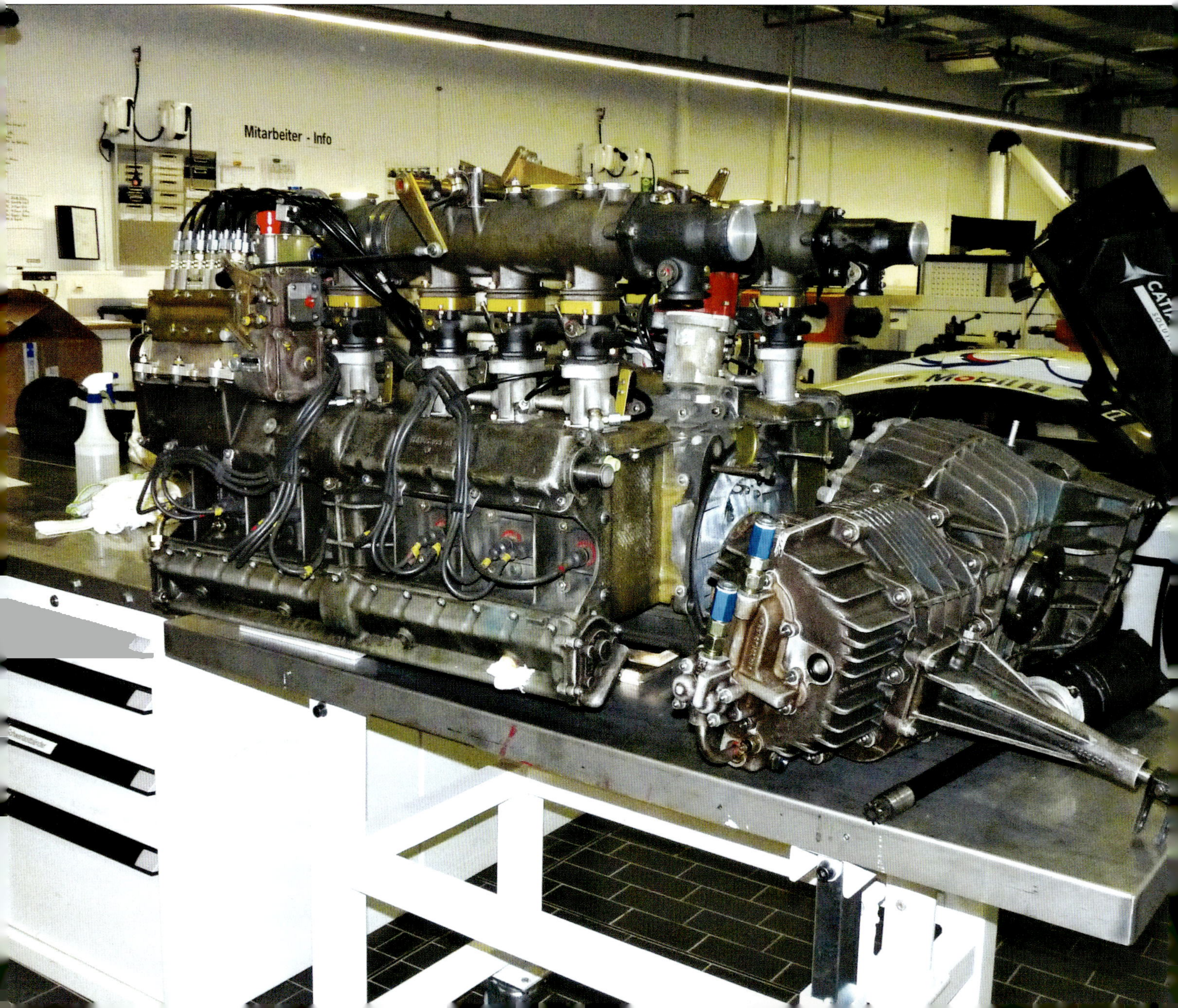

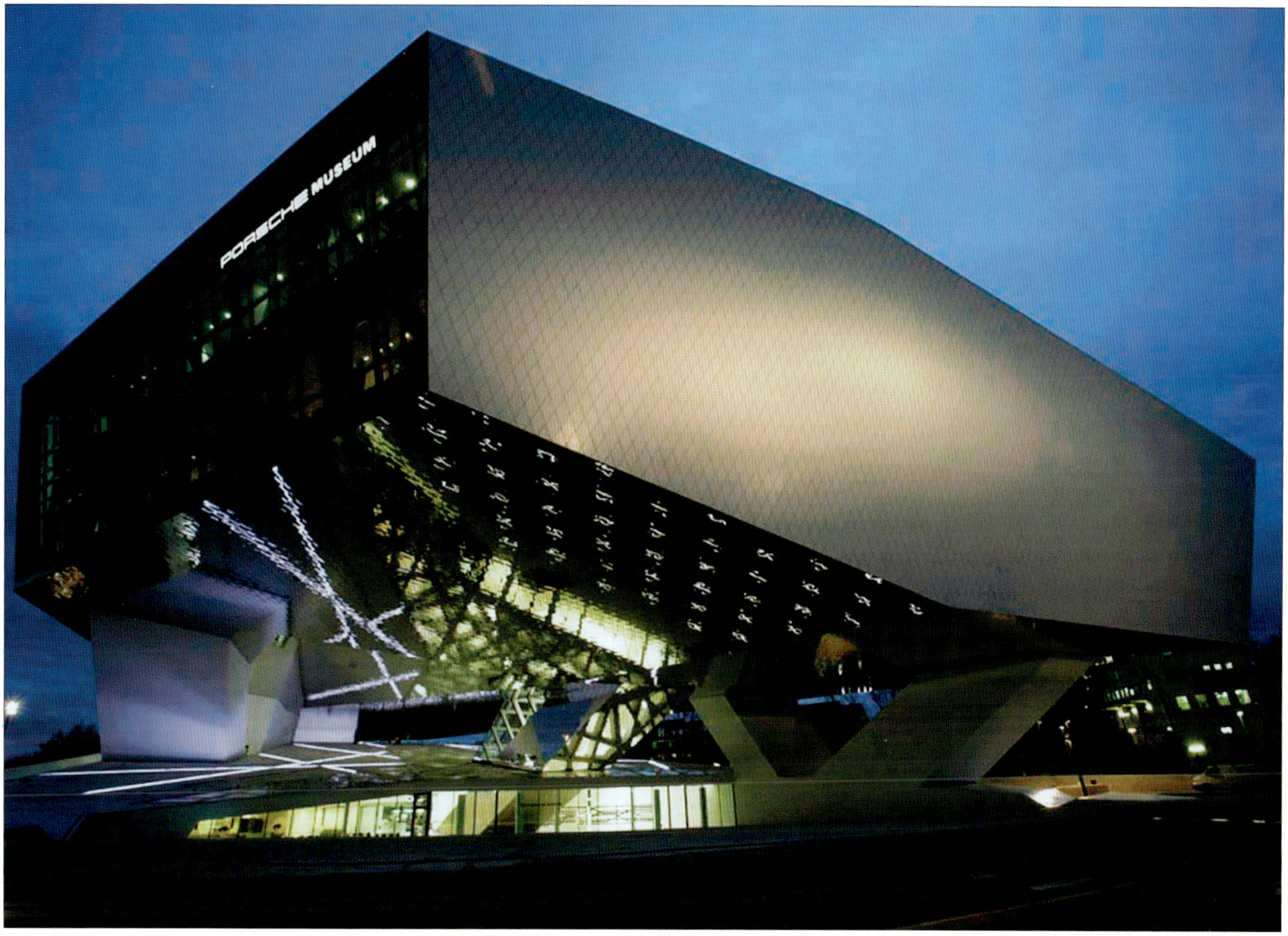

The Porsche Museum literally and figuratively stands very tall among the factory's many buildings in Stuttgart. It's highly dramatic day or night. (Photo Courtesy Corporate Archives Porsche AG)

If you need a mechanically fuel-injected, flat 6-cylinder engine for a GT-1, Porsche may or may not be able to provide one. You can certainly tune and service yours here if you have one.

INDEX

PORSCHE
Spyder
S GO 1302

MICHELIN